BIBLICAL FOUNDATIONS FOR
MANHOOD AND WOMANHOOD

FOUNDATIONS FOR THE FAMILY SERIES

BIBLICAL FOUNDATIONS FOR MANHOOD AND WOMANHOOD

WAYNE GRUDEM,

EDITOR

CROSSWAY BOOKS

A DIVISION OF
GOOD NEWS PUBLISHERS
WHEATON, ILLINOIS

Cover design: David LaPlaca

Cover photo: Josh Dennis

First printing 2002

Printed in the United States of America

Unless otherwise indicated, Scripture quotations are as follows:

Chapters 1, 3, 5, 7: The Holy Bible, English Standard Version, copyright © 2001 by Crossway Bibles, a division of Good News Publishers. Used by permission. All rights reserved.

Chapters 2, 4, 6, 9, 10: The Holy Bible: New International Version,® © 1973, 1978, 1984 by International Bible Society. Used by permission of Zondervan Publishing House. All rights reserved. The "NIV" and "New International Version" trademarks are registered in the United States Patent and Trademark Office by International Bible Society. Use of either trademark requires the permission of International Bible Society.

Chapter 8: The New American Standard Bible, © 1960, 1962, 1963, 1968, 1971, 1972, 1975, 1977 by The Lockman Foundation. Used by permission.

Library of Congress Cataloging-in-Publication Data
Biblical foundations for manhood and womanhood / Wayne Grudem, editor.
    p.   cm. — (Foundations for the family series)
    Includes bibliographical references.
    ISBN 1-58134-409-0
    1. Women—Biblical teaching. 2. Men—Biblical teaching. 3. Man-woman relationships—Biblical teaching. I. Grudem, Wayne A. II. Series.
BS680.W7 B53   2002
261.8'343—dc21
                                     2002001697
                                         CIP

15	14	13	12	11	10	09	08	07	06	05	04	03	02
15	14	13	12	11	10	9	8	7	6	5	4	3	2	1

To Dennis Rainey
Stalwart defender of God's plan for the family,
and faithful friend

CONTENTS

THE CONTRIBUTORS

Daniel Doriani is Dean of the Faculty and Professor of New Testament at Covenant Theological Seminary in St. Louis, Missouri. An ordained minister in the Presbyterian Church in America (PCA), Doriani earned a Ph.D. and M.Div. from Westminster Theological Seminary and an S.T.M. from Yale University and has twice been a research fellow at Yale (1981, 1995). Doriani has written five books: *The Life of a God-Made Man* (Crossway, 2001); *Putting the Truth to Work: The Theory and Practice of Biblical Interpretation* (Presbyterian and Reformed, 2001); *Getting the Message, a Plan for Interpreting and Applying the Bible* (Presbyterian and Reformed, 1996), *David the Anointed* and *Teach the Nations* (Great Commission, 1984 and 1991). In addition to academic articles, he has contributed chapters to several books on family issues, including *Women in the Church: A Fresh Analysis of 1 Timothy 2:11-15* (Baker, 1995), *Christian Perspectives on Sexuality and Gender* (Eerdmans, 1996), and *Biblical Foundations for Building Strong Families* (Crossway, 2002). Doriani speaks frequently at Christian conferences, enjoys various sports, and coached college tennis for two years. He and his wife Deborah, a musician, have three teenage daughters, Abigail, Sarah, and Beth.

Wayne Grudem is Research Professor of Bible and Theology at Phoenix Seminary in Scottsdale, Arizona. Prior to Phoenix Seminary he taught for twenty years at Trinity Evangelical Divinity School, Deerfield, Illinois, where he was chairman of the Department of Biblical and Systematic Theology. He received a B.A. from Harvard University, an M.Div. from Westminster Seminary, Philadelphia, and a Ph.D. (in New Testament) from the University of Cambridge, England. He has published eight books, including *Systematic Theology: An Introduction to Biblical Doctrine* (Zondervan), *Recovering Biblical*

Manhood and Womanhood (Crossway; co-edited with John Piper), and *The Gift of Prophecy in the New Testament and Today* (Crossway). He is a past president of the Evangelical Theological Society, a co-founder and past president of the Council on Biblical Manhood and Womanhood, and a member of the Translation Oversight Committee for the English Standard Version of the Bible. He and his wife, Margaret, are members of the FamilyLife speaker team (a division of Campus Crusade for Christ). They have been married since 1969 and have three adult sons.

Daniel R. Heimbach is Professor of Christian Ethics at Southeastern Baptist Theological Seminary. Born in China of missionary parents and educated at the U.S. Naval Academy, Trinity Evangelical Divinity School, and Drew University, Dr. Heimbach served President George Bush at the White House and the Pentagon before he began teaching full-time in 1993. Dr. Heimbach served Focus on the Family as lead scholar for a project on sexual morality and is a member of the Council for Biblical Manhood and Womanhood. He lives with his wife Anna and two sons in Wake Forest, North Carolina, near the seminary where he teaches.

Richard W. Hove (M. Div., Trinity Evangelical Divinity School) has been on staff with Campus Crusade for Christ for twenty-three years. Presently he directs the ministry at Duke University. He is the author of *Equality in Christ? Galatians 3:28 and the Gender Dispute*, published by Crossway Books, 1999. He teaches Biblical Interpretation/ Communication classes for Campus Crusade and has helped develop several theological tools for the national campus ministry, including the gospel presentation *Life@Large* and the book *The Ultimate Road Trip: How to Lead a Small Group*, which is used all over the country to train small-group leaders. Rick and his wife Sonya have three children.

Peter Jones holds an M.Div. from Gordon-Conwell Theological Seminary, a Th.M. from Harvard Divinity School, and a Ph.D. from Princeton Theological Seminary. From 1973-1991 he was a missionary with the Presbyterian Church in America, serving as Professor of New Testament at La Faculté Libre de Théologie Reformée in Aix-en-Provence, France. In 1991 he moved to Escondido, California, where he is Professor of New Testament at Westminster Theological Seminary in California. He has authored *The Gnostic Empire Strikes Back*, *Pagans in the Pews*, and *Gospel Truth/Pagan Lies*, as well as many articles. He is married to Rebecca (Clowney) Jones. Peter and Rebecca have seven children and four grandchildren. Many of their writings are posted at their website, www.spirit-wars.com.

John Piper, pastor of Bethlehem Baptist Church in Minneapolis since 1980, is the author of numerous books, including *Desiring God, A Hunger for God, The Hidden Smile of God,* and *Seeing and Savoring Jesus Christ.* He received his doctorate in theology from the University of Munich and taught biblical studies for six years at Bethel College, St. Paul, before becoming a pastor. He and his wife, Noël, live in Minneapolis and have four sons, a daughter, and two grandchildren.

Bruce A. Ware (Ph.D. from Fuller Seminary) is Senior Associate Dean of the School of Theology and Professor of Christian Theology at The Southern Baptist Theological Seminary, Louisville, Kentucky. Previously Dr. Ware taught at Bethel Theological Seminary, Western Seminary, and Trinity Evangelical Divinity School. He also serves as president of the Council on Biblical Manhood and Womanhood and as the editor of the *Journal for Biblical Manhood and Womanhood.* He has recently written *God's Lesser Glory: The Diminished God of Open Theism,* published with Crossway Books. Bruce is married to Jodi, his wife of twenty-three years, and they have two daughters, Bethany and Rachel.

PREFACE

—∞∞—

Since the publication of *Recovering Biblical Manhood and Womanhood* (edited by John Piper and Wayne Grudem; Wheaton, IL: Crossway Books, 1991), the ongoing debate over the biblical understanding of men and women has brought new challenges to the perspective we presented there, as well as new insights from ongoing scholarly investigation of Scripture and of trends in the culture.

Several speakers at a conference in Dallas, Texas, held March 20-22, 2000, addressed those new challenges and new insights as they related to manhood and womanhood in marriage. The conference, "Building Strong Families in Your Church," was co-sponsored by the Council on Biblical Manhood and Womanhood and by FamilyLife (a division of Campus Crusade for Christ). The conference was designed to inform and challenge pastors and other Christian leaders regarding recent developments in the manhood-womanhood controversy, and we are grateful to Crossway Books for publishing four volumes with the contents of the messages delivered by speakers at that conference. This volume contains the messages that had a more scholarly focus, messages that thus provided the "Biblical Foundations" for manhood and womanhood in the home.

In the first chapter I present an overview of the manhood-womanhood controversy, discussing six "key issues" that need to be kept in mind in present-day discussions: (1) our equality in value and dignity as men and women, (2) our different roles in marriage as established by God before the Fall, (3) the relationship between the Trinity and our equality and differences as men and women, (4) the goodness of our equality and differences, (5) the importance of this issue as a matter of obedience to the Bible, and (6) the deep connections between the manhood-womanhood controversy and all of life.

In Chapter 2 Bruce Ware explores the meaning of our creation as male and female in the image of God. He shows that we were created equal before God, but also different from the moment of creation, different in ways that allow us to complement each other and fulfill God's purposes together. Finally, he applies these insights to singleness as it finds expression in the fellowship of the church.

In Chapter 3 John Piper shows how marriage is not an end in itself but must always be lived for the glory of God. He argues that God expects us to love Him more than our marriage partners, and that this does not diminish but enriches our marriages. He challenges us by saying that if we want strong marriages in our churches, we need to preach less about marriage and more about the greatness of God.

Then in Chapter 4 Rick Hove summarizes the results of his groundbreaking research into Galatians 3:28, "There is neither Jew nor Greek, slave nor free, male nor female, for you are all one in Christ Jesus." Those on the other side of this question, those who are called "egalitarians" or "evangelical feminists," often claim Galatians 3:28 as the primary biblical support for their position. But Hove, drawing on the results of numerous computer searches in ancient Greek literature, demonstrates that Galatians 3:28 does not teach male-female "sameness" or the interchangeability of male-female roles, but rather male-female *unity* in Christ, a unity that assumes and preserves our differences.

After that, in Chapter 5 I return once again to the meaning of the Greek term *kephalē* ("head"), especially as it pertains to Ephesians 5:23, "For the husband is the *head* of the wife even as Christ is the head of the church," and 1 Corinthians 11:3, "the *head* of a wife is her husband." I give three strands of evidence to show that "head" in these verses has to mean "person in authority over": first, a number of previously unnoticed citations from the early church fathers, second, an examination of recently published studies of *kephalē*, and third, a private letter from Peter G. W. Glare, the editor of the *Liddell-Scott Greek-English Lexicon: Supplement* and probably the preeminent living lexicographer of ancient Greek. (This chapter is identical to my article in *Journal of the Evangelical Theological Society* 44/1 [March 2001], with the exception of the added interaction, on pages 194-199, with Anthony Thiselton's new commentary on 1 Corinthians.)

But what has been the historic position of the church on the roles of men and women in marriage? In Chapter 6 Daniel Doriani traces the history of interpretation of Ephesians 5:22-33. Doriani considers the egalitarian claim that "be subject to one another" in Ephesians 5:21 teaches a kind of "mutual submission" that negates male headship in marriage. After a survey of about a hundred commentaries throughout the history of the church, he finds that "feminist interpretations of Ephesians 5 begin to appear in commentaries around 1970." He finds that the feminist understanding of Ephesians 5:21 is a "historical novelty."

In Chapter 7 I also consider Ephesians 5:21 and argue that it is a mistake to claim that "submitting to one another" in that verse teaches "mutual submission," because neither the context nor the meanings of the words will bear that interpretation.

Bruce Ware takes up recent disputes over the doctrine of the Trinity in Chapter 8, interacting first with feminist claims that we should no longer refer to God as "Father, Son, and Holy Spirit" but rather with the non-male-oriented terms *Creator, Redeemer,* and *Sustainer.* Then Ware goes on to interact with evangelical feminists who have begun to deny the eternal submission of the Son to the Father and to advocate instead an eternal "mutual submission" within the Trinity. Ware shows that they are not being faithful either to the Bible or to the historic position of the church, and they are in fact "tampering with the Trinity."

In the last two chapters we turn to an examination of broader historical and cultural trends. In Chapter 9 Peter Jones helps us understand why sexual perversion is so common in modern culture. Jones argues that this is the inevitable result of a society turning away from Christian convictions about the nature of God and the nature of reality. In a wide-ranging and alarming study of attitudes toward sexuality and religion in ancient and modern cultures, Jones unmasks the underlying theme of "monism" (the idea that all is one) and shows how it denies the existence of the God of the Bible and inevitably results in homosexuality, a demand for total sexual license, and an androgyny that demands the ultimate emasculation of men and defeminization of women. Jones sees deep spiritual opposition at work in our culture to destroy biblical teachings on manhood and womanhood.

Finally, in Chapter 10 Daniel Heimbach examines a view popular in secular academic circles, the idea that our sexual identity is not fixed but is "plastic," and individuals are thus free to shape their sexual identity in any way they choose. So the idea that someone is a "man" or a "woman" is just a societal construct, and any individual who wishes to reject it can do so and choose another sexual identity. Lest we think this is an academic fad, Heimbach warns that it is infecting modern culture, and he sees ominous parallels in the thinking of evangelical feminists. In response, Heimbach argues that manhood and womanhood are grounded in God's good creation before the Fall, that our sexual identity is something essential to our humanity, and that we will exist as men and women forever.

The focus of our Dallas conference, and therefore of the four volumes in this series, was manhood and womanhood in the family. Though some chapters occasionally touch on related areas such as the church or society, those areas are not treated extensively in these volumes.

I am grateful to Susanne Henry and Sharon Sullivan for excellent secretarial help in producing this book, to Travis Buchanan for careful work in compiling the indexes, to several generous donors (who will here remain unnamed) for providing financial support for the 2000 Dallas conference that gave birth to this book, to Kevin Hartman for competently and graciously overseeing the details of that Dallas conference, and to my wife, Margaret, for her unfading support, encouragement, counsel, and patience in my writing and editing (which always seem to take longer than either of us expects).

Finally, I have dedicated this book to Dennis Rainey, the wise, godly, and amazingly energetic director of FamilyLife. He is a stalwart defender of God's plan for the family, and he understands deeply how important it is to teach true biblical manhood and womanhood if we want to maintain healthy families in our hostile culture. He and the FamilyLife staff provided outstanding planning, publicity, and event management skills for our joint FamilyLife-CBMW conference in Dallas. I count Dennis's friendship as a special gift from God, and I hope that this volume will provide additional foundational material that will support and strengthen the good work that is being done by him and the FamilyLife team.

Thanks be to God for the excellence of His wonderful creation! "Male and female he created them . . . . and behold, *it was very good*" (Gen. 1:27, 31, ESV).

Wayne Grudem
April 2002

I

OVERVIEW

———∞∞∞———

1

THE KEY ISSUES IN THE MANHOOD-WOMANHOOD CONTROVERSY, AND THE WAY FORWARD

Wayne Grudem

KEY ISSUE 1: MEN AND WOMEN ARE EQUAL IN VALUE AND DIGNITY

KEY ISSUE 1: MEN AND WOMEN ARE EQUAL IN VALUE AND DIGNITY

Very early in the Bible we read that both men and women are "in the image of God." In fact, the very first verse that tells us that God created human beings also tells us that both "male and female" are in the image of God:

> *So God created man in his own image, in the image of God he created him;* male and female he created them.
> —GEN. 1:27, emphasis added

To be in the image of God is an incredible privilege. It means *to be like God* and *to represent God*.[1] No other creatures in all of creation, not even the powerful angels, are said to be in the image of God. It is a privilege given only to us as men and women. We are more like God than any other creatures in the universe, for we alone are "in the image of God."[2]

---

[1]For further discussion, see Wayne Grudem, *Systematic Theology: An Introduction to Biblical Doctrine* (Leicester, England: Inter-Varsity Press, and Grand Rapids, MI: Zondervan, 1994), 442-450.

[2]God created us so that our likeness to Him would be seen in our moral judgment and actions, in our spiritual life and ability to relate to God who is spirit, in our reasoning ability, our use of language, our awareness of the distant past and future, our creativity, the complexity and variety of our emotions, the depth of our interpersonal relationships, our equality and differences

Any discussion of manhood and womanhood in the Bible must start here. Every time we look at each other or talk to each other as men and women, we should remember that the person we are talking to is a creature of God who is *more like God than anything else in the universe*, and men and women share that status equally. Therefore we should treat men and women with equal dignity, and we should think of men and women as having equal value. We are *both* in the image of God, and we have been so since the very first day that God created us. "In the image of God he created him; *male and female he created them*" (Genesis 1:27). Nowhere does the Bible say that men are more in God's image than women.[3] Men and women share equally in the tremendous privilege of being in the image of God.

The Bible thus almost immediately corrects the errors of male dominance and male superiority that have come as the result of sin and that have been seen in nearly all cultures in the history of the world. Wherever men are thought to be better than women, wherever husbands act as selfish dictators, wherever wives are forbidden to have their own jobs outside the home or to vote or to own property or to be educated, wherever women are treated as inferior, wherever there is abuse or violence against women or rape or female infanticide or polygamy or harems, the biblical truth of equality in the image of God is being denied. To all societies and cultures where these things occur, we must proclaim that the very beginning of God's Word bears a fundamental and irrefutable witness against these evils.[4]

---

in marriage and other interpersonal relationships, our rule over the rest of creation, and in other ways. All of these aspects are distorted by sin and manifest themselves in ways that are *unlike* God and are displeasing to Him, but all of these areas of our lives are also being progressively restored to greater Godlikeness through the salvation that is ours in Christ, and they will be completely restored in us when Christ returns.

For a fuller discussion of what it means to be in the image of God, see Bruce Ware's chapter, "Male and Female Complementarity and the Image of God" elsewhere in this volume (Chapter 2).

[3]In 1 Corinthians 11:7 Paul says, "A man ought not to cover his head, since he is the image and glory of God, but woman is the glory of man." He is not denying here that woman was created in the image of God, for that is clearly affirmed in Genesis 1:27. Nor does he say that woman is the image of man. Rather, Paul is simply saying that *in the relationship between man and woman*, man in particular reflects something of the excellence of the God who created him, and woman *in that relationship* reflects something of the excellence of the man from whom she was created. Yet Paul goes on almost immediately to say that men and women are interdependent (see vv. 11-12), and that we could not exist without each other. He does not say in this passage that man is more in the image of God than woman is, nor should we derive any such idea from this passage.

[4]A tragic example of male dominance was reported on the front page of *USA Today: International Edition* (Sept. 6, 1994): "No girls allowed: Abortion for sex selection raises moral questions" was the caption on a photo of a doctor performing an ultrasound on a pregnant woman in India. The cover story, "Asians' Desire for Boys Leaves a Deadly Choice," reported that according to

Yet we can say even more. If men and women are equally in the image of God, then we are equally important *to God* and equally valuable *to Him*. We have equal worth before Him *for all eternity*, for this is how we were created. This truth should exclude all our feelings of pride or inferiority and should exclude any idea that one sex is "better" or "worse" than the other. In contrast to many non-Christian cultures and religions, no one should feel proud or superior because he is a man, and no one should feel disappointed or inferior because she is a woman. If God thinks us to be equal in value, then that settles forever the question of personal worth, for God's evaluation is the true standard of personal value for all eternity.

Further evidence of our equality in the image of God is seen in the New Testament church, where the Holy Spirit is given in new fullness to both men and women (Acts 2:17-18), where both men and women are baptized into membership in the body of Christ (Acts 2:41)[5], and where both men and women receive spiritual gifts for use in the life of the church (1 Cor. 12:7, 11; 1 Pet. 4:10). The apostle Paul reminds us that we are not to be divided into factions that think of themselves as superior and inferior (such as Jew and Greek, or slave and free, or male

---

Dr. Datta Pai, a Bombay obstetrician, "99% of those found to be carrying female fetuses aborted their unborn children" (2A). The story explained that "modern technology, the strong cultural desire for boys and pressure to reduce population have joined forces in a deadly combination in India, China and much of Asia to produce a booming business in sex selection . . . the practice of aborting female fetuses appears common judging by emerging statistics that show lopsided sex ratios throughout Asia and into North Africa. Nor is the practice of sex selection limited to abortion. Female infanticide, the abandonment of baby girls, and the preferential feeding and health care of boys contribute greatly to the imbalanced ratios" (1A-2A). The story goes on to quote Harvard professor Amartya Sen as saying that there are now more than 100,000,000 women "missing" in the population of the world, including 44,000,000 fewer women in China and 37,000,000 fewer in India than should be alive according to normal sex ratios at birth (2A).

This is a tragedy of unspeakable proportions. In addition to the harm of these lost lives, we must think of the destructive consequences in the lives of those women who survive. From their earliest age they receive the message from their families and indeed from their whole society, "Boys are better than girls," and "I wish you were a boy." The devastation on their own sense of self-worth must be immense. Yet all of this comes about as a result of a failure to realize that men and women, boys and girls have equal value in God's sight and should have equal value in our sight as well. The first chapter of the Bible corrects this practice and corrects any lurking sense in our own hearts that boys are more valuable than girls, when it says we are both created in the image of God.

[5]The fact that both men and women are baptized stands in contrast to the Old Testament, where the outward sign of inclusion in the community of God's people was circumcision. Circumcision by its nature was only administered to men. By contrast, both men and women are baptized in the New Testament church. In this way, every baptism should remind us of our equality in the image of God.

and female), but rather that we should think of ourselves as united because we are all "one" in Christ Jesus (Gal. 3:28).

By way of application to marriage, whenever husbands and wives do not listen respectfully and thoughtfully to each other's viewpoints, do not value the wisdom that might be arrived at differently and expressed differently from the other person, or do not value the other person's different gifts and preferences as much as their own, this teaching on equality in the image of God is being neglected.

Speaking personally, I do not think I listened very well to my wife Margaret early in our marriage. I did not value her different gifts and preferences as much as my own, or her wisdom that was arrived at or expressed differently. Later we made much progress in this area, but looking back, Margaret told me that early in our marriage she felt as though her voice was taken away, and as though my ears were closed. I wonder if there are other couples in many churches where God needs to open the husband's ears to listen and needs to restore the wife's voice to speak.[6]

A healthy perspective on the way that equality manifests itself in marriage was summarized as part of a "Marriage and Family Statement" issued by Campus Crusade for Christ in July 1999. After three paragraphs discussing both equality and differences between men and women, the statement says the following:

> In a marriage lived according to these truths, the love between husband and wife will show itself in listening to each other's viewpoints, valuing each other's gifts, wisdom, and desires, honoring one another in public and in private, and always seeking to bring benefit, not harm, to one another.[7]

Why do I list this as a key issue in the manhood-womanhood con-

---

[6]I realize there is an opposite mistake, in which the husband "listens" so much and the wife has so great a "voice" that in effect the wife becomes the governing partner in the relationship. I am not advocating that mistake either, and in what follows I will argue for the necessity of a male leadership role in decision-making within marriage.

[7]Policy statement announced and distributed to Campus Crusade staff members at a biannual staff conference, July 28, 1999, at Moby Arena, Colorado State University, Fort Collins, Colorado. The statement was reported in a Religion News Service dispatch July 30, 1999, a Baptist Press story by Art Toalston on July 29, 1999 (www.baptistpress.com), and an article in *World* magazine September 11, 1999 (32), and it was also quoted in full in James Dobson's monthly newsletter *Family News from Dr. James Dobson* (Sept. 1999, 1-2). The statement is also reproduced and discussed in Dennis Rainey, *Ministering to Twenty-First Century Families* (Nashville: Word, 2001), 39-56.

troversy? Not because we differ with egalitarians[8] on this question, but because we differ at this point with sinful tendencies in our own hearts. And we differ at this point with the oppressive male chauvinism and male dominance that has marred most cultures throughout most of history.

Why do I list this as a key issue? Because anyone preaching on manhood and womanhood has to start here—where the Bible starts—not with our differences, but with our *equality* in the image of God.

And to pastors who wish to teach on biblical manhood and womanhood in their churches, I need to say that if you don't start here in your preaching, affirming our equality in the image of God, you simply will not get a hearing from many people in your church. And if you don't start here, with male-female equality in the image of God, your heart won't be right in dealing with this issue.

There is yet one more reason why I think this is a key issue, one that speaks especially to men. I personally think that one reason God has allowed this whole controversy on manhood and womanhood to come into the church at this time is so that we could correct some mistakes, change some wrongful traditions, and become more faithful to Scripture in treating our wives and all women with dignity and respect. The first step in correcting these mistakes is to be fully convinced in our hearts that women share equally with us men in the value and dignity that belongs to being made in the image of God.

KEY ISSUE 2: MEN AND WOMEN HAVE DIFFERENT ROLES IN MARRIAGE AS PART OF THE CREATED ORDER

When the members of the Council on Biblical Manhood and Womanhood wrote the "Danvers Statement" in 1987, we included the following affirmations:

> 1. Both Adam and Eve were created in God's image, equal before God as persons and distinct in their manhood and womanhood.

---

[8]Throughout this chapter, I use the word *egalitarian* to refer to those within the evangelical world who say that no differences in the roles of men and women should be based on their gender alone. In particular, egalitarians deny that there is any unique male leadership role in marriage or in the church. Sometimes I use the phrase *evangelical feminists* to mean the same thing as egalitarians.

2. Distinctions in masculine and feminine roles are ordained by God as part of the created order, and should find an echo in every human heart.

3. Adam's headship in marriage was established by God before the Fall, and was not a result of sin.[9]

The statement adopted by the Southern Baptist Convention in June 1998 and affirmed (with one additional paragraph) by Campus Crusade in July 1999 also affirms God-given differences:

The husband and wife are of equal worth before God, since both are created in God's image. The marriage relationship models the way God relates to his people. A husband is to love his wife as Christ loved the church. *He has the God-given responsibility to provide for, to protect, and to lead his family. A wife is to submit herself graciously to the servant leadership of her husband* even as the church willingly submits to the headship of Christ. *She being in the image of God as is her husband and thus equal to him, has the God-given responsibility to respect her husband and serve as his helper in managing the household and nurturing the next generation.*[10]

By contrast, egalitarians do not affirm such created differences. In fact, the "statement on men, women and Biblical equality" published by Christians for Biblical Equality (CBE) says:

1. The Bible teaches that both man and woman were created in God's image, had a direct relationship with God, and *shared jointly the responsibilities of bearing and rearing children and having dominion over the created order (Gen. 1:26-28)*. . . .

5. The Bible teaches that the rulership of Adam over Eve resulted from the Fall and was, therefore, *not a part of the original created order*. . . .

10. The Bible defines the function of leadership as the empowerment of others for service rather than as the exercise of power over them (Matt. 20:25-28, 23:8; Mark 10:42-45; John 13:13-17; Gal. 5:13; 1 Pet 5:2-3).

---

[9]The Danvers Statement was prepared by several evangelical leaders at a Council on Biblical Manhood and Womanhood meeting in Danvers, MA, in December 1987. It was first published in final form by the CBMW in Wheaton, IL, in November 1988. See Appendix 1 for the full text of this statement.

[10]The entire statement in the form adopted by Campus Crusade for Christ is available at www.baptistpress.com, in the archives for July 29, 1999 (italics added).

11. The Bible teaches that husbands and wives are heirs together of the grace of life and that they are bound together in a relationship of mutual submission and responsibility (1 Cor. 7:3-5; Eph. 5:21; 1 Pet. 3:1-7; Gen. 21:12). The husband's function as "head" (*kephalē*) is to be understood as self-giving love and service within this relationship of mutual submission (Eph. 5:21-33; Col. 3:19; I Pet. 3:7).[11]

So which position is right? Does the Bible really teach that men and women had different roles from the beginning of creation?

When we look carefully at Scripture, I think we can see at least ten reasons indicating that God gave men and women distinct roles before the Fall, and particularly that there was male headship in marriage before the Fall.

Ten Reasons Showing Male Headship in Marriage Before the Fall

1. *The order*: Adam was created first, then Eve (note the sequence in Gen. 2:7 and Gen. 2:18-23). We may not think of this as very important today, but it was important to the biblical readers, and the apostle Paul sees it as important: He bases his argument for different roles in the assembled New Testament church on the fact that Adam was created prior to Eve. He says, "I permit no woman to teach or to have authority over men. . . . For Adam was formed first, then Eve" (1 Tim. 2:12-13). According to Scripture itself, then, the fact that Adam was created first and then Eve has implications not just for Adam and Eve themselves, but for the relationships between men and women generally throughout time, including the church age.[12]

2. *The representation*: Adam, not Eve, had a special role in representing the human race.

Looking at the Genesis narrative, we find that Eve sinned first, and then Adam sinned (Gen. 3:6: "she took of its fruit and ate; and she also

---

[11]The entire statement is available from the website of Christians for Biblical Equality, www.cbeinternational.org (italics added as quoted above). I should add that the CBE statement regularly portrays a non-egalitarian position in pejorative language such as "the rulership of Adam over Eve" and fails to even mention a third alternative—namely, loving, humble headship. (For a discussion of repeated ambiguities in the CBE statement see John Piper and Wayne Grudem, "Charity, Clarity, and Hope," in *Recovering Biblical Manhood and Womanhood* (Wheaton, IL: Crossway Books, 1991), 403-422.)

[12]Bruce Ware adds yet another reason related to this temporal priority in creation—namely, that woman was created "from" or "out of" man. See his discussion elsewhere in this volume, Chapter 2. Although I have not listed it separately here, this could be counted as an eleventh reason along with the ten I list.

gave some to her husband who was with her, and he ate"). Since Eve sinned first, we might expect that the New Testament would tell us that we inherit a sinful nature because of Eve's sin, or that we are counted guilty because of Eve's sin. But this is not the case. In fact, it is just the opposite. We read in the New Testament, "For as *in Adam* all die, so also *in Christ* shall all be made alive" (1 Cor. 15:22). The New Testament does not say, "as *in Eve* all die, so also in Christ shall all be made alive."

This is further seen in the parallel between Adam and Christ, where Paul views Christ as the "last Adam":

> *Thus it is written, "The first man Adam became a living being"; the last Adam became a life-giving spirit. . . . The first man was from the earth, a man of dust; the second man is from heaven. . . . Just as we have borne the image of the man of dust, we shall also bear the image of the man of heaven.*
>
> —1 COR. 15:45-49 (see also ROM. 5:12-21,
> where another relationship between
> Adam and Christ is developed)

It is unmistakable, then, that Adam had a leadership role in representing the entire human race, a leadership role that Eve did not have. Nor was it true that Adam and Eve *together* represented the human race. It was *Adam alone* who represented the human race, because he had a particular leadership role that God had given him, a role that Eve did not share.

3. *The naming of woman*: When God made the first woman and "brought her to the man," the Bible tells us,

> *Then the man said, "This at last is bone of my bones and flesh of my flesh; she shall be called Woman, because she was taken out of Man."*
>
> —GEN. 2:23

When Adam says, "she shall be called Woman," he is giving a name to her. This is important in the context of Genesis 1—2, because in that context the original readers would have recognized that the person doing the "naming" of created things is always the person who has authority over those things.

In order to avoid the idea that Adam's naming of woman implies male leadership or authority, some egalitarians (such as Gilbert

Bilezikian) deny that Adam gives a name to his wife in Genesis 2:23.[13] But his objection is hardly convincing when we see how Genesis 2:23 fits into the pattern of naming activities throughout these first two chapters of Genesis. We see this when we examine the places where the same verb (the Hebrew verb *qārā'* ["to call"]) is used in contexts of naming in Genesis 1—2:

> *Genesis 1:5: "God called the light Day, and the darkness he called Night."*

> *Genesis 1:8: "And God called the expanse Heaven."*

> *Genesis 1:10: "God called the dry land Earth, and the waters that were gathered together he called Seas."*

> *Genesis 2:19: So out of the ground the LORD God formed every beast of the field and every bird of the heavens and brought them to the man to see what he would call them. And whatever the man called every living creature, that was its name."*

> *Genesis 2:20: "The man gave names to all livestock and to the birds of the heavens and to every beast of the field."*

> *Genesis 2:23: "Then the man said, 'This at last is bone of my bones and flesh of my flesh; she shall be called Woman, because she was taken out of Man.'"*

In each of these verses prior to Genesis 2:23, the same verb, the Hebrew verb *qārā'*, had been used. Just as God demonstrated His sovereignty over day and night, heavens, earth, and seas by assigning them names, so Adam demonstrated his authority over the animal kingdom by assigning them names. The pattern would have been eas-

---

[13]See Gilbert Bilezikian, *Beyond Sex Roles*, 2nd ed. (Grand Rapids, MI: Baker, 1990), 259, where he says, "No mention of 'giving a name' is made in reference to the woman in verse 23." He also says, "The contrast between Genesis 2:23 and 3:20 bears out the fact that there was no act of naming in the first instance. When Eve actually receives her *name*, the text uses that very word, 'The man called his wife's *name* Eve'" (261).

Bilezikian apparently thinks that where the word "name" (the Hebrew noun *shem*) is not used, no act of naming occurs. But he takes no account of the fact that the noun *shem* is not used in Genesis 1:5, 8, or 10 either, where God names the "Day" and the "Night" and "Heaven" and "Earth" and "Seas." The idea of naming can be indicated by the verb *qārā'* without the noun "name" being used.

ily recognized by the original readers, and they would have seen a continuation of the pattern when Adam said, "she shall be *called* Woman."

The original readers of Genesis and of the rest of the Old Testament would have been familiar with this pattern, a pattern whereby people who have authority over another person or thing have the ability to assign a name to that person or thing, a name that often indicates something of the character or quality of the person. Thus parents give names to their children (see Gen. 4:25-26; 5:3, 29; 16:15; 19:37-38; 21:3). And God is able to change the names of people when He wishes to indicate a change in their character or role (see Gen. 17:5, 15, where God changes Abram's name to Abraham and where He changes Sarai's name to Sarah). In each of these passages we have the same verb as is used in Genesis 2:23 (the verb *qara'*), and in each case the person who gives the name is one in authority over the person who receives the name. Therefore when Adam gives to his wife the name "Woman," in terms of biblical patterns of thought this indicates a kind of authority that God gave to Adam, a leadership function that Eve did not have with respect to her husband.

We should notice here that Adam does not give the personal name "Eve" to his wife until Genesis 3:20 ("the man *called* [Hebrew *qārā'*] his wife's name Eve, because she was the mother of all living"). This is because in the creation story in Genesis 2 Adam is giving a broad category name to his wife, indicating the name that would be given to womanhood generally, and he is not giving specific personal names designating the character of the individual person.[14]

4. *The naming of the human race*: God named the human race "Man," not "Woman." Because the idea of naming is so important in the Old Testament, it is interesting what name God chose for the human race as a whole. We read: "When God created man, he made him in the likeness of God. Male and female he created them, and he blessed them and *named them Man* when they were created" (Gen. 5:1-2).

In the Hebrew text, the word that is translated "Man" is the Hebrew word *'ādām*. But this is by no means a gender-neutral term in

---

[14]Similarly, because God is having Adam examine and name the entire animal kingdom, it is likely that Adam gave names to one representative of each broad category or type of animal in Genesis 2:19-20 (such as "dog," "cat," "deer," or "lion," to use English equivalents). We hardly expect that he would have given individual, personal names (such as "Rover" or "Tabby" or "Bambi" or "Leo"), because those names would not have applied to others of the same kind. This distinction is missed by Gilbert Bilezikian (*Beyond Sex Roles*, 259-261) when he objects that Adam did not name Eve until Genesis 3:20, after the Fall. Adam did give her a specific personal name ("Eve") after the Fall, but he also gave her the general category name "Woman" before the Fall.

the eyes of the Hebrew reader at this point, because in the four chapters prior to Genesis 5:2, the Hebrew word *'ādām* has been used many times to speak of a male human being in distinction from a female human being. In the following list the roman word *man* represents this same Hebrew word *'ādām* in every case:

> *Genesis 2:22: "And the rib that the LORD God had taken from the* man *he made into a woman and brought her to the* man.*" (We should notice here that it does not say that God made the rib into another* 'ādām, *another "man," but that He made the rib into a "woman," which is a different Hebrew word.)*

> *Genesis 2:23: "Then the* man *said, 'This at last is bone of my bones and flesh of my flesh; she shall be called Woman. . . .'"*

> *Genesis 2:25: "And the* man *and his wife were both naked and were not ashamed."*

> *Genesis 3:8: " . . . and the* man *and his wife hid themselves from the presence of the LORD God . . ."*

> *Genesis 3:9: "But the LORD God called to the* man *and said to him, 'Where are you?'"*

> *Genesis 3:12: "The* man *said, 'The woman whom you gave to be with me, she gave me fruit of the tree, and I ate.'"*

> *Genesis 3:20: "The* man *called his wife's name Eve."*

When we come, then, to the naming of the human race in Genesis 5:2 (reporting an event before the Fall), it would be evident to the original readers that God was using a name that had clear male overtones or nuances. In fact, in the first four chapters of Genesis the word *'ādām* had been used thirteen times to refer not to a human being in general but to a male human being. In addition to the eight examples mentioned above, it was used a further five times as a proper name for Adam in distinction from Eve (Gen. 3:17, 21; 4:1, 25; 5:1).[15]

---

[15]There are actually more than thirteen instances where the Hebrew word *'ādām* referred to a male human being, because prior to the creation of Eve there are twelve additional instances where references to "the man" spoke only of a male person whom God had created: see Genesis 2:5, 7 (twice), 8, 15, 16, 18, 19 (twice), 20 (twice), 21. If we add these instances, there are twenty-five examples of *'ādām* used to refer to a male human being prior to Genesis 5:2. The male connotations of the word could not have been missed by the original readers.

We are not saying here that the word *'ādām* in the Hebrew Bible always refers to a male human being, for sometimes it has a broader sense and means something like "person." But here in the early chapters of Genesis the connection with the man in distinction from the woman is a very clear pattern. God gave the human race a name that, like the English word *man*, can either mean a male human being or can refer to the human race in general.

Does this make any difference? It does give a hint of male leadership, which God suggested in choosing this name. It is significant that God did not call the human race "Woman." (I am speaking, of course, of Hebrew equivalents to these English words.) Nor did he give the human race a name such as "humanity," which would have no male connotations and no connection with the man in distinction from the woman. Rather, he called the race "man." Raymond C. Ortlund rightly says, "God's naming of the race 'man' whispers male headship."[16]

While it is Genesis 5:2 that explicitly reports this naming process, it specifies that it is referring to an event prior to sin and the Fall: "When God created man, he made him in the likeness of God. Male and female he created them, and he blessed them and named them Man *when they were created*" (Gen. 5:1-2).

And, in fact, the name is already indicated in Genesis 1:27: "So God created *man* in his own image, in the image of God he created him; male and female he created them."

If the name *man* in English (as in Hebrew) did not suggest male leadership or headship in the human race, there would be no objection to using the word *man* to refer to the human race generally today. But it is precisely the hint of male leadership in the word that has led some people to object to this use of the word *man* and to attempt to substitute other terms instead.[17] Yet it is that same hint of male leadership that makes this precisely the best translation of Genesis 1:27 and 5:2.

5. *The primary accountability*: God spoke to Adam first after the Fall. After Adam and Eve sinned, they hid from the Lord among the

---

[16]Raymond C. Ortlund, Jr. in *Recovering Biblical Manhood and Womanhood*, 98.

[17]It is interesting to notice that several gender-neutral Bible translations have changed the word "man," which was standard in earlier English translations. The word "humankind" is used in the *New Revised Standard Version* in Genesis 1:26-27. The *New Living Translation* uses the word "people," while the inclusive language edition of the *New International Version* uses the phrase "human beings." In Genesis 5:2, various gender-neutral substitutes replace the name "man": "humankind" (NRSV), "human" (NLT), or "human beings" (*NIV—Inclusive Language Edition*, CEV, NCV).

trees of the garden. Then we read, "But the LORD God called to *the man* and said to *him*, 'Where are *you*?'" (Gen. 3:9).

In the Hebrew text, the expression "the man" and the pronouns "him" and "you" are all singular. Even though Eve had sinned first, God first summoned Adam to give account for what had happened. This suggests that Adam was the one primarily accountable for what had happened in his family.

An analogy to this is seen in the life of a human family. When a parent comes into a room where several children have been misbehaving and have left the room in chaos, the parent will probably summon the oldest and say, "What happened here?" This is because, though all are responsible for their behavior, the oldest child bears the primary responsibility.

In a similar way, when God summoned Adam to give an account, it indicated a primary responsibility for Adam in the conduct of his family. This is similar to the situation in Genesis 2:15-17, where God had given commands to Adam alone before the Fall, indicating there also a primary responsibility that belonged to Adam. By contrast, the serpent spoke to Eve first (Gen. 3:1), trying to get her to take responsibility for leading the family into sin, and inverting the order that God had established at creation.

6. *The purpose*: Eve was created as a helper for Adam, not Adam as a helper for Eve.

After God had created Adam and gave him directions concerning his life in the Garden of Eden, we read, "Then the LORD God said, 'It is not good that the man should be alone; I will make him a helper fit for him'" (Gen. 2:18).

It is true that the Hebrew word here translated "helper" (*'ezer*) is often used of God who is our helper elsewhere in the Bible. (See Ps. 33:20; 70:5; 115:9; etc.) But the word "helper" does not by itself decide the issue of what God intended the relationship between Adam and Eve to be. The nature of the activity of helping is so broad that it can be done by someone who has greater authority, someone who has equal authority, or someone who has lesser authority than the person being helped. For example, I can help my son do his homework.[18] Or I can help my neighbor move his sofa. Or my son can help me clean the garage. Yet the fact remains that *in the situation under consideration*, the person doing

---

[18]I am taking this analogy from Raymond C. Ortlund, Jr., in *Recovering Biblical Manhood and Womanhood*, 104.

the helping puts himself in a subordinate role to the person who has primary responsibility for carrying out the activity. Thus, even if I help my son with his homework, the primary responsibility for the homework remains his and not mine. I am the helper. And even when God helps us, with respect to the specific task at hand He still holds us primarily responsible for the activity, and He holds us accountable for what we do.

But Genesis 2 does not merely say that Eve functions as Adam's "helper" in one or two specific events. Rather, it says that God made Eve for the purpose of providing Adam with help, one who *by virtue of creation* would function as Adam's "helper": "Then the LORD God said, 'It is not good that the man should be alone; I will make him a helper fit for him'" (Gen. 2:18).

The Hebrew text can be translated quite literally as, "I will make *for him* [Hebrew *lo*] a helper fit for him." The apostle Paul understands this accurately because in 1 Corinthians 11 he writes, "for indeed man was not created for the woman's sake, but woman for the man's sake" (v. 9, NASB). Eve's role, and the purpose that God had in mind when He created her, was that she would be "for him . . . a helper."

Yet in the same sentence God emphasizes that she is not to help Adam as one who is inferior to him. Rather, she is to be a helper "fit for him," and here the Hebrew word *kenegdô* means "a help corresponding to him," that is, "equal and adequate to himself."[19] So Eve was created as a helper, but as a helper who was Adam's equal. She was created as one who differed from him, but who differed from him in ways that would exactly complement who Adam was.

7. *The conflict*: The curse brought a distortion of previous roles, not the introduction of new roles.

After Adam and Eve sinned, God spoke words of judgment to Eve:

> To the woman he said, "I will surely multiply your pain in childbearing; in pain you shall bring forth children. Your desire shall be for your husband, and he shall rule over you."
>
> —GEN. 3:16

The word translated "desire" is an unusual Hebrew word, *teshûqāh*. What is the meaning of this word? In this context and in this construction, it probably implies an aggressive desire, perhaps a desire to conquer or rule

---

[19]This is the definition given in Frances Brown, S. R. Driver, and Charles A. Briggs, *A Hebrew and English Lexicon of the Old Testament* (Oxford: Clarendon Press, 1968), 617.

over, or else an urge or impulse to oppose her husband, an impulse to act "against" him. This sense is seen in the only other occurrence of *teshûqāh* in all the books of Moses (Genesis, Exodus, Leviticus, Numbers, Deuteronomy), and the only other occurrence of *teshûqāh* plus the preposition *'el* in the whole Bible. That occurrence of the word is in the very next chapter of Genesis, in 4:7. God says to Cain, "Sin is crouching at the door, and its *desire* is for you, but you must master it" (NASB). Here the sense is very clear. God pictures sin as a wild animal waiting outside Cain's door, waiting to attack him, even to pounce on him and overpower him. In that sense, sin's "desire" or "instinctive urge" is "against" him.[20]

The striking thing about that sentence is what a remarkable parallel it is with Genesis 3:16. In the Hebrew text, six words are the same and are found in the same order in both verses. It is almost as if this other usage is put here by the author so that we would know how to understand the meaning of the term in Genesis 3:16. The expression in 4:7 has the sense, "desire, urge, impulse *against*" (or perhaps "desire to conquer, desire to rule over"). And that sense fits very well in Genesis 3:16 also.[21]

Some have assumed that "desire" in Genesis 3:16 refers to sexual desire. But that is highly unlikely because (1) the entire Bible views

---

[20]The ESV margin translates *teshûqāh* plus *'el* in Genesis 3:16 and 4:7 as "Or *against*." This seems to me to be the most accurate rendering. The preposition *'el* can take the meaning "against," as is clear from the next verse, Genesis 4:8, where "Cain rose up *against* (*'el*) his brother Abel and killed him." BDB gives sense 4 for *'el* as: "Where the motion or direction implied appears from the context to be of a hostile character, *'el* = *against*." They cite Genesis 4:8 and several other verses.

[21]The only other occurrence of the word *teshûqāh* in the entire Hebrew Old Testament is found in Song of Solomon 7:10 (v. 11 in Hebrew): "I am my beloved's, and his *desire* is for me" (emphasis added). There the word does not indicate a hostile or aggressive desire but indicates the man's sexual desire for his wife.

I have previously argued elsewhere that a positive kind of "desire to conquer" could be understood in Song 7:10, whereby it indicates the man's desire to have a kind of influence over his beloved that is appropriate to initiating and consummating the sexual relationship, an influence such that she would receive and yield to his amorous advances. This sense would be represented by the paraphrase, "His desire is to have me yield to him."

However, I am now inclined to think that the word *teshûqāh* itself does not signify anything so specific as "desire to conquer," but rather something more general such as "urge, impulse." (The word takes that sense in Mishnaic Hebrew, as indicated by David Talley in the following footnote.) In that case, Genesis 3:16 and 4:7 have the sense "desire, urge, impulse *against*," and Song 7:10 has the sense, "desire, urge, impulse *for*." This seems to me to fit better with the context of Song 7:10.

The difference in meaning may also be signaled by a different construction. The Genesis and Song of Solomon examples are not exactly parallel linguistically, because a different preposition follows the verb in Song of Solomon, and therefore the sense may be somewhat different. In Song 7:11 [10, English], *teshûqāh* is followed by *'al*, but it is followed by *'el* in Genesis 3:16 and 4:7.

(The preposition *'al* is misprinted as *'el* in Song 7:11 [10, English] as cited in BDB, 1003. BDB apparently does this because it follows the *Biblia Hebraica Stuttgartensia* editors (1334), who in the margin suggest changing the Hebrew text to *'el*, but this is mere conjecture with no

sexual desire within marriage as something positive, not as something evil or something that God imposed as a judgment; and (2) surely Adam and Eve had sexual desire for one another prior to their sin, for God had told them to "be fruitful and multiply" (Gen. 1:28), and certainly in an unfallen world, along with the command, God would have given the desire that corresponded to it. So "your desire shall be for your husband" cannot refer to sexual desire. It is much more appropriate to the context of a curse to understand this as an aggressive desire *against* her husband, one that would bring her into conflict with him.

Then God says with regard to Adam, "and he shall *rule* over you" (Gen. 3:16). The word here translated "rule" is the Hebrew term *māshal*. This term is common in the Old Testament, and it regularly, if not always, refers to ruling by greater power or force or strength. It is used of human military or political rulers, such as Joseph ruling over the land of Egypt (Gen. 45:26), or the Philistines ruling over Israel (Judg. 14:4; 15:11), or Solomon ruling over all the kingdoms that he had conquered (1 Kings 4:21). It is also used to speak of God ruling over the sea (Ps. 89:9) or God ruling over the earth generally (Ps. 66:7). Sometimes it refers to oppressive rulers who cause the people under them to suffer (Neh. 9:37; Isa. 19:4). In any case, the word does not signify one who leads among equals, but rather one who rules by virtue of power and strength, and sometimes even rules harshly and selfishly.

Once we understand these two terms, we can see much more clearly what was involved in the curse that God brought to Adam and Eve as punishment for their sins.

· One aspect of the curse was imposing *pain on Adam's particular area of responsibility*, raising food from the ground: "cursed is the ground because of you; in pain you shall eat of it all the days of your life; thorns and thistles it shall bring forth for you. . . . By the sweat of your face you shall eat bread, till you return to the ground" (Gen. 3:17-19). Another aspect of the curse was to impose *pain on Eve's particular area of responsibility*, the bearing of children: "I will surely multiply your pain in childbearing; in pain you shall bring forth children" (Gen. 3:16).

---

manuscript support. The LXX confirms the difference, translating with *pros* for *'el* in Genesis 3:16 and 4:7 but with *epi* for *'al* in Song 7:11 [10, English], which is what we would expect with a very literal translation.)

In any case, while the sense in Song 7:10 (11) is different, both the context and the construction are different, and this example is removed in time and authorship from Genesis 3:16 and must be given lower importance in understanding the meaning of the word in Genesis. Surely the sense cannot be "sexual desire" in Genesis 4:7, and it seems very unlikely in the context of Genesis 3:16 as well.

A third aspect of the curse was to introduce *pain and conflict into the relationship* between Adam and Eve. Prior to their sin, they had lived in the Garden of Eden in perfect harmony, yet with a leadership role belonging to Adam as the head of his family. But after the Fall, God introduced conflict in that Eve would have an inward urging and impulsion to oppose Adam, to resist Adam's leadership (the verb *teshûqāh*). "Your impulse, your desire, will be *against* your husband." And Adam would respond with a rule over Eve that came from his greater strength and aggressiveness, a rule that was forceful and at times harsh (the verb *māshal*). "And he because of his greater strength will rule over you." There would be pain in tilling the ground, pain in bearing children, and pain and conflict in their relationship.

It is crucial at this point for us to realize that *we ourselves are never to try to increase or perpetuate the results of the curse*. We should never try to promote or advocate Genesis 3:16 as something good! In fact, the entire Bible following after Genesis 3 is the story of God's working to overcome the effects of the curse that He in His justice imposed. Eventually God will bring in new heavens and a new earth, in which crops will come forth abundantly from the ground (Isa. 35:1-2; Amos 9:13; Rom. 8:20-21) and in which there is no more pain or suffering (Rev. 21:4).

So we ourselves should *never* try to perpetuate the elements of the curse! We should not plant thorns and weeds in our garden but rather overcome them. We should do everything we can to alleviate the pain of childbirth for women. And we should do everything we can to undo the conflict that comes about through women desiring to oppose or even control their husbands and their husbands ruling harshly over them.

Therefore Genesis 3:16 should never be used as a direct argument for male headship in marriage. But it does show us that the Fall brought about a *distortion* of previous roles, not the introduction of new roles. The distortion was that Eve would now rebel against her husband's authority, and Adam would misuse that authority to rule forcefully and even harshly over Eve.[22]

---

[22]The understanding of Genesis 3:16 as a hostile desire, or even a desire to rule over, has gained significant support among Old Testament commentators. It was first suggested by Susan T. Foh, "What Is the Woman's Desire?" in *Westminster Theological Journal* 37 (1975), 376-383. David Talley says the word is attested in Samaritan and Mishnaic Hebrew "with the meaning urge, craving, impulse" and says of Foh, "Her contention that the desire is a contention for leadership, a negative usage, seems probable for Gen. 3:16" (*New International Dictionary of New Testament Theology and Exegesis*, 5 vols., ed., Willem Van Gemeren, Vol. 4 [Grand Rapids, MI: Zondervan, 1991], 341, with reference to various commentators).

8. *The restoration*: When we come to the New Testament, salvation in Christ reaffirms the creation order.

If the previous understanding of Genesis 3:16 is correct, as we believe it is, then what we would expect to find in the New Testament is a reversal of this curse. We would expect to find an *undoing* of the wife's hostile or aggressive impulses against her husband and the husband's response of harsh rule over his wife.

In fact, that is exactly what we find. We read in the New Testament: "Wives, *be subject to your husbands*, as is fitting in the Lord. Husbands, *love your wives, and do not be harsh with them*" (Col. 3:18-19, NIV).

This command is an undoing of the impulse to oppose (Hebrew *teshûqāh*) and the harsh rule (Hebrew *māshal*) that God imposed at the curse.

What God does in the New Testament is reestablish the beauty of the relationship between Adam and Eve that existed from the moment they were created. Eve was subject to Adam as the head of the family. Adam loved his wife and was not harsh with her in his leadership. That is the pattern that Paul commands husbands and wives to follow.[23]

9. *The mystery*: Marriage from the beginning of creation was a picture of the relationship between Christ and the church.

When the apostle Paul discusses marriage and wishes to speak of the relationship between husband and wife, he does not look back to any sections of the Old Testament telling about the situation after sin came into the world. Rather, he looks all the way back to Genesis 2, prior to the Fall, and uses that creation order to speak of marriage:

"For this reason a man shall leave his father and mother and be joined to his wife, and the two shall become one flesh." [This is a quote from Gen. 2:24.] This mystery is a profound one, and I am saying that it refers to Christ and the church.

—EPH. 5:31-32, RSV

Now a "mystery" in Paul's writing is something that was understood only very faintly, if at all, in the Old Testament, but that is now made clearer in the New Testament. Here Paul makes clear the meaning of the

---

[23]There was a foreshadowing of these New Testament commands in the godly marriages found in the Old Testament and the honor given to women in passages such as those in Ruth, Esther, and Proverbs 31. But in the unfolding of God's plan of redemption, He waited until the New Testament to give the full and explicit directions for the marriage relationship that we find in Ephesians 5, Colossians 3, and 1 Peter 3.

"mystery" of marriage as God created it in the Garden of Eden. Paul is saying that the "mystery" of Adam and Eve, the meaning that was not previously understood, was that marriage "refers to Christ and the church."

In other words, although Adam and Eve did not know it, their relationship represented the relationship between Christ and the church. They were *created* to represent that relationship, and that is what all marriages are supposed to do. In that relationship Adam represents Christ, and Eve represents the church, because Paul says, "for the husband is the head of the wife *even as Christ is the head of the church*" (Eph. 5:23).

Now the relationship between Christ and the church is not culturally variable. It is the same for all generations. And it is not reversible. There is a leadership or headship role that belongs to Christ that the church does not have. Similarly, in marriage as God created it to be, there is a leadership role for the husband that the wife does not have. And for our purposes it is important to notice that this relationship was there from the beginning of creation, in the beautiful marriage between Adam and Eve in the Garden.

10. *The parallel with the Trinity*: The equality, differences, and unity between men and women reflect the equality, differences, and unity in the Trinity.

Though I list this here as the tenth reason why there were differences in roles between men and women from creation, I will not explain it at this point because by itself it constitutes "Key Issue #3" that I discuss below.

Conclusion: Here then are at least ten reasons showing differences in the roles of men and women before the Fall. Some reasons are not as forceful as others, though all have some force. Some of them whisper male headship, and some shout it clearly. But they form a cumulative case showing that Adam and Eve had distinct roles before the Fall, and that this was God's purpose in creating them.

But How Does It Work in Practice?

Perhaps I could say something at this point about how male-female equality together with male headship work out in actual practice. The situation I know best is my own marriage, so I will speak about that briefly.

In our marriage, Margaret and I talk frequently and at length about many decisions. Sometimes these are large decisions (such as buying a house or a car), and sometimes they are small decisions (such as where we should go for a walk together). I often defer to her wishes, and she often defers to mine, because we love each other. In almost every case, each of us has some wisdom and insight that the other does not have, and we have learned to listen to each other and to place much trust in each other's judgment. Usually we reach agreement on the decision. Very seldom will I do something that she does not think to be wise. She prays, she loves God, she is sensitive to the Lord's leading and direction, and I greatly respect her and the wisdom God gives her.

But in every decision, whether large or small, and whether we have reached agreement or not, the responsibility to make the decision still rests with me. I do not agree with those who say that male headship only makes a difference once in ten years or so when a husband and wife can't reach agreement. I think that male headship makes a difference in every decision that the couple makes every day of their married life. If there is genuine male headship, there is a quiet, subtle acknowledgment that the focus of the decision-making process is the husband, not the wife. And even though there will often be much discussion, and though there should be much mutual respect and consideration of each other, yet ultimately the responsibility to make the decision rests with the husband. And so in our marriage, the responsibility to make the decision rests with me.

This is not because I am wiser or a more gifted leader. It is because I am the husband, and God has given me that responsibility. In the face of cultural pressures to the contrary, I will not forsake this male headship, I will not deny this male headship, I will not be embarrassed by it.

This is something that is God-given. It is very good. It brings peace and joy to our marriage, and both Margaret and I are thankful for it.

Yet there are dangers of distortion in one direction or another. Putting this biblical pattern into practice in our daily lives is a challenge, because we can err in one direction or the other. There are errors of passivity, and there are errors of aggressiveness. This can be seen in the following chart:

	Errors of passivity	Biblical ideal	Errors of aggressiveness
Husband	Wimp	Loving, humble headship	Tyrant
Wife	Doormat	Joyful, intelligent submission	Usurper

The biblical ideal, in the center column, is loving, humble headship on the part of the husband, following Ephesians 5:23-33. The biblical ideal on the part of the wife is joyful, intelligent submission to and support of her husband's leadership, in accordance with Ephesians 5:22-24 and 31-33.

On the right side of the chart, the errors of aggressiveness are those that had their beginning, as we saw, in Genesis 3:16. The husband can become selfish, harsh, and domineering and act like a tyrant. This is not biblical headship but a tragic distortion of it. A wife can also demonstrate errors of aggressiveness when she resists and continually struggles against her husband's leadership, not supporting it, but fighting against it and creating conflict every step of the way. She can become a usurper, something that is a tragic distortion of the biblical pattern of equality in the image of God.

On the other hand, on the left side of the chart, are the opposite errors, the errors of passivity. A husband can abdicate his leadership and neglect his responsibilities. He does not discipline his children, and he sits and watches TV and drinks his beer and does nothing. The family is not going to church regularly, and he is passive and does nothing. The family keeps going further into debt, and he closes his eyes to it and does nothing. Some relative or friend is verbally harassing his wife, and he does nothing. This also is a tragic distortion of the biblical pattern. He has become a wimp.

A wife also can commit errors of passivity. Rather than participating actively in family decisions, rather than contributing her wisdom and insight that is so much needed, her only response to every question is, "Yes, dear, whatever you say." She knows her husband and her children are doing wrong, and she says nothing. Or her husband becomes verbally or physically abusive, and she never objects to him and never seeks church discipline or civil governmental intervention to bring about an end to the abuse. Or she never really expresses her own preferences with regard to friendships or family vacations or her own opinions regarding people or events, and she thinks what is required is that she be "submissive" to her husband. But this also is a tragic distortion of biblical patterns. She has become a doormat.

Now, we all have different backgrounds, personalities, and temperaments. We also have different areas of life in which sanctification is less complete. Therefore, some of us tend to be more prone toward errors of aggressiveness, and others of us tend to be more prone toward errors of passivity. We can even fall into errors of aggressiveness in our own homes and errors of passivity when we visit our in-laws! Or it can be the other way around. In order to maintain a healthy, biblical balance, we need to keep reading God's Word each day and continue to pray for God's help each day and continue to follow Christ in obedience to God's Word as best we can.

The Man's Responsibility to Provide for and Protect, and the Woman's Responsibility to Care for the Home and to Nurture Children

There are other differences in roles in addition to headship and submission. Two other aspects of male headship in marriage are the husband's responsibility to provide for his wife and family and to protect them. A corresponding responsibility on the part of the wife is to have primary responsibility to care for home and children. Each can help the other, but there remains a primary responsibility that is not shared equally. These responsibilities are mentioned in both the "Danvers Statement" and the Southern Baptist Convention/Campus Crusade for Christ statement. I will not discuss these in detail at this point but simply note that these additional aspects of differing roles are established in Scripture. Biblical support for the husband having the primary responsibility to provide for his family and the wife having primary responsibility to care for the household and children is found in Genesis 2:15 with 2:18-23; 3:16-17 (Eve is assumed to have the primary responsibility for childbearing, but Adam for tilling the ground to raise food, and pain is introduced into both of their areas of responsibility); Proverbs 31:10-31, especially vv. 13, 15, 21, 27; Isaiah 4:1 (shame at the tragic undoing of the normal order); 1 Timothy 5:8 (the Greek text does not specify "any man," but in the historical context that would have been the assumed referent except for unusual situations like a household with no father); 1 Timothy 5:10; 1 Timothy 5:3-16 (widows, not widowers, are to be supported by the church); Titus 2:5. I believe that a wife's created role as a "helper fit for him" (Gen. 2:18) also supports this distinction of roles. I do not think a wife would be fulfilling her role as "helper" if she became the permanent primary breadwinner, for then the husband would be the primary "helper."

Biblical support for the idea that the man has the primary responsibility to protect his family is found in Deuteronomy 20:7-8 (men go forth to war, not women, here and in many Old Testament passages); 24:5; Joshua 1:14; Judges 4:8-10 (Barak does not get the glory because he insisted that a woman accompany him into battle); Nehemiah 4:13-14 (the people are to fight for their brothers, homes, wives, and children, but it does not say they are to fight for their husbands!); Jeremiah 50:37 (it is the disgrace of a nation when its warriors become women); Nahum 3:13 ("Behold, your troops are women in your midst" is a taunt of derision); Matthew 2:13-14 (Joseph is told to protect Mary and baby Jesus by taking them to Egypt); Ephesians 5:25 (a husband's love should extend even to a willingness to lay down his life for his wife, something many soldiers in battle have done throughout history, to protect their families and homelands); 1 Peter 3:7 (a wife is a "weaker vessel," and therefore the husband, as generally stronger, has a greater responsibility to use his strength to protect his wife).

In addition, there is the complete absence of evidence from the other side. Nowhere can we find Scripture encouraging women to be the primary means of support while their husbands care for the house and children. Nowhere can we find Scripture encouraging women to be the primary protectors of their husbands. Certainly women can help in these roles as time and circumstances allow (see Gen. 2:18-23), but they are not the ones primarily responsible for them.

Finally, there is the evidence of the internal testimony from both men's and women's hearts. There is something in a man that says, "I don't want to be dependent on a woman to provide for me in the long term. I want to be the one responsible to provide for the family, the one my wife looks to and depends on for support." Personally, I have never met a man who does not feel some measure of shame at the idea of being supported by his wife in the long term. (I recognize that in many families there is a temporary reversal of roles due to involuntary unemployment or while the husband is getting further education for his career, and in those circumstances these are entirely appropriate arrangements; yet the longer they go on, the more strain they put on a marriage. I also recognize that permanent disability on the part of the husband, or the absence of a husband in the home, can create a necessity for the wife to be the primary provider; but every family in which that happens will testify to the unusual stress it brings and to the fact that they wish it did not have to be so.) On the other hand, there is something in a woman that says, "I want my husband to provide for me, to give me the security of knowing that we will have enough to buy groceries and pay the bills. It feels right to me to look to him and depend on him for that responsibility." Personally, I have never met a woman who did not want her husband to provide that sense of security for her.[24]

Some Egalitarian Objections to Male Headship in Marriage

Egalitarians raise a number of objections to the idea that men and women have different roles in marriage as part of the created order, different roles that should find expression in marriages today as well. At this point I will mention three of the most common objections:

> 1. Galatians 3:28 abolishes role distinctions in marriage.
> 2. Mutual submission in Ephesians 5:21 nullifies male authority in marriage.
> 3. "The husband is the head of the wife" (Eph. 5:23) does not indicate authority for the husband, because "head" means "source" or something else, but not "person in authority."

I will consider these three objections briefly at this point, since they are treated more extensively elsewhere.[25]

OBJECTION #1: GALATIANS 3:28 ABOLISHES ROLE DISTINCTIONS IN MARRIAGE

In this verse Paul says, "There is neither Jew nor Greek, there is neither slave nor free, there is neither male nor female, for *you are all one in Christ Jesus.*" Egalitarians frequently claim that if there is "neither male nor female," then distinctions in role based on our gender are abolished because we are now "all one in Christ Jesus."

The problem is that this is not what the verse says. To say that we are "one" means that we are *united*, that there should be no factions or divisions among us, that there should be no sense of pride and superiority or jealousy and inferiority between these groups that viewed themselves as so distinct in the ancient world. Jews should no longer think themselves superior to Greeks, freed men should not think themselves superior to slaves, and men should no longer think them-

---

[24]For some further discussion, see John Piper, "A Vision of Biblical Complementarity: Manhood and Womanhood Defined According to the Bible," in *Recovering Biblical Manhood and Womanhood*, 31-59. See also Dorothy Patterson, "The High Calling of Wife and Mother in Biblical Perspective," 364-377 in the same volume.

[25]See Richard W. Hove, "Does Galatians 3:28 Negate Gender-Specific Roles?" in this present volume (Chapter 4), and also his book *Equality in Christ? Galatians 3:28 and the Gender Dispute* (Wheaton, IL: Crossway Books, 1999).

selves superior to women. They are all parts of one body in Christ, and all share in equal value and dignity as members of one body in Christ.

But, as Richard Hove has demonstrated in detail elsewhere in this volume,[26] when the Bible says that several things are "one," it never joins things that are exactly the same. Rather, it says things that are different, things that are diverse, share some kind of unity. So in Romans 12:4-5 we read:

> For as in one body we have many members, and the members do not all have the same function, so we, though many, are one body in Christ, and individually members one of another. (emphasis added)

Paul does not mean to say that all the members of the body are the *same*, for, as anyone can see, a body has hands and feet and eyes and ears, and all the "members" are different, and they have different functions, though they are "one body."

Similarly, using the same construction,[27] Hove found that Paul can say, "*Now he who plants and he who waters are one*; but each will receive his own reward according to his own labor" (1 Cor. 3:8, NASB). Now planting and watering are two different activities done by different persons in Paul's example. Those persons are not reduced to sameness, nor are they required to act in exactly the same way; but they are still "one" because they have a kind of unity of purpose and goal.

And so Galatians 3:28 simply says that we have a special kind of *unity* in the body of Christ. Our differences as male and female are not obliterated by this unity; rather, the unity is beautiful in God's sight particularly because it is a unity of different kinds of people.

Surely this verse cannot abolish all differences between men and women, not only because Paul himself elsewhere commands husbands and wives to act differently according to their different roles, but also because marriage in Scripture from beginning to end is intended by God to be only between one man and one woman, not between one man and another man or one woman and another woman. If Galatians

---

[26]See Hove, *Equality in Christ*, and his essay, "Does Galatians 3:28 Negate Gender-Specific Roles?" mentioned in the footnote above.

[27]Hove ran forty-five computer searches on Greek literature near the time of the New Testament. He reports finding sixteen examples of Greek expressions from the New Testament and other ancient literature that use the verb "to be" (*eimi*) plus the number "one" (Greek *heis/mia/hen*) and finds that the expression is never used to indicate unity among things that are identical, but always among things that are different and have different functions but that also share something in common that gives them a kind of unity (72-76).

3:28 truly abolished all differences between men and women, then how could anyone say that homosexual marriage was wrong? But homosexual conduct is surely forbidden by Scripture (see Rom. 1:26-27; 1 Cor. 6:9; 1 Tim. 1:10). (And our egalitarian friends within the evangelical world agree that homosexual conduct is prohibited by Scripture.) Therefore Galatians 3:28 does not abolish differences in roles between men and women.

The egalitarian objection from Galatians 3:28, therefore, is not persuasive. Egalitarians are simply trying to make the verse say something it does not say and never has said and never will say. Galatians 3:28 tells us that we are united in Christ and that we should never be boastful or arrogant against others and should never feel inferior or without value in the body of Christ. But the verse does not say that men and women are the same or that they have to act the same.

OBJECTION #2: MUTUAL SUBMISSION IN EPHESIANS 5:21 NULLIFIES MALE AUTHORITY IN MARRIAGE

Ephesians 5:21 says, "Be subject to one another out of reverence for Christ" (RSV). Egalitarians say that this verse teaches "mutual submission," and that means that just as wives have to submit to their husbands, *so husbands have to submit to their wives.* Doesn't the text say that we have to submit "to one another"? And this means there is no unique kind of submission that a wife owes to her husband, and no unique kind of authority that a husband has over his wife.

Sometimes egalitarians will say something like this: "Of course I believe that a wife should be subject to her husband. And a husband should also be subject to his wife." Or an egalitarian might say, "I will be subject to my husband as soon as he is subject to me." And so, as egalitarians understand Ephesians 5:21, there is no difference in roles between men and women. There is no unique leadership role, no unique authority, for the husband. There is simply "mutual submission."[28]

I have to affirm at the outset that people can mean different things by "mutual submission." There is a sense of the phrase *mutual submission* that is different from an egalitarian view and that does not nullify the husband's authority within marriage. If "mutual submission"

---

[28]In fact, our egalitarian friends have a journal called *Mutuality*, published by the organization Christians for Biblical Equality.

means being considerate of one another and caring for one another's needs and being thoughtful of one another, then of course I would agree that mutual submission is a good thing.

However, egalitarians mean something so different by this phrase, and they have used this phrase so often to nullify male authority within marriage, that I think the expression *mutual submission* only leads to confusion if we go on using it.[29]

In previous generations some people did speak about "mutual submission," but never in the sense in which egalitarians today understand it. In his study of the history of the interpretation of Ephesians 5:21, Daniel Doriani has demonstrated that a number of earlier writers thought there was a kind of "mutual submission" taught in the verse, but that such "submission" took very different forms for those *in authority* and for those *under authority*. They took it to mean that those in authority should govern wisely and with sacrificial concern for those under their authority. But Doriani found no author in the history of the church prior to the advent of feminism in the last half of the twentieth century who thought that "be subject to one another" in Ephesians 5:21 nullified the authority of the husband within marriage.[30]

What exactly is wrong with understanding Ephesians 5:21 to teach mutual submission? I have addressed that question in some detail in another essay in this volume, but I could say briefly at this point that the egalitarian view is inconsistent with the patterns of submission to authority that Paul specifies in this very context (wives to husbands, children to parents, and servants to masters), does not fit with the strongly established meaning of *hypotassō*, which always indicates submission to an authority, is inconsistent with the parallel to the church's submission to Christ in Ephesians 5:24, and is inconsistent with the

---

[29]When the Southern Baptist Convention was debating its statement on marriage and the family, I am told there was a motion from the floor to add "mutual submission" to the statement, and that Dorothy Patterson, a member of the drafting committee for the statement and one of the original members of the Council on Biblical Manhood and Womanhood, spoke against the motion and explained how egalitarians have used it to deny any sense of male authority within marriage. The motion was defeated, and appropriately so. If "mutual submission" had been added to the Southern Baptist statement, in effect it would have torpedoed the whole statement, because it would have watered it down so much that people from almost any position could sign it, and it would have affirmed no unique male authority within marriage. (These events were reported to me by friends who were present when the statement was being debated on the floor of the Southern Baptist Convention in the summer of 1998.)

[30]See Doriani, "The Historical Novelty of Egalitarian Interpretations of Ephesians 5:21," Chapter 6 in this volume.

other directives to wives to be subject to their husbands in Colossians 3:18, Titus 2:5, and 1 Peter 3:1.[31]

I conclude, in that longer study, that we can paraphrase Ephesians 5:21 as follows: "Be subject to others in the church who are in positions of authority over you."[32] I do not believe any idea of mutual submission is taught in Ephesians 5:21. The idea itself is self-contradictory if *hypotassō* means here (as it does everywhere else) "be subject to an authority."

With respect to your own churches, if you want to add a statement on men and women in marriage to your governing document or publish it as a policy statement (as did the Southern Baptist Convention and Campus Crusade for Christ), and if in the process someone proposes to add the phrase "mutual submission" to the document, I urge you strongly not to agree to it. In the sense that egalitarians understand the phrase *mutual submission*, the idea is found nowhere in Scripture, and it actually nullifies the teaching of significant passages of Scripture.

How then should we respond when people say they favor mutual submission? We need to find out what they mean by it, and if they do not wish to advocate an egalitarian view, we need to see if we can suggest alternative wording that would speak to their concerns more precisely. Some people who hold a fully complementarian view of marriage do use the phrase *mutual submission* and intend it in a way that does not nullify male leadership in marriage. I have found that some people who want to use this language may simply have genuine concerns that men should not act like dictators or tyrants in their marriages. If this is what they are seeking to guard against by the phrase *mutual submission*, then I suggest trying this alternative wording, which is found in the Campus Crusade for Christ statement:

> In a marriage lived according to these truths, the love between husband and wife will show itself in listening to each other's viewpoints, valuing each other's gifts, wisdom, and desires, honoring one another in public and in private, and always seeking to bring benefit, not harm, to one another.

---

[31]See Wayne Grudem, "The Myth of Mutual Submission As an Interpretation of Ephesians 5:21," Chapter 7 in this volume.

[32]It is interesting that the King James Version showed an understanding of the sense of *allēlous* in this passage. It translated the verse, "submitting yourselves *one to another* in the fear of God." In fact, when *allēlous* takes the sense "some to others," the King James Version often signaled that by phrases such as "one to another."

OBJECTION #3: "THE HUSBAND IS THE HEAD OF THE WIFE" DOES NOT
INDICATE AUTHORITY FOR THE HUSBAND, BECAUSE "HEAD" MEANS
"SOURCE" OR SOMETHING ELSE, BUT NOT "PERSON IN AUTHORITY"

In 1 Corinthians 11:3 Paul says:

Now I want you to realize that the head *[Greek* kephalē*] of every
man is Christ, and the* head *of the woman is man, and the* head *of
Christ is God. (NIV)*

And in Ephesians 5:23 Paul makes this statement:

For the husband is the head *of the wife just as Christ is the* head *of the
church, his body, and is himself its Savior.*

It is important to realize the decisive significance of these verses,
and particularly of Ephesians 5:23, for the current controversy. If the
word "head" means "person in authority over," then there is a unique
authority that belongs to the husband in marriage and is parallel to
Christ's authority over the church, and then the egalitarians have lost
the debate.[33]

So what have egalitarians done to give a different meaning to the
statement, "The husband is the head of the wife just as Christ is the
head of the church"? The most common approach has been to say that
the word translated "head" (Greek *kephalē*) does not mean "person in
authority over" but has some other meaning, especially the meaning
"source." Thus the husband is the *source* of the wife (an allusion to the
creation of Eve from Adam's side in Gen. 2), as Christ is the *source* of
the church. The problem of this interpretation is that it does not fit the
evidence.

In 1985 I looked up 2,336 examples of the word "head" (*kephalē*)
in ancient Greek literature, using texts from Homer in the eighth century B.C. up to some church fathers in the fourth century A.D. I found
that in those texts the word *kephalē* was applied to many people in
authority (when it was used in a metaphorical sense to say that person
A was the head of person or persons B), but it was never applied to a

---

[33]I realize that a few egalitarians claim that Paul's teaching only applied to his time in history
and is not applicable to us today. This particular position is not affected by disputes over the
meaning over the word "head," but it is very difficult to sustain in light of the parallel with Christ
and the church, and in light of Paul's tying it to the statements about marriage before there was
sin in the world (Eph. 5:31-32, quoting Gen. 2:24).

person without governing authority. Several studies took issue with part or all of my conclusions, and I have considered those in two subsequent studies, with my fundamental claims about the meaning of *kephalē*, it seems to me, further established by additional new evidence. I have given more detail on those studies in another chapter in this volume.[34]

The fact remains that no one has yet produced one text in ancient Greek literature (from the eighth century B.C. to the fourth century A.D.) where a person is called the *kephalē* ("head") of another person or group *and that person is not the one in authority over that other person or group.* The alleged meaning "source without authority," now seventeen years after the publication of my 1985 study of 2,336 examples of *kephalē*, has still not been supported with *any* citation of *any* text in ancient Greek literature. Over fifty examples of *kephalē* meaning "ruler, authority over" have been found, but no examples of the meaning of "source without authority."

The question is this: Why should we give *kephalē* in the New Testament a sense that it is nowhere attested to have, and that, when applied to persons, no Greek lexicon has ever given to it?

So the egalitarian objection also fails to be convincing, and we are right to conclude that the Bible gives husbands the responsibility of a unique leadership role, a unique authority, in the marriage.

KEY ISSUE 3: THE EQUALITY AND DIFFERENCES BETWEEN MEN AND WOMEN REFLECT THE EQUALITY AND DIFFERENCES IN THE TRINITY

This point may sound obscure, but it is at the heart of the controversy, and it shows why much more is at stake than the meaning of one or two words in the Bible, or one or two verses. Much more is at stake even than how we live in our marriages. Here we are talking about the nature of God Himself.

In 1 Corinthians 11 Paul writes, "But I want you to understand

---

[34]For details, see Wayne Grudem, "The Meaning of κεφαλή ('Head'): An Evaluation of New Evidence, Real or Alleged," Chapter 5 in this present volume. That chapter is a reprint with only slight modifications of my article, "The Meaning of *kephalē* ('Head'): An Analysis of New Evidence, Real and Alleged," *JETS* 44/1 (March 2001), 25-65.

My two earlier studies on the meaning of *kephalē* were "The Meaning of *kephalē* ('Head'): A Response to Recent Studies," *Trinity Journal* 11 NS (Spring 1990), 3-72 (reprinted in *Recovering Biblical Manhood and Womanhood: A Response to Evangelical Feminism,* 425-468) and "Does *kephalē* ('Head') Mean 'Source' or 'Authority Over' in Greek Literature? A Survey of 2,336 Examples," Appendix in *The Role Relationship of Men and Women* (rev. ed.), George W. Knight III (Chicago: Moody, 1985), 49-80 (also printed in *Trinity Journal* 6 NS [Spring 1985], 38-59).

that the *head* of every man is Christ, the *head* of a wife is her husband, and the *head* of Christ is God" (v. 3).

In this verse, the word "head" refers to one who is in a position of authority over the other, as this Greek word (*kephalē*) uniformly does whenever it is used in ancient literature to say that one person is "head of" another person or group.[35] So Paul is here referring to a relationship of authority between God the Father and God the Son, and he is making a parallel between that relationship in the Trinity and the relationship between the husband and wife in marriage. This is an important parallel because it shows that there can be equality and differences between persons at the same time. We can illustrate that in the following diagram, where the arrows indicate authority over the person to whom the arrow points:

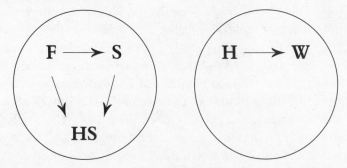

Just as the Father and Son are equal in deity and are equal in all their attributes, but different in role, so husband and wife are equal in personhood and value, but are different in the roles that God has given them. Just as God the Son is eternally subject to the authority of God the Father, so God has planned that wives would be subject to the authority of their own husbands.

Scripture frequently speaks of the Father-Son relationship within the Trinity, a relationship in which the Father "gave" His only Son (John 3:16) and "sent" the Son into the world (John 3:17, 34; 4:34; 8:42; Gal. 4:4; etc.), a relationship in which the Father "predestined" us to be conformed to the image of His Son (Rom 8:29; cf. 1 Pet. 1:2) and "chose us" in the Son "before the foundation of the world" (Eph. 1:4). The Son is obedient to the commands of the Father (John 12:49) and says that He comes to do "the will of him who sent me" (John 4:34; 6:38).

---

[35]See my extended discussion of the meaning of *kephalē* as indicated in footnote 34 above.

These relationships are never reversed. Never does Scripture say that the Son sends the Father into the world, or that the Holy Spirit sends the Father or the Son into the world, or that the Father obeys the commands of the Son or the Holy Spirit. Never does Scripture say that the Son predestined us to be conformed to the image of the Father. The role of planning, directing, sending, and commanding the Son belongs to the Father only.

And these relationships are eternal, for the Father predestined us in the Son "before the foundation of the world" (Eph. 1:4), requiring that the Father has eternally been Father, and the Son has eternally been Son. If the Father's love is seen in that He "gave his only Son" (John 3:16), then the Father had to be Father and the Son had to be Son before He came into the world. The Father did not give someone who was just another divine person in the Trinity; He gave the one who was His only Son, the one who eternally had been His Son.

It was also this way in the creation of the world, where the Father initiated and commanded and created through the Son. The Son was the powerful Word of God who carried out the commands of the Father, for "all things were made through him" (John 1:3). The Son is the one "through whom" God "created the world" (Heb. 1:2). All things were created by the Father working through the Son, for "there is one God, the Father, *from* whom are all things . . . and one Lord, Jesus Christ, *through* whom are all things" (1 Cor. 8:6, emphasis added). Nowhere does Scripture reverse this and say that the Son created "through" the Father.

The Son sits at the Father's right hand (Rom. 8:34; Heb. 1:3, 13; 1 Pet. 3:22; etc.); the Father does not sit at the Son's right hand. And for all eternity the Son will be subject to the Father, for after the last enemy, death, is destroyed, "the Son himself will also be subjected to him who put all things under him, that God may be everything to every one" (1 Cor. 15:28, RSV).

We see from these passages then that *the idea of headship and submission within a personal relationship* did not begin with the Council on Biblical Manhood and Womanhood in 1987. Nor did it begin with some writings of the apostle Paul in the first century. Nor did it begin with a few patriarchal men in a patriarchal society in the Old Testament. Nor did the idea of headship and submission begin with Adam and Eve's fall into sin in Genesis 3. In fact, the idea of headship and submission did not even begin with the creation of Adam and Eve in Genesis 1—2.

No, the idea of headship and submission existed *before creation*. It began in the relationship between the Father and Son in the Trinity. The Father has eternally had a leadership role, an authority to initiate and direct, that the Son does not have. Similarly, the Holy Spirit is subject to both the Father and Son and plays yet a different role in creation and in the work of salvation.

When did the idea of headship and submission begin then? *The idea of headship and submission never began!* It has *always existed* in the eternal nature of God Himself. And in this most basic of all authority relationships, authority is not based on gifts or ability (for the Father, Son, and Holy Spirit are equal in attributes and perfections). It is just there. Authority belongs to the Father not because he is wiser or because He is a more skillful leader, but just because he is the Father.

Authority and submission between the Father and the Son, and between both Father and Son and the Holy Spirit, is the fundamental difference between the persons of the Trinity. They don't differ in any attributes, but only in how they relate to each other. And that relationship is one of leadership and authority on the one hand and voluntary, willing, joyful submission to that authority on the other hand.

We can learn from this relationship among the members of the Trinity that submission to a rightful authority is a noble virtue. It is a privilege. It is something good and desirable. It is the virtue that has been demonstrated by the eternal Son of God *forever*. It is His glory, the glory of the Son as He relates to His father.

In modern society, we tend to think in this way: If you are a person who has authority over another, that's a good thing. If you are someone who has to submit to an authority, that's a bad thing. But that is the world's viewpoint, and it is not true. Submission to a rightful authority is a good and noble and wonderful thing, because it reflects the interpersonal relationships within God Himself.

We can say then that a relationship of authority and submission between equals, with mutual giving of honor, is the most fundamental and most glorious interpersonal relationship in the universe. Such a relationship allows interpersonal differences without "better" or "worse," without "more important" and "less important."

And when we begin to dislike *the very idea of authority and submis-*

sion—not distortions and abuses, but the very idea—we are tampering with something very deep. We are beginning to dislike God Himself.

Now this truth about the Trinity creates a problem for egalitarians within the church. They try to force people to choose between equality and authority. They say, if you have male headship, then you can't be equal. Or if you are equal, then you can't have male headship. And our response is that you can have both—just look at the Trinity. Within the being of God, you have both equality and authority.

In reply to this, egalitarians should have said, "Okay, we agree on this much. In God you *can* have equality and differences at the same time." In fact, some egalitarians have said this very thing.[36] But some prominent egalitarians have taken a different direction, one that is very troubling. Both Gilbert Bilezikian and Stanley Grenz have now written that they think there is "mutual submission" within the Trinity. They say that the Father also submits to the Son.[37] This is their affirmation even though no passage of Scripture affirms such a relationship, and even though this has never been the orthodox teaching of the Christian church throughout 2,000 years. But so deep is their commitment to an egalitarian view of men and women within marriage that they will modify the doctrine of the Trinity and remake the Trinity in the image of egalitarian marriage if it seems necessary to maintain their position.

KEY ISSUE 4: THE EQUALITY AND DIFFERENCES BETWEEN MEN AND WOMEN ARE VERY GOOD

This is a key issue because in today's hostile culture, we might be embarrassed to talk about God-given differences between men and women. We don't want to be attacked or laughed at by others. Perhaps

---

[36]See Craig Keener's affirmation of an eternal subordination of the Son to the Father in "Is Subordination Within the Trinity Really Heresy? A Study of John 5:18 in Context," *Trinity Journal* 20 NS (1999), 39-51.

[37]For a fuller discussion of egalitarian tampering with the doctrine of the Trinity see Bruce Ware, "Tampering with the Trinity: Does the Son Submit to His Father?," Chapter 8 in this volume. The primary statements by Bilezikian and Grenz are found in Gilbert Bilezikian, "Hermeneutical Bungee-Jumping: Subordination in the Godhead," *Journal of the Evangelical Theological Society* (JETS), 40/1 (March 1997), 57-68; and Stanley J. Grenz, "Theological Foundations for Male-Female Relationships," JETS 41/4 (December 1998), 615-630.

A survey of historical evidence showing affirmation of the eternal subordination of the Son to the authority of the Father is found in Stephen D. Kovach and Peter R. Schemm, Jr., "A Defense of the Doctrine of the Eternal Subordination of the Son," in JETS 42/3 (Sept. 1999), 461-476. See also Wayne Grudem, *Systematic Theology* (Leicester: IVP, and Grand Rapids, MI: Zondervan, 1994), 248-252.

we fear that someone will take offense if we talk clearly about God-given differences between men and women. (However, there is more acknowledgment of male/female differences in the general culture today than there was a few years ago. A number of secular books such as John Gray's *Men Are from Mars, Women Are from Venus* have once again made it acceptable to talk about *at least some differences* between men and women, though the idea of a husband's authority and the wife's submission within marriage still seems to be taboo in the general culture.)[38]

The fundamental statement of the excellence of the way God made us as men and women is found in Genesis 1:31: "And God saw everything that he had made, and behold, *it was very good.*" Just four verses after the Bible tells us that God made us "male and female," it tells us that God looked at everything He had made, *including Adam and Eve created in His image,* and His evaluation of what He saw was that it was "very good." The way God created us as men and women, equal in His image and different in roles, was very good. And if it is very good, then we can make some other observations about the created order.

This created order is *fair.* Our egalitarian friends argue that it's "not fair" for men to have a leadership role in the family simply because they are men. But if this difference is based on God's assignment of roles from the beginning, then it *is* fair. Does the Son say to the Father, "It's not fair for You to be in charge simply because You are the Father"? Does the Son say to the Father, "You've been in charge for fifteen billion years, and now it's My turn for the next fifteen billion"? No! Absolutely not! Rather, He fulfilled the Psalm that said, "I desire to do your will, O my God; your law is within my heart" (Ps. 40:8; compare Heb. 10:7). And of his relationship with the Father, He said, "I always do the things that are pleasing to him" (John 8:29). He said, "I have come down from heaven, not to do my own will but the will of him who sent me" (John 6:38). The order of relationships within the Trinity is fair. And the order of relationships established by God for marriage is fair.

This created order is also *best for us,* because it comes from an all-wise Creator. This created order truly honors men and women. It does not lead to abuse but guards against it, because both men and women are equal in value before God. It does not suppress women's gifts and

---

[38]See John Gray, *Men Are from Mars, Women Are from Venus* (New York: HarperCollins, 1992), and several other books written by Gray on a similar theme; see also Debra Tannen, *You Just Don't Understand: Women and Men in Conversation* (New York: Ballantine Books, 1990).

wisdom and insight, as people have sometimes done in the past, but it encourages them.

This created order is also a *mystery*. I have been married to one very wonderful woman for thirty-two years. I cannot understand her. Just when I think I understand her, she surprises me again. Marriage is a challenge! And it's also fun. But in our relationships with each other as men and women, I think in this life there will always be elements of surprise, always elements of mystery, always aspects of difference that we cannot fully understand but simply enjoy.

This created order is also *beautiful*. God took delight in it and thought it was "very good." When it is functioning in the way that God intended, we will enjoy this relationship and will delight in it, because there is a Godlike quality about it. And in fact, though some elements of society have been pushing in the opposite direction for several decades, there is much evidence from natural law—from our observation of the world and our inner sense of right and wrong—that men and women have a sense that different roles within marriage are *right*. This is what we meant when we said in the "Danvers Statement," "Distinctions in masculine and feminine roles are ordained by God and should find an echo in every human heart" (Affirmation 2). God's created order for marriage is beautiful because it is God's way to bring amazing *unity* to people who are so *different* as men and women.

The beauty of God's created order for marriage finds expression in our sexuality within marriage. "Therefore a man shall leave his father and his mother and hold fast to his wife, and they shall become one flesh"(Gen. 2:24). From the beginning God designed our sexuality so that it reflects unity and differences and beauty all at the same time. As husband and wife, we are most attracted to the parts of each other that are the most different. Our deepest unity—physical and emotional and spiritual unity—comes at the point where we are most different. In our physical union as God intended it, there is no dehumanization of women and no emasculation of men, but there is equality and honor for both the husband and the wife. And there is one of our deepest human joys and our deepest expression of unity.

This means that sexuality within marriage is precious to God. It is designed by Him to show *equality* and *difference* and *unity* all at the same time. It is a great mystery how this can be so, and it is also a great blessing and joy. Moreover, God has ordained that from that sexual union

comes the most amazing, the most astounding event—the creation of
a new human being in the image of God!

Within this most intimate of human relationships, we show
equality and *difference* and *unity,* and much Godlikeness all at once. Glory
be to God!

KEY ISSUE 5: THIS IS A MATTER OF OBEDIENCE TO THE BIBLE

Why did the Southern Baptist Convention in June 1998, for the first
time since 1963, add to its statement of faith and include in that addition a statement that men and women are equal in God's image but different in their roles in marriage?[39] Why, shortly after that, did over 100
Christian leaders sign a full-page ad in *USA Today* saying, "Southern
Baptists, you are right. We stand with you"[40]? Why did Campus Crusade
for Christ, after forty years of no change in their doctrinal policies,
endorse a similar statement as the policy of their organization in 1999?[41]

---

[39]This is the text of the June 1998 addition to the Southern Baptist Convention's statement,
"The Baptist Faith and Message":

XVIII. The Family

God has ordained the family as the foundational institution of human society. It is composed of persons related to one another by marriage, blood, or adoption.

Marriage is the uniting of one man and one woman in covenant commitment for a life-
time. It is God's unique gift to reveal the union between Christ and His church and to provide for the man and the woman in marriage the framework for intimate companionship,
the channel of sexual expression according to biblical standards, and the means for procreation of the human race.

The husband and wife are of equal worth before God, since both are created in God's
image. The marriage relationship models the way God relates to His people. A husband is
to love his wife as Christ loved the church. He has the God-given responsibility to provide
for, to protect, and to lead his family. A wife is to submit herself graciously to the servant
leadership of her husband even as the church willingly submits to the headship of Christ.
She, being in the image of God as is her husband and thus equal to him, has the God-given
responsibility to respect her husband and to serve as his helper in managing the household
and nurturing the next generation.

Children, from the moment of conception, are a blessing and heritage from the Lord.
Parents are to demonstrate to their children God's pattern for marriage. Parents are to teach
their children spiritual and moral values and to lead them, through consistent lifestyle example and loving discipline, to make choices based on biblical truth. Children are to honor and
obey their parents.

Genesis 1:26-28; 2:15-25; 3:1-20; Exodus 20:12; Deuteronomy 6:4-9; Joshua 24:15; 1
Samuel 1:26-28; Psalms 51:5; 78:1-8; 127; 128; 139:13-16; Proverbs 1:8; 5:15-20; 6:20-22;
12:4; 13:24; 14:1; 17:6; 18:22; 22:6, 15; 23:13-14; 24:3; 29:15, 17; 31:10-31; Ecclesiastes 4:9-
12; 9:9; Malachi 2:14-16; Matthew 5:31-32; 18:2-5; 19:3-9; Mark 10:6-12; Romans 1:18-32;
1 Corinthians 7:1-16; Ephesians 5:21-33; 6:1-4; Colossians 3:18-21; 1 Timothy 5:8, 14; 2
Timothy 1:3-5; Titus 2:3-5; Hebrews 13:4; 1 Peter 3:1-7.

In addition, in June 2000, the SBC also added the following sentence to Article VI, "The
Church": "While both men and women are gifted for service in the church, the office of pastor is limited to men as qualified by Scripture."

[40]*USA Today,* August 26, 1998, 5D.

[41]See above for a discussion of the Campus Crusade policy statement.

All of this is because many Christian leaders are beginning to say, "The egalitarian view just *cannot* be proven from Scripture."

Twenty-five years ago there were many questions of differences in interpretation, and both the egalitarian position and the complementarian position were found within evangelical groups. Over the last twenty-five years, we have seen extensive discussion and argument, and we have seen hundreds of articles and books published.

But now it seems to me that people are beginning to look at the situation differently. The egalitarian viewpoint, which was novel within evangelicalism twenty-five years ago, has had great opportunity to defend itself. The arguments are all out on the table, and the detailed studies of words of the Bible, the technical questions of grammar, and the extensive studies of background literature and history have been carried out. There are dozens and dozens of egalitarian books denying differences in male and female roles within marriage, but they now seem to be repeating the same arguments over and over. The egalitarians have not had any new breakthroughs, any new discoveries that lend substantial strength to their position.

So now it seems to me that many people in leadership are deciding that the egalitarian view is just not what the Bible teaches. And they are deciding that it will not be taught in their churches. And then they add to their statements of faith. Then the controversy is essentially over, for that group at least, for the next ten or twenty years.

James Dobson saw the wisdom of this. After Campus Crusade announced its policy in June 1999, Dr. Dobson's newsletter in September 1999, on the front page, said, "We applaud our friends at Campus Crusade for taking this courageous stance." He quoted the statement in full, and then he said:

> It is our prayer that additional denominations and parachurch organizations will join with SBC in adopting this statement on marriage and the family. Now is the time for Christian people to identify themselves unreservedly with the truths of the Bible, whether popular or not.[42]

Our egalitarian friends did not appreciate this statement by Dr. Dobson. In fact, they were greatly troubled by it. In the Spring 2000 issue of CBE's newsletter *Mutuality*, there was an article by Kim Pettit,

---

[42]*Family News from Dr. James Dobson*, September 1999, 1-2.

"Why I Disagree With Dobson and the SBC." In the article she objected that "endorsement of the SBC statement by an increasing number of Christian organizations means dissenters are excluded as this becomes a confessional issue."[43]

Personally, I do not think that the SBC statement or others like it will mean that people who hold another view will be *excluded* from fellowship in the church. But I do think it means that people who hold an egalitarian view *will be excluded from many teaching and governing positions within the denomination.* Because I think that the egalitarian view is both harmful and contrary to Scripture, I think this is an appropriate result, and I think it is the one that was intended by those who added this statement to the "Baptist Faith and Message."

People who are right in the middle of turning points in history do not always realize it. I believe that today we are in the middle of a turning point in the history of the church. Organizations right now are making commitments and establishing policies. Some organizations are affirming biblical principles, as the Southern Baptists did. Others are establishing egalitarian principles as part of their policies, as Willow Creek Community Church near Chicago, Illinois, has done.[44] There is a sifting, a sorting, a dividing going on within the evangelical world, and I believe that institutions that adopt an egalitarian position on this issue will drift further and further from faithfulness to the Bible on other issues as well.

What is "the way forward" regarding biblical manhood and womanhood? I believe the way forward is to add a clear statement to the governing document of your church, your denomination, or your parachurch organization.

Why should we do this? First, because it affects so much of life. As Christians, we can differ over issues of the Tribulation or the Millennium and still live largely the same way in our daily lives. But differences over this issue affect people's lives and result in "increasingly destructive consequences in our families, our churches, and the culture at large," to use the words of the "Danvers Statement" (Affirmation 10). Where biblical patterns are not followed, husbands and wives have no clear guidance on how to act within their marriages,

---

[43]*Mutuality* (Spring 2000), 17.

[44]See Wayne Grudem, "Willow Creek Enforces Egalitarianism: Policy Requires All Staff and New Members to Joyfully Affirm Egalitarian Views," in *CBMW NEWS* 2:5 (Dec. 1997), 1, 3-6. This article also responds to Willow Creek's main arguments.

and there is increasing stress that brings harmful and even destructive consequences to families.

The second reason I believe that organizations should add statements to their governing documents is that egalitarians have run out of new exegetical arguments, and they simply are not winning the debate on the basis of the biblical text. As a result, it seems that their books increasingly deal not with detailed analysis of the words and sentences of Scripture, but with broad generalizations about Scripture, then with arguments from experience or arguments from philosophical concepts like fairness, or from the supposed negative results of a complementarian position (such as spousal abuse, which they wrongly attribute to our position, but which we strongly oppose and condemn as well).[45] But it seems to me, and increasingly it seems to many others, that the egalitarian position has simply lost the arguments based on the meaning of the biblical text, and they have no more arguments to be made.

A third reason why I think organizations should add a statement on biblical manhood and womanhood to their governing documents is that I believe this is a "watershed issue." Many years ago Francis Schaeffer called the doctrine of biblical inerrancy a "watershed issue" because the position that people took regarding inerrancy determined where their teachings would lead in succeeding years. Schaeffer said that the first people who make a mistake on a watershed issue take only a very small step, and in all other areas of life they are godly and orthodox; and this was the case with a number of scholars who denied inerrancy in principle but did not change their beliefs on much of anything else. However, the next generation of leaders and scholars who came after them took the error much further. They saw the implications of the change, and they were consistent in working it out with regard to other matters of doctrine and practice, and they fell into greater and greater deviation from the teachings of the Bible.

I believe it is the same with this issue today. This controversy is the key to deeper issues and deeper commitments that touch every part of life. Though many of our egalitarian friends today do not adopt the

---

[45]I still regret, and still cannot understand, why the Board of Directors of Christians for Biblical Equality declined to issue a joint statement with the Council on Biblical Manhood and Womanhood on the issue of abuse. CBMW adopted the statement in November 1994 and has continued to distribute it widely through its literature and its website: www.cbmw.org. The letter from CBE in which they declined to issue a statement jointly with us can be found in *CBMW News* 1:1 (Aug. 1995), 3 and is also available at the CBMW website.

other implications of their view, their followers will, and the next generation of leaders will go much further in the denial of the truths of Scripture or their failure to be subject to Scripture in other parts of life.

I said earlier that I believe one reason God allowed this controversy into the church at this time is so that we could correct wrongful male chauvinism in our churches and families. Now I need to say that I think there is another reason God has allowed this controversy into the church, and that is to test our hearts. Will we be faithful to Him and obey His Word or not? This is another reason God often allows false teaching to spread among His people: It is a means of testing us, to see what our response will be.

In the Old Testament, God allowed false prophets to come among the people, but He had told them, "you shall not listen to the words of that prophet or to that dreamer of dreams. *For the LORD your God is testing you,* to know whether you love the LORD your God with all your heart and with all your soul" (Deut. 13:3). Now I am certainly not saying that egalitarians are the same as those who advocated the serving of other gods in the Old Testament, for egalitarians within evangelicalism do worship Jesus Christ as their Savior. But I am saying that there is a principle of God's actions in history that we can see in Deuteronomy 13:3, and that is that God often allows various kinds of false teaching to exist in the church, probably in every generation, and by these false teachings God tests His people, to see whether they will be faithful to His Word or not. In this generation, one of those tests is whether we will be faithful to God in the teaching of His Word on matters of manhood and womanhood.

A similar idea is found in 1 Corinthians 11:19: "For there must be factions among you in order that those who are genuine among you may be recognized." When divisions and controversies arise in the church, people who make the right choices about the division eventually become "recognized" or are made "evident" (NASB). Others make wrong choices and thereby disqualify themselves from leadership. Charles Hodge wrote about this verse, "By the prevalence of disorders and other evils in the church, God puts his people to the test. They are tried as gold in the furnace, and their genuineness is made to appear."[46] Today, by the controversy over manhood and womanhood, God is test-

---

[46]Charles Hodge, *An Exposition of 1 and 2 Corinthians* (Wilmington, DE: Sovereign Grace, 1972; first published 1857), 125.

ing all of His people, all of His churches. The egalitarian alternative would be so easy to adopt in today's culture, and it can appear on the surface to make so little difference. But will we remain faithful to the Word of God?

KEY ISSUE 6: THIS CONTROVERSY IS MUCH BIGGER THAN WE REALIZE, BECAUSE IT TOUCHES ALL OF LIFE

I believe that the question of biblical manhood and womanhood is the focal point in a tremendous battle of worldviews. In that battle, biblical Christianity is being attacked simultaneously by two opponents with awesome power over the dominant ideas in the cultures of the world. Opponent #1, on the left, may be called No Differences, and its slogan would be, "All is one." Opponent #2, on the right side, may be called No Equality, and its slogan would be, "Might makes right."[47]

The chart on the following pages (see pp. 62-63) shows how a biblical view of men and women ("the complementarian middle") stands in contrast to the opponent No Differences on the far left and to the opponent No Equality on the far right. In the middle column, a biblical view of God includes *equality* and *differences* and *unity*. God is a Trinity where the Father, Son, and Holy Spirit have *equal* value and *different* roles, and They have absolute *unity* in the one being of God.

The Left Column—No Differences: On the far left, the differences in the persons of God are abolished, and the differences between God and the creation are abolished because "all is one." God then is viewed as equal to the creation, and people will worship the earth or parts of the earth as God (or as our "Mother"). Much New Age worship takes this form, as does much eastern religion where the goal is to seek unity with the universe.

When we follow the theme that there are "No Differences" into the area of manhood and womanhood, the attempt to obliterate differences leads to the emasculation of men and the defeminization of women. Men become more like women, and women become more like men, because "All is one."

Within marriage, if there are no differences, then same-sex "marriages" would be approved. Women who reject feminine roles will support abortion. Since there are no distinct roles for a child's father and

---

[47]The groundbreaking ideas of Peter Jones and Daniel Heimbach, fellow members of the Council on Biblical Manhood and Womanhood, provided the fundamental concepts that led to the following material. I am grateful for their contributions, though the specific applications that follow are my own. See the chapters (9, 10) by Jones and Heimbach in this volume.

mother within the family, there's really no longer any need to have children raised by the family; "society" can take care of raising children. Within the realm of sexuality, homosexuality and lesbianism will be approved. The chart goes on to detail how the idea that there should be "no differences" but that "all should be one" will also work out in feminized religion within churches, in hatred of authority (if someone has more authority, then all is not one), in no competition in sports (if we have "winners" and "losers," then all is not one), in no respect for authority and in the civil realm (with an increase in rampant crime), in attempts to abolish private property and equalize possessions (no one can be different, but all should be one), and in attempts to prohibit all-male or all-female schools or to prohibit educating boys and girls separately. These are the tendencies that follow once we adopt the conviction that "all is one" and there are no differences of persons in the being of God, and thus there should be no differences between men and women either.

The Egalitarian Column: Remove Many Differences: What concerns me about the egalitarian viewpoint within evangelicalism is that it tends toward this direction in many areas of life. It tends to remove or deny many differences between men and women. Egalitarians have begun to deny eternal personal distinctions among the Father, Son, and Holy Spirit in the Trinity and argue rather for "mutual submission" within the Trinity. They deny that there are any gender-based role differences in marriage.[48] Within marriage an egalitarian view tends toward abolishing differences and advocates "mutual submission," which often results in the husband acting as a wimp and the wife as a usurper. Because there is a deep-seated opposition to most authority, the drive toward sameness will often result in children being raised with too little discipline and too little respect for authority. Within the family there will be a tendency toward sharing all responsibilities equally between husband and wife, or to dividing responsibilities according to gifts and

---

[48]There was an amusing but very revealing suggestion for a new title to the book *Men Are from Mars, Women Are from Venus* in the CBE publication *Mutuality*: In an imaginary conversation in a bookstore, the writer suggested that a better title for a book about men and women would be, *Men Are from Mars, Women Are from Venus, But Some Men Are from Venus and Some Women Are from Mars, and All of God's Children Have Both Mars and Venus Qualities Within Them So Why Not Just Say That Men and Women Are from the Earth, and Let's Get About the Business of Developing the Unique God-given Mars/Venus Qualities That God Has Given All of Us for the Sake of the Kingdom* (article by Jim Banks in *Mutuality* [May 1998], 3). What was so revealing about this humorous suggestion was the way it showed that egalitarians seem to feel compelled to oppose any kinds of differences between men and women other than those that are purely physical.

	THE EFFEMINATE LEFT — NO DIFFERENCES "All is one"	EGALITARIANISM — Removing or denying many differences between men & women	THE COMPLEMENTARIAN MIDDLE — EQUALITY and UNITY (Emphasizing both equality and differences between men & women)	EQUALITY and DIFFERENCES	MALE DOMINANCE — Over-emphasizing the differences between men and women	THE VIOLENT RIGHT — NO EQUALITY "Might makes right"
God	God = creation / God as Mother / Sophia worship / New Age worship	Mutual submission in the Trinity [diagram: F ↔ S, HS]	God as Trinity [diagram: F ↔ S, HS]	Father, Son, Holy Spirit: equal value, different roles	Arianism (Son and Holy Spirit not fully God) [diagram: F, S, HS]	God as one person, not a Trinity, not three persons. Harsh, unloving warrior-God (Allah)
Man / Woman	Emasculation of men / Defeminization of women	No gender-based role differences in marriage (no "Mars-Venus" differences)	[diagram: H → W]	Husband, wife equal value, different roles	Men are better than women / Excessive competitiveness to show women as inferior	Men as brutes / Women as objects / Dehumanization of women
Marriage	Same-sex "marriages" approved	"Mutual submission" Often: husband as "wimp," wife as "usurper"	Husband: loving, humble headship / Wife: intelligent, joyful submission to husband		Husband as harsh, selfish, "dictator" / Wife as "doormat"	Polygamy, harems, female infanticide
Children	Children murdered: abortion supported by women who reject feminine roles	Children raised with too little discipline, little respect for authority	Children loved, cared for, valued / Children raised with discipline and love		Children raised with harsh discipline, little love or compassion	Children murdered: abortion supported by men who reject masculine responsibility for family
Family Responsibilities	No family—just "society"	All responsibilities shared equally between husband and wife, or divided according to gifts and interests	Husband: responsible to lead, provide for, protect / Wife: responsible to help husband by managing household and nurturing children		Wives forbidden to have own job outside home, or to vote or own property, etc.	Men have all power, women and children are to serve them
Sex	Homosexuality / Lesbianism	Men become un-masculine, unattractive to women / Women become un-feminine, unattractive to men	Monogamous, equally fulfilling intercourse as deepest expression of a great "mystery": equality and differences and unity!		Pornography / Lust / Adultery	Violence against women / Rape
	Violent opposition to God's plan for sex as only between man and woman	Ambivalence toward sex	Delight in God's plan for sexual expression restrained by bonds of lifelong marriage		Excessive attention to sex	Violent opposition to God's plan for sex as only within marriage

Natural Desires	Temptation: unlimited same-sex sexual activity	Moving "contrary to nature" (Rom. 1:26)	Natural desires fulfilled Men and women have deep sense of acting as God made them to act	Moving in exaggeration and distortion of nature	Temptation: unlimited unequal sexual activity
Religion	Feminized religion in churches Pantheism	No governing or teaching roles in church reserved for men	Some governing and teaching roles in church restricted to men	All ministry done by men; women's gifts squelched; Crusades	Militant forms of Islam Religion advanced by violence
Authority	Hatred of authority	Suspicion of authority	Authority exercised within boundaries	Over-use of authority	Abuse of authority
Sports	No competition "everybody wins"	Anti-competition	Competition with fairness and rules Winners honored, losers respected	Excessive competition Losers humiliated	Violent harm to opponents Gladiators fight to death WWF wrestling
Crime	No respect for authority, rampant crime, especially by frustrated, angry men	Criminal seen as victim to be helped, not punished; punishment long delayed	Punishment is speedy, fair; aims at justice plus restoration of criminal	Repressive government, little freedom, debtors' prisons	Excessive punishment, dehumanization of criminals (cut off hand of thief); little crime, but no freedom
Property	No private property; all possessions equalized	No one is allowed to be very rich; large-scale dependence on welfare state and government	Laws protect private property *and* care for poor; more work and skill earns more wealth; equal opportunity for all	Women cannot own property	Slavery; dehumanization of the poor and weak; all property in hands of few
Education	All-male schools prohibited by law; prohibitions against educating boys and girls separately	Systematic pressure to make boys and girls do equally well in all subjects	Boys and girls both educated, but different preferences, abilities, and sense of calling respected	Boys given preferential treatment in schools	Girls not allowed to be educated

Please note: This chart contains many generalizations and is only meant to show broad tendencies. Most people and many religious systems hold mixed views and have inconsistencies in thinking. Moreover, conscience, social pressure, and the Bible often restrain people from adopting all aspects of non-biblical views. Therefore this chart certainly *does not* imply that every person or religious system within each column holds to everything in that column. *This chart may be duplicated for teaching purposes without charge.*

interests, not according to roles as specified by Scripture. Within the realm of human sexuality, tendencies to deny the differences between men and women will often result in men becoming unmasculine and unattractive to women and women becoming unfeminine and unattractive to men. There will often be ambivalence toward sex.

The chart goes on to show how within the realm of religion the egalitarian view tends toward removing or denying many differences between men and women and would support the idea that no governing or teaching roles within the church should be reserved for men. Within sports, this viewpoint that attempts to deny differences would tend to be opposed to competition and think of it as evil rather than good. With respect to crime, the criminal would be seen as a victim to be helped and not punished, and punishment would be long delayed. As far as private property is concerned, because there are tendencies to abolish differences, no one would be allowed to be very rich, and there would be large-scale dependence on the welfare state and on government. Within education, there would be systematic pressure to make boys and girls participate equally and do equally well in all subjects and all activities, attempting to forcibly eradicate any patterns of natural preferences and aptitudes for some kinds of activities by boys and some kinds by girls. All of this would tend toward a denial of differences between men and women.

The Far Right Column: No Equality: But there are opposite errors as well. The opponent on the far right side of the chart is No Equality, and the dominant idea from this perspective is that there is no equality between persons who are different. Rather, the stronger person is more valuable, and the weaker person is devalued, for "might makes right." In this view God is not seen as a Trinity but as one person who is all-powerful. Often God can be viewed as a harsh, unloving warrior God, as in a common Islamic view of Allah. In this perspective, since "might makes right" and the weaker person is viewed as inferior, the relationships between men and women are distorted as well. Men begin to act as brutes and to treat women as objects. This view results in a dehumanization of women. Whereas the No Differences error on the far left most significantly results in the destruction of men, this No Equality error on the far right most significantly results in the destruction of women.

Within marriage, the idea that there is no equality in value between men and women will lead to polygamy and harems in which one man will have many wives. There is no concern to value women equally, for "might makes right," and men are stronger. This view will also lead to female infanticide in which girls are put to death because people prefer to have boys. With regard to children, in this No Equality viewpoint, men who reject masculine responsibility to care for their families will support abortion, and unborn children will be murdered with the encouragement of men. Within the family, if there is no equality in value before God, men will have all the power, and women and children will simply exist to serve them. Within the realm of sexuality, the No Equality error results in violence against women and rape.

The chart goes on to explain how this viewpoint also works out in terms of religion, where religion is advanced by violence and force (as in militant forms of Islam). The view that there need be no equality of value between persons results in the destruction of people who have less power or less authority; so authority is abused as a result. Within sports, this viewpoint will lead to violent harm to opponents, and even to gladiators fighting to the death. (The increasing popularity of violent and harmful wrestling programs on television is a manifestation of this tendency.) As far as criminal justice, this viewpoint will lead to excessive punishment and dehumanization of criminals (such as cutting off the hand of a thief or putting people to death for expressing different religious beliefs). There will often be little outward crime in the society, but there will be little freedom for people as well. As far as private property is concerned, there will be slavery and dehumanization of the poor and weak, while all property is held in the hands of a few who are very powerful. In education, the No Equality viewpoint would result in girls not being allowed to obtain an education.

The Male Dominance Column: Overemphasizing the Differences and Neglecting Equality: There have been disturbing tendencies leading in the direction of No Equality and advocating that "might makes right" whenever a "male dominance" view has found expression within the church or society. This viewpoint would overemphasize the differences between men and women and would not treat women as having equal value to men; nor would it treat those under authority as having equal value to those who have authority. With respect to a view of God, this view, which might be called the "domineering right," would be parallel to Arianism (the view that the Son and Holy Spirit are not fully God in the sense that the Father is God, but are lesser beings that were created at one time). In relationships between men and women, this viewpoint would have an attitude that men are better than women and would result in excessive competitiveness in which a man feels he always has to win in any sport or any argument, in order to show that women are inferior.

Within marriage, this "male dominance" error would result in a husband being harsh and selfish and acting as a dictator or a tyrant, and the wife acting as a doormat.

Because there is too great an emphasis on authority, this viewpoint would tend toward a system where children are raised with harsh discipline but with little love or compassion. As far as family responsibilities, wives would be forbidden to have their own jobs outside the home or to vote or to own property, for there is no thought of treating them as equal.

Within the realm of sexuality, a "male dominance" view would result in pornography and adultery and hearts filled with lust. There would be excessive attention given to sex, with men focusing excessively on their own sexual desires. People may wonder why involvement with pornography often leads to violence against women, but this chart makes the connection clear: Pornography is *looking at* women as objects for sexual gratification, not as persons equal in God's sight; violence against women just takes that idea one step further and begins to *treat* them as objects that are unworthy of being treated with dignity and respect.

The chart goes on to point out how "male dominance," the view that overemphasizes differences between men and women, would work out in a religious system where all ministry is done by men, and women's gifts are suppressed and squelched. This view would also lead to things like the Crusades, the mistaken military expeditions in the eleventh, twelfth, and thirteenth centuries that were carried out to regain control of the Holy Land from the Muslims by force. Within sports, there would be excessive competition, and losers would be humiliated. Within crime, there would be a repressive government with little freedom, and things like debtors' prisons would dehumanize the poor. Within such a viewpoint, women would not be permitted to own property, and boys would be given preferential treatment in schools.

The Complementarian Middle: Equality and Differences and Unity All Maintained: In contrast to these errors in both directions, the biblical picture is one that emphasizes *equality* and *differences* and *unity* at the same time. In parallel to the equality and differences among the members of the Trinity, within a complementarian view men and women are equal in value but have different roles. Within marriage, a husband will manifest loving, humble headship, and a wife will manifest intelligent, joyful submission to her husband's leadership. Children will be loved and cared for and valued, and they will be raised with both discipline and love. Children will respect the authority of their parents, but their parents will respect the dignity of children as having equal value because they are persons created in the image of God. Within the family, there will be a division of responsibilities in which the husband is primarily responsible to lead, provide for, and protect his family. The wife, on the other hand, will be primarily responsible to help her husband by managing the household and nurturing the children, though both husband and wife will often participate willingly in helping the other person with his or her area of primary responsibility.

In the realm of sexuality, a complementarian view will result in monogamous, lifelong marriage and in equally fulfilling experiences of sex as the deepest expression of a great "mystery" created by God: We are equal, and we are different, and we are one! There will be a delight in God's plan for sexual expression, but it will be restrained by the bonds of lifelong marriage and lifelong faithfulness to one's marriage partner. Men and women will have then a deep sense of acting in the way that God created them to act in all these areas.

The lower rows of the chart go on to explain how a complementarian viewpoint works out in religion, where some governing and teaching roles in the church are restricted to men, but women's gifts are also honored and used fully in the ministries of the church. In all areas of life, authority will be exercised within boundaries, so that the person under authority is treated with respect and dignity and as someone who shares equally in the image of God. Within sports, there will be an appreciation for competition with fairness and rules, and winners will be honored while losers are respected. Equality. Differences. Unity.

As far as crime is concerned, punishment will be speedy and fair and will aim at the satisfaction of justice as well as the restoration of the criminal. As far as private property, laws will protect private property but will also reflect care for the poor. People will be rewarded according to their work and skill, and there will be a desire to have equal opportunity for all in the economic realm. Within education, boys and girls will both be educated, but the different preferences and abilities and senses of calling that boys and girls may have will be respected, and no quotas will be imposed to force an artificial equality in the number of participants in every activity where that would not have resulted from allowing boys and girls to choose activities freely of their own accord. Equality. Differences. Unity.

I realize, of course, that any chart like this has generalizations, and people who hold one viewpoint or another at some point on the chart may not hold all the viewpoints represented within a particular column. Nevertheless, I think the chart has significant value in showing that we will continually face two opposing challenges in trying to uphold a biblical view of manhood and womanhood. People on the domineering right will continue to think of us as weak and yielding too much to the demands of feminism. People on the egalitarian left will continue to see us as harsh and overemphasizing the differences between men and women. And we must steadfastly and patiently hold to the middle, with the help of God.

Now I think it is plain why I say that this controversy is much bigger than we realize. The struggle to uphold equality *and* differences *and* unity between men and women has implications for all areas of life.

Moreover, there are strong spiritual forces invisibly warring against us in this whole controversy. I am not now focusing on the egalitarian left or the domineering right, but on the far left column and the far right column, the effeminate left and the violent right. I do not think that we can look at those two columns for long without realizing that behind the attempt to abolish all differences and make everything "one," and behind the attempt to destroy those who are weaker and make the stronger always "right," there is a deep spiritual evil. At both extremes we see the hand of the enemy seeking to destroy God's idea of sex, of marriage, and of manhood and womanhood. We see the hand of the enemy seeking to destroy everything that glorifies God and especially seeking to destroy the beauty of our sexual differences that wonderfully reflect God's glory. We see the hand of the enemy who hates everything that God created as good and hates everything that brings glory to God Himself.

So in the end, this whole controversy is really about God and how His character is reflected in the beauty and excellence of manhood and womanhood as He created it. Will we glorify God through manhood and womanhood lived according to His Word? Or will we deny His Word and give in to the pressures of modern culture? That is the choice we have to make.

II

THE GLORY OF MAN AND WOMAN AS CREATED BY GOD

———⟡———

2

MALE AND FEMALE COMPLEMENTARITY AND THE IMAGE OF GOD[1]

Bruce A. Ware

———

INTRODUCTION

And God said, "Let the land produce living creatures according to their kinds: livestock, creatures that move along the ground, and wild animals, each according to its kind." And it was so. God made the wild animals according to their kinds, the livestock according to their kinds, and all the creatures that move along the ground according to their kinds. And God saw that it was good. Then God said, "Let us make man in our image, in our likeness, and let them rule over the fish of the sea and the birds of the air, over the livestock, over all the earth, and over all the creatures that move along the ground." So God created man in his own image, in the image of God he created him; male and female he created them. God blessed them and said to them, "Be fruitful and increase in number; fill the earth and subdue it. Rule over the fish of the sea and the birds of the air and over every living creature that moves on the ground." Then God said, "I give you every seed-bearing plant on the face of the whole earth and every tree that has fruit with seed in it. They will be yours for food. And to all the beasts of the earth and all the birds of the air and all the creatures that move on the ground—everything that has the breath of life in it—I give every green plant for food." And it was so. God saw all that he had made, and it was very good. And there was evening, and there was morning—the sixth day.

—GEN. 1:24-31

---

[1] This chapter was first delivered as a paper at the "Building Strong Families" conference, Dallas, Texas, March 20-22, co-sponsored by FamilyLife and The Council on Biblical Manhood and Womanhood, and will be published in a forthcoming issue of the *Journal for Biblical Manhood and Womanhood.*

Everyone agrees: Whatever being created in the image of God means, it is very, very significant! Clearly, in Genesis 1, the progression of creation builds throughout the six days, culminating in the final creative act, in the second part of the sixth day—the creation of man as male and female in the image of God. Some key internal indicators signal the special significance of man's creation: 1) As just noted, man is the pinnacle of God's creative work, only after which God *then* says of all He has made that it is "very good" (1:31). 2) The creation of man is introduced differently than all others, with the personal and deliberative expression, "Let Us make man in Our image, according to Our likeness" (NASB). 3) The one God who creates man as male and female deliberately uses plural references for Himself (e.g., "Let *Us*," "*Our* image," "*Our* likeness") as the creator of singular "man" who is plural ("male and female"). 4) The phrase "image of God" is stated three times in 1:26-27 in relation to man as male and female, but never in relation to any other part of creation. 5) The special term for God's unique creative action, *bārā*, is used three times in 1:27 for the creation of man in His image as male and female. 6) Man is given a place of rulership over all other created beings on the earth, thus indicating the higher authority and priority of man in God's created design. 7) Only the creation of man as male and female is expanded and portrayed in detail as recorded in Genesis 2.

What does it mean, though, that man as male and female has been created in the image and likeness of God? What does this tell us about the nature of manhood and womanhood as both male and female exhibit full and equal humanness as the image of God while also being distinguished as male (not female) and female (not male)? And what relevance do these truths have for complementarian male/female relations with God and with one another?

This chapter will focus on these three questions. First, attention will be given to the question of what the image of God is. Obviously this issue must be settled with some degree of confidence if we are to proceed. Second, we will explore the particular question of what it might mean that male and female are created in the image of God, stressing both their full human equality and gender distinctiveness. And third, we will suggest some ways in which this understanding makes a difference in how we understand the complementarian nature of our lives as male and female both before God and with each other.

THE MEANING OF THE CREATION OF MAN IN THE IMAGE OF GOD

Through the history of the church, there have been many and varying proposals as to what it means that man is created in God's image. While one would hope to find more agreement, this is not the case. No doubt this lack of agreement is owing, in significant part, to the fact that Scripture declares but does not explain clearly just what it means that man is created in God's image.

Traditional Understandings of the Image of God

While varied, the main proposals offered throughout history may be grouped under three broad headings.

Structural views. The prevailing kind of approach reasoned as follows: The image of God in man must relate to some way or ways in which we humans are like God but unlike the other created animals. After all, since humans and other animals are all created beings, those aspects that we share in *common* with them cannot constitute what *distinguishes* us from them. And since we are made in the image of *God*, this must refer to some resemblance to God in particular that God imparted to humans and is not shared by the animals. So there must be some aspect or aspects of the *structure/substance* of our *human nature* that shows we are created in the image of God. Here are some examples:

1. Irenaeus (c. 130-200) distinguished the image (*şelem*) and likeness (*demûth*) of God in man. He argued that the *image* of God is our reason and volition, and the *likeness* of God is our holiness and spiritual relation to God. As a result, the likeness of God is lost in the Fall and regained in redemption, but all humans are in the image of God by their capacities of reason and will.[2]

2. Augustine (354-430) understood the image of God as the reflection of the triune persons of God mirrored in the distinct yet unified intellectual capacities of memory, intellect, and will. While stopping short of calling these an exact analogy of the Trinity, he did suggest that the triune Godhead is what is reflected in us when we are called the image of God.[3]

3. Thomas Aquinas (1224-1274) locates the image of God squarely in man's reason, by which we have the capacity to know and love God.

---

[2]Irenaeus, *Against Heresies*, in *Ante-Nicene Fathers*, Vol. 1, eds. A. Roberts and J. Donaldson (Grand Rapids, MI: Eerdmans, 1953).

[3]St. Augustine, *The Trinity*, trans. Edmund Hill, *The Works of St. Augustine*, Vol. 5 (Brooklyn, NY: New City Press, 1991).

Angels, says Thomas, are even more perfectly in God's image because of their more perfect understanding and love of God. While fallen men lose the added gift of the grace of God (*donum superadditum*), so they no longer know or love God as they should, they still retain this rational capacity and some natural knowledge of God, and hence they likewise retain the image of God.[4]

4. John Calvin (1509-1564) sees the human soul as comprising the image of God. By soul, Calvin meant both the mind and heart of man by which he could know and love God. Because fallen man has turned to deception and rebellion in regard to God, the image of God has been deformed greatly in the souls of depraved men. Yet even in fallen man there are some "remaining traces" of God's image, since man retains the distinctive human capacities of reason and will.[5]

Relational views. Only more recently has another very prominent understanding been developed. Rather than seeing the image of God as referring to some aspect(s) of our human nature, God's image is reflected in our relation to one another and to God. So while it is true that God has given us reason, soul, volition, and other capacities of our nature, none of these constitutes the image of God. Rather, it is the use of these capacities in relation with God and others that reflects most clearly what it means to be created in God's image.

1. Karl Barth (1886-1968) was very critical of the entire history of the doctrine of the image of God in man. Barth complained that little attention had been given to what Scripture actually says when it speaks of man created in the image of God. In Genesis 1:26-27 (cf. 5:1-2), as Barth notes, God deliberately speaks of Himself in the plural as creating man who is likewise plural as male and female. The image of God should best be seen as the relational or social nature of human life as God created us. That both male and female together are created in His image signals the relational meaning of the image of God in man.[6]

2. Emil Brunner (1889-1966) distinguished formal and material senses of the image of God. The *formal* image of God in man is his capacity to relate to God through his knowledge and love of God; the *material* image is manifest through his actually seeking, knowing, and loving God. For Brunner, then, the formal image is retained after the

---

[4]Thomas Aquinas, *Summa Theologica*, I.93.

[5]John Calvin, *Institutes of the Christian Religion*, ed. J. T. McNeill, trans. F. L. Battles (Philadelphia: Westminster, 1960), I.15.

[6]Karl Barth, *Church Dogmatics*, trans. G. Bromiley (Edinburgh: T. & T. Clark, 1960), III.2.

Fall, but the material image is lost altogether. While it is important for Brunner that God made us with the capacity to know and love Him (i.e., the formal image), the heart of the concept of the image of God has to do with our relationship with God, in which we express real longing for God, trust in Him, and a desire to know and love Him (i.e., the material image).[7]

Functional views. While this view can be traced through the centuries, only recently has it been urged with increasing forcefulness. Here it is not our inner capacities of nature, nor our human or Godward relationality that comprise the image of God, but it is the functioning of man who is responsible to act as God's representative over creation that shows us as His images. Advocates such as Leonard Verduin[8] and D. J. A. Clines[9] have argued that the double reference in Genesis 1:26-28 of man "rul[ing] over" the fish of the sea and the birds of the air, etc., cannot be accidental. Rather, this links the concept of the image of God with the fact that God places man over the rest of earthly creation in order to rule on His behalf. Creation stewardship as God's vice-regents, then, is at the heart of what it means to be in the image of God.

Evaluation of These Traditional Understandings of the Image of God

Clearly, we should affirm with Karl Barth that our understanding of the image of God should be directed as fully as possible by the text of Scripture. One of the main problems with much of the traditional understandings (particularly with the variations of the structural view) is that these proposals were led more by speculation regarding how men are like God and unlike animals than by careful attention to indications in the text of Scripture itself as to what may constitute this likeness. While it is not wrong to ask and ponder this question, what confidence can we have that when we have answered it we have also answered the question of what the image of God in man is? The relevant passages, particularly Genesis 1:26-28, need to be far more central and instructive than most of the tradition has allowed them to be.

A major attraction of both the relational and functional views is their care to notice features of Genesis 1:26-28, where we are instructed

---

[7]Emil Brunner, *The Christian Doctrine of Creation and Redemption*, trans. O. Wyon (Philadelphia: Westminster, 1953).

[8]Leonard Verduin, *Somewhat Less Than God* (Grand Rapids, MI: Eerdmans, 1970).

[9]D. J. A. Clines, "The Image of God in Man," *Tyndale Bulletin* (1968), 53-103.

clearly and forcefully that man is created in God's image. The relational view rightly points to the fact that God creates male and female, not isolated and individual man. And yet one wonders whether the point of mentioning "male and female" was to say that the image of God was *constituted* by their social relatedness, or might the point more simply be that *both man and woman* are created in God's image? Barth's proposal, in particular, runs into some difficulties. First, if relationality is constitutive of the image of God, then how do we account for the teaching of Genesis 9:6 where the murder of an individual human being is a capital offense precisely because the one killed was made in the image of God? Relationality has no place in this prohibition against murder. Every individual human person is an image of God and is therefore to be treated with rightful respect (e.g., in Genesis 9:3 man can kill animals for food, but in 9:6 man cannot wrongfully kill another man). Second, Jesus is "the image of the invisible God" (Col. 1:15), and yet this is said of Him as an individual person. Third, all single individuals, including Jesus, John the Baptist, and Paul, are fully the image of God, yet they never entered into the male-female union spoken of the first pair of humans in Genesis 2. I hesitate, then, to follow a strict version of the relational model, though, as will be apparent, it still contributes to a holistic understanding of man created in God's image.

The functional view also has merit biblically in that it rightly points to the double imperative in Genesis 1:26-28 of man to rule over the earthly creation. I agree with those who say that this connection cannot be accidental; it rather must play a central role in our understanding of what it means to be created in the image of God. Yet, function always and only follows essence. Put differently, what something can *do* is an expression of what it *is*. So, obviously to the extent that humans being made in the image of God has to do with their *functioning* a certain way, behind this must be truth about their *being made* a certain way, by which (and *only* by which) they are able to carry out their God-ordained functioning.

Functional Holism as the Image of God

One of the finest recent discussions of the image of God has been done by Anthony Hoekema.[10] I agree fully with the implication of Hoekema's questions when he asks:

---

[10]Anthony A. Hoekema, *Created in God's Image* (Grand Rapids, MI: Eerdmans, 1986).

Must we think of the image of God in man as involving only what man is and not what he does, or only what he does and not what he is, or both what he is and what he does? Is "image of God" only a description of the way in which the human being functions, or is it also a description of the kind of being he or she is?[11]

Hoekema defends and develops a view of the image of God in which humans are seen to be made by God with certain structural capacities (to "mirror" God) in order that they might function in carrying out the kinds of responsibilities in relationship He has given them in particular to do (to "represent" God). The stress, then, is on the functional and relational responsibilities, while the structural capacities provide the created conditions necessary for that functioning to be carried out. Furthermore, Hoekema describes the relational elements of this functioning in terms of how we are to relate to God, to others, and to the world God has made. So God has made us a particular way and has done so in order for us to function in this threefold arena of relationality, and this together constitutes what it means to be created in the image of God. Hoekema summarizes his view as follows:

> The image of God, we found, describes not just something that man *has*, but something man *is*. It means that human beings both mirror and represent God. Thus, there is a sense in which the image includes the physical body. The image of God, we found further, includes both a structural and a functional aspect (sometimes called the broader and narrower image), though we must remember that in the biblical view structure is secondary, while function is primary. The image must be seen in man's threefold relationship: toward God, toward others, and toward nature.[12]

Another treatment of the image of God has contributed much to the discussion and supports this same holistic understanding, with a particular stress on the functional responsibilities man has as created in God's image.[13] D. J. A. Clines considered Genesis 1:26-28 in light of the Ancient Near Eastern (ANE) usage of "image of God." Clines notes that the concept of image of God was used widely in ANE literature. Many times inanimate objects (e.g., stones, trees, crafted

---

[11]Ibid., 69.
[12]Ibid., 95.
[13]Clines, "Image of God in Man."

idols) were considered images of the gods, and when this was the case, they were seen as possessing some divine substance that gave them certain powers. But also often (and more important to the background of Genesis 1:26-28), the image of the god was a king or another royal official. When this was the case, Clines noted three characteristics. First, the god would put into the king some divine substance (e.g., some fluid or wind or breath) that would give the king extraordinary powers, thus making him like the god, to some degree, and able to represent the god to the people. Second, the king was to function as the representative of the god and rule as the vice-regent of the god, acting as the god would, in his place. Third, it was only the king or other high official who was the image of the god; ordinary people were never the image of the god.

When applied to Genesis 1—2, it appears reasonable that the author may have had this background in mind. At least, one must wonder why the author does not define "image of God" when it is apparent to all that this is a term of extraordinary importance. Perhaps the meaning was widely understood. If so, as Clines suggests, the phrase "image of God" in Genesis 1—2 contains three elements that are parallel yet not identical to the three characteristics of the ANE understanding of image of a god. First, man was created with such a nature that divine enablement was given him to *be* what he must be in order to *do* what God would require him to do. Clines points to the breathing into Adam the breath of life in Genesis 2:7 as indication that his formation included this divine empowerment requisite to function as God's image. Second, immediately upon creating man in Genesis 2, God puts *man* to work, stewarding and ruling in the world that is *God's* own creation. Man is given responsibility to cultivate the garden, and man is called upon to name the animals. So, while the garden in which man dwells is God's, God gives to man the responsibility to steward it. And, importantly, while the animals are God's, God gives to man the right and responsibility to name them (note especially the statement in Genesis 2:19 that whatever the *man* called the living creature, "that was its name"). By this, man shows his God-derived authority over creation, for to cultivate the garden and especially to name the animals is to manifest his rightful yet derived rulership over the rest of creation. Third, the place where Genesis 1:26-28 departs from the pattern of the ANE usage is that *both* male and female are created in God's image. While the ANE king or royal official *only* is the image of the god, in the creation of man, *all* men, *both male and female*, are fully the image of God. Man and woman, then, both are fully the image of God and together share the responsibility to steward the earthly creation God has made.

Hoekema's and Clines's proposals are complementary insofar as they both stress that the structural, relational, and functional elements need to be brought together to understand what it means in Genesis 1:26-28 to be made in the image of God. Yet, while all three are needed, the *structural* serves the purpose of the *functional* being carried out in *relationship*. One might think of this proposal, then, as advocating a "functional holism" view of the image of God. That is, while all three aspects are involved, priority is given to the God-ordained functioning of human beings in carrying out the purposes He has for them. Perhaps our summary statement of what it means to be made in God's image could employ this language:

> The image of God in man as functional holism means that God made human beings, both male and female, to be created and finite *representations* (images *of* God) of God's own nature, that in *relationship* with Him and each other they might be His *representatives* (imaging God) in carrying out the *responsibilities* He has given to them. In this sense, we are *images of God* in order *to image God* and His purposes in the ordering of our lives and the carrying out of our God-given responsibilities.

Our Lord Jesus surely exhibited this expression of the image of God in His own human, earthly life. Made fully human and filled with the Holy Spirit, He was a fully faithful representation of God through His human and finite nature (as He was, of course, intrinsically and perfectly in His infinite divine nature). In relationship with God and others, He then sought fully and only to carry out the will of the Father who sent Him into the world.[14] More than any other man, Jesus exhibited this as His uniform and constant desire. He represented God in word, attitude, thought, and action throughout the whole of His life and ministry. So the responsibilities God gave Him, He executed fully. Clearly, a functional holism was at work in Jesus as the image of God. As such, Jesus was in human nature the *representation* of God so that, in

---

[14]Over thirty times in John's Gospel we are told that Jesus was sent into this world to carry out the will of the Father who sent Him. See, e.g., John 4:34; 5:23, 30, 37; 6:37-38, 57; and 12:49.

relation to God and others, He might *represent* God in fulfilling His God-given *responsibilities* as He functioned, always and only, to do the will of His Father.

MALE AND FEMALE AS THE IMAGE OF GOD
Male and Female Equality as the Image of God

Complementarians and egalitarians have agreed that the creation of male and female as the image of God indicates the equal value of women with men as being fully human, with equal dignity, worth, and importance. While Genesis 1:26-27 speaks of God creating "man" in His image, the passage deliberately broadens at the end of verse 27 to say, "male and female He created them" (NASB). Hear again these central verses:

> *Then God said, "Let us make man in our image, in our likeness, and let them rule over the fish of the sea and the birds of the air, over the livestock, over all the earth, and over all the creatures that move along the ground." So God created man in his own image, in the image of God he created him; male and female he created them.*

Clearly the intention of the text is to say both that the man and the woman share a common humanity and equal worth before God (hence, both are "man"), and yet they do so not as identical (hence they are distinctly "male and female").

Genesis 5:1-2 only confirms and reinforces this understanding. Here we read: "This is the written account of Adam's line. When God created man, he made him in the likeness of God. He created them male and female and blessed them. And when they were created, he called them 'man.'" As with Genesis 1:26-27, we see the common identity of male and female, both named "man," and yet the male and the female is each a distinct expression of this common and equally possessed nature of "man." As is often observed, since this was written in a patriarchal cultural context, it is remarkable that the biblical writer chose to identify the female along with the male as of the exact same name and nature as "man." Male and female are equal in essence and so equal in dignity, worth, and importance.

Another clear biblical testimony to this equality is seen in the position of redeemed men and women in Christ. Galatians 3:28 ("There is neither Jew nor Greek, slave nor free, male nor female, for you are all one in Christ Jesus") makes clear that gender distinctions (along with race and class distinctions) are irrelevant in relation to the standing and benefits we have in Christ.[15] As Paul had said in the previous verse, *all* who are baptized into Christ have been clothed with Christ. So men and women alike who by faith are sons of God (v. 26) enter fully into the promise of Christ and all that entails (v. 29). This same idea is echoed by Peter when he instructs believing husbands to show their believing wives honor as fellow heirs with them of the grace of life in Christ (1 Pet. 3:7). Christian wives and husbands stand on exactly equal footing in Christ: both saved by faith, both fully united with Christ, and both fully heirs of all the riches of Christ. These New Testament passages reflect the Bible's clear teaching that as male and female are equal in their humanity (Gen. 1:26-27), so they are equal in their participation of the fullness of Christ in their redemption (Gal. 3:28).

Male and Female Differentiation as the Image of God

After affirming the complete essential equality of men and women as created in the image of God, an obvious observation must be made that has important implications: While male is fully human, male is also *male*, not female; and while female is fully human, female is also *female*, not male. That is, while God did intend to create male and female as *equal* in their essential nature as human, He also intended to make them *different expressions* of that essential nature, as male and female reflect different ways, as it were, of being human. Now, the question before us is whether any of these male/female differences relate to the question of what it means for men and women to be created in the image of God.

Some might reason that since Genesis 1:26-27 and 5:1-2 speak of both male and female created fully in the image of God, any male/female *differences* one might point to cannot bear any relationship to the *united* sense in which they possess, equally and fully, the image of God. That they both are the image of God equally and fully manifests not their *differences* but their *commonality* and *equality*. Yes, male and female are different, but they are not different, some might argue, in any sense as being the images of God; we have to look elsewhere to locate the basis for their differences.

Let me suggest that this distinction may not reflect the whole of

---

[15]See Richard Hove, *Equality in Christ? Galatians 3:28 and the Gender Dispute* (Wheaton, IL: Crossway Books, 1999).

biblical teaching. I will here propose that it may be best to understand the original creation of male and female as one in which the male was made the image of God first, in an unmediated fashion, as God formed him from the dust of the ground, and the female was made the image of God second, in a mediated fashion, as God chose, not more earth, but the very rib of Adam by which He would create the woman fully and equally the image of God. So, while both are *fully* the image of God, and both are *equally* the image of God, it may be the case that both are not constituted as the image of God in the identical way. Scripture gives some clues that there is a God-intended temporal priority[16] bestowed upon the man as the original image of God, through whom the woman, as the image of God formed from the male, comes to be.

Consider the following biblical indicators of a male priority in male and female as God's images. First, does it not stand to reason that the *method* by which God fashions first the man and then the woman is meant to communicate something important about their respective identities? Surely this is the case considering the simple observation that Adam was created first. Some might think that the creation of the male prior to the female is insignificant in itself, and surely irrelevant for deriving any theological conclusions; whether God created the woman first or the man first might be thought of as nothing more than a sort of tossing of a divine coin. But as we know, the apostle Paul knew differently. In 1 Timothy 2:13 and 1 Corinthians 11:8,[17] Paul demonstrates that the very ordering of the creative acts of God in the formation of male, then female, has significant theological meaning. Male headship is rooted in part on what might otherwise seem to have been an optional or even arbitrary temporal ordering of the formation of man and woman.

Given the significance of the mere temporal ordering of the cre-

---

[16]When I speak in this section of the "priority" of the male in God's creation of male and female equally as His image-bearers, readers should understand that I do not intend to communicate any sense of greater value, dignity, worth, human personhood, or sharing in the image of God that the male possesses over the female; in fact, the preceding section should make clear that I believe Scripture clearly teaches the complete equality of female with male as being bearers of the image of God. As will become clear, just as children become fully and equally the image of God through the God-ordained reproductive expression of their parents, so the woman becomes the image of God second, and she does so fully and equally to the image of God in Adam, although she is deliberately formed by God as the image of God from Adam's rib, not from the dust of the ground as was Adam.

[17]As will be seen below, while both of these texts stress the temporal priority of the creation of the male, they are not identical in how they state this historical reality, and an interesting difference can be noted in the wording used in these verses respectively.

ation of man as male and female, ought we not also consider it significant that while God formed Adam from dust, He intentionally formed the woman from Adam's rib? Surely, if God wanted to convey an absolute and unequivocal identity in *how* man and woman respectively are constituted as human beings in the image of God, He could have created each in the same manner. That is, after fashioning the man from the dust of the ground as His image-bearer (Gen. 2:7), God then could have taken more of the same dust to form the woman, who would then come to be also His image-bearer in the identically same fashion as the man had come into existence. But this is not what occurred. Instead, God intentionally took, not more dust, but Adam's rib as the material out of which He would fashion the woman. The theology of this is clear. As the man himself puts it in Genesis 2:23, her identity is as bone of *his* bones and flesh of *his* flesh; she is called woman (*'ishshāh*) because she was *taken out of* man (*'îsh*). In the very formation of the woman, it was to be clear that her life, her constitution, her nature, was rooted in and derived from the life, constitution, and nature of the man. Now, surely God could have created a female human being from the dust, to parallel in her formation the male human being He had made from the dust. And surely had He done so, they would be seen as equally human. But God wanted to convey *two theological truths* (not just one) in the formation of the woman from the rib of Adam: Since the woman was taken out of the man, 1) she is *fully and equally human* since she has come from his bones and his flesh, and 2) her very human nature is constituted, not in parallel fashion to his with both formed from the same earth, but as *derived from his own nature*, so showing a God-chosen dependence upon him for her origination.

This understanding seems confirmed by the wording Paul uses in 1 Corinthians 11:8 in particular to describe the creation of the woman ("For man did not come from woman, but woman from man"). Here he says that the woman comes "from" or "out of" (*ek*) the man, and not merely that man was created prior to the woman. Of course, this more basic truth (i.e., that man was created before the woman) is entailed by what Paul says in this verse. But his primary point concerns the very derivation of the woman's own existence and nature as "from man." So notice then that whereas 1 Timothy 2:13 ("For Adam was formed first, then Eve") states the more basic and simple truth that the man was created first (indicating temporal priority strictly), 1 Corinthians 11:8 indicates more fully a God-intended derivation of her very being as "from" the man. It seems clear, then, that Genesis 2 intends for us to understand the formation of the woman as both fully *like the man in his humanity*, while attributing the *derivation* of her very nature to God's formation of her, not from common dust of the ground, but specifically from the rib of Adam, and so *from the man*.

Second, in Genesis 5:2 God chooses to name *both* male and female with a name that functions as a masculine generic (i.e., the Hebrew term *'ādām* is a masculine term that can be used exclusively for a man, especially in Genesis 1—4, but here is used as a generic term in reference to male and female together). In Genesis 5:2 we read that God created man in the likeness of God, as male and female, and "when they were created he called *them* '*man*'" (emphasis added). It appears that God intends the identity of *both* to contain an element of priority given to the male, since God chooses as their *common* name a name that is purposely *masculine* (i.e., a name that can be used also of the man alone, as distinct altogether from the woman, but never of the woman alone, as distinct altogether from the man). As God has so chosen to create man as male and female, by God's design the woman's identity as female is inextricably tied to and rooted in the prior identity of the male.[18]

God's naming male and female "man" indicates simultaneously, then, the *distinctiveness* of female from male, and the *unity* of the female's nature as it is identified with the prior nature of the first-created man, from which she now has come. Since this is so, we should resist the movement today in Bible translation that would customarily render instances of *'ādām* with the fully non-gender-specific term "human being."[19] This misses the God-intended implication conveyed by the masculine generic "man," viz., that woman possesses her common human nature only through the prior nature of the man. Put differently, she is woman as God's image by sharing in the man who is himself previously God's image. A male priority is indicated, then, along with full male-female equality, when God names male and female "man."

Third, consider the difficult statement of Paul in 1 Corinthians 11:7. Here he writes, "A man ought not to cover his head, since he is

---

[18]This is not to say that, in principle, God could not have created the female differently, perhaps independently from the male, and perhaps even as created first and existing (for a time anyway) without the male. But the point is that this is not how God actually did create woman. Rather, He formed her as she is *from* the man (Gen. 2:23; 1 Cor. 11:8), and this is signified by the use of the masculine generic term *'ādām* in Genesis 5:2.

[19]See Vern S. Poythress and Wayne A. Grudem, *The Gender-Neutral Bible Controversy: Muting the Masculinity of God's Words* (Nashville: Broadman & Holman, 2000).

the image and glory of God; but the woman is the glory of man."
Notice two contextual factors that relate to the interpretation of this
verse. First, 11:7 is followed by two explanatory statements, each beginning with *gar* ("for") in verses 8 and 9 (although the NIV fails to translate the *gar* that begins verse 9), which give the reason for Paul's
assertion and admonition in verse 7. In verses 8-9 Paul writes, "For
man did not come from woman, but woman from man; [for] neither
was man created for woman, but woman for man." One thing that is
clear from verses 8-9 is that Paul is arguing for the headship of man
over woman (cf. 1 Cor. 11:3). Man is not to cover his head, but the
woman should *because* the woman came from man, not the reverse
(11:8), and *because* the woman was created for the man, not the reverse
(v. 9). These two explanations, both beginning with *gar*, indicate Paul's
reasoning for his admonition in 11:7.

Second, notice that both explanatory statements have to do with
the *origination* of the man and the woman respectively. First Corinthians
11:8 points specifically to the fact that the man was created first and the
woman second, as she was crafted out of man's own being (see Gen.
2:21-23 and the discussion under the second point above), and 11:9
indicates that the purpose of woman's creation was to provide a fitting
service and help to the man (see Gen. 2:18, 20). So it is evident that Paul
is thinking specifically about the *woman's origination* vis-à-vis the man's,
and he reflects here on the importance of the man's prior creation, out
of whose being and for whose purpose the woman's life now comes.

Given the case he makes from 11:8-9, it appears that Paul's assertion in 11:7 (that the man is the image and glory of God, and the
woman the glory of the man) must be speaking about relative differences in the origination of man and woman respectively. His point, I
believe, is this: Because man was created by God in His image *first*, man
alone was created in a *direct* and *unmediated* fashion as the image of God,
manifesting, then, the glory of God. But in regard to the woman, taken
as she was *from* or *out of* man and made for the purpose of being a *helper*
suitable to him, her created glory is a *reflection* of the man's.[20] Just as the
man, created directly by God, is the image and glory of God, so the
woman, created out of the man, has her glory through the man. Now,
what Paul does not also here explicitly say but does seem to imply is

---

[20]See Hans Conzelmann, *1 Corinthians: A Commentary on the First Epistle to the Corinthians*, trans.
J. W. Leitch, Hermeneia Series (Philadelphia: Fortress Press, 1975).

this: In being created as the glory of the man, the woman likewise, in being formed through the man, is thereby created in the image and glory of God. At least this much is clear: As God chose to create her, the woman was not formed to be the human that she is *apart from* the man but *only through* the man. Does it not stand to reason, then, that her humanity, including her being the image of God, occurs as God forms her from the man as "the glory of man"?

To see it this way harmonizes what otherwise might appear contradictory—viz., that Genesis 1:26-27 and 5:1-2 teach the woman is created in the image of *God*, but 1 Corinthians 11:7 says only that she is "the glory of *man*." Paul's point, I believe, is that her glory comes through the man, and as such (implied in 1 Corinthians 11:7) she too possesses her full, yet derivative, human nature. But, of course, since her human nature comes to be "from man," so does her being the image of God likewise come only as God forms her from Adam, whose glory she now is. So there is no contradiction between Genesis 1:27 and 1 Corinthians 11:7. Woman *with* man is created in the image of God (Gen. 1:27), but woman *through* man has her true human nature and hence her glory (1 Cor. 11:7b), the glory of the man who himself is the image and glory of God (1 Cor. 11:7a).

Fourth, consider another passage that helps in our consideration of this issue. Genesis 5:3 makes the interesting observation that Adam, at 130 years of age, "had a son in his own likeness, in his own image; and he named him Seth." The language here is unmistakably that of Genesis 1:26. While the order of "image" and "likeness" is reversed, it appears that what is said earlier of man being created in the image and likeness of God (Gen. 1:26) is said here as Seth is brought forth in the likeness and image of Adam. Notice two things. First, since the author of Genesis had just been speaking, as we saw, of both male and female (5:2: "He created them male and female and blessed them. And when they were created, he called them 'man'"), it would have been natural to speak of Seth as being born in the likeness and image of *Adam and Eve*. But instead the author specifically states that Seth is in the likeness and image of Adam (only). Second, the parallel nature of this language with Genesis 1:26 likely has the effect of indicating that Seth is born in the image of Adam, who is himself the image of God, so that Seth, by being in the image of Adam, is likewise in the image of God. At least we know this: Man after Adam and Eve continues to be made in the image of God. When Genesis 9:6 forbids murder, the basis for this prohibition is that the one murdered is created in the image of God. So it appears that those born become the image of God because they are born through those who are the image of God. But Genesis 5:3 would lead us to speak with more precision. Seth was born in the image of God, it would appear, because he was born through the fatherhood of *Adam* (specifically Adam is mentioned and not Eve). So as Seth is born in the likeness and image of Adam, he is born in the image and likeness of God.

Understood this way, we see a conceptual parallel between Genesis 5:3 and 1 Corinthians 11:7. What is true in both texts, of Seth's and the woman's formation respectively, is that they derive their human natures, as Scripture specifically indicates, *through* the man. Another parallel is clear and is significant: Both Seth and Eve are *fully and equally* the image of God when compared to Adam, who is the image of God. So the present discussion reaffirms and reinforces our earlier declaration that *all human beings*, women as well as men, children as well as parents, are fully and equally the image of God. But having said this, Scripture indicates in addition to this important point another: God's design regarding *how* the woman and *how* a child become the image of God seems to involve inextricably and intentionally the role of the man's prior existence as the image of God.

It appears, then, that just as Seth becomes the image of God through his origination from his father, being born in the likeness and image of Adam (Gen. 5:3), so too does the woman become the image of God that she surely is (Gen. 1:27) through (and, by God's intentional design, *only* through) her origination from the man and as the glory of the man (Gen. 2:21-23; 1 Cor. 11:7-9). This suggests, then, that not only is the concept of male headship relevant to the question of how men and women are to relate and work together, but it seems also true that male headship is a part of the very constitution of the woman being created in the image of God. Man is a human being made in the image of God first; woman becomes a human being bearing the image of God only through the man. While both are fully and equally the image of God, there is a built-in priority given to the male that reflects God's design of male headship in the created order.

MALE AND FEMALE COMPLEMENTARITY AS THE IMAGE OF GOD

Thus far we have observed three central ideas. First, we have seen that the image of God in man involves God's creation of divine representations (images of God) who, in relationship with God and each other, function to represent God (imaging God) in carrying out God's designated responsibilities. Second, we observed that Scripture clearly teaches the full human and essential equality of man and woman as created in the image of God. And third, we saw that while male and female are equally the image of God, there is a priority given to the male as the one through whom the female is herself constituted as the image of God, for she is created as the glory of the man who is himself the image and glory of God. Now it is time for us to ask how these three elements of male and female complementarity as the image of God may be employed in living as the images God created us to be. Consider five aspects of this complementarian vision.

First, since priority in the concept of the image of God must go to our *functioning* as God's representatives who carry out our God-given responsibilities, we must see that it is essential that man and woman learn to work together in a unified manner to achieve what God has given them to do. There can be no competition, no fundamental conflict of purpose if we are to function as the image of God. Adversarial posturing simply has no place between the man and woman who are *both* the image of God. The reason for this is simple: Both man and woman, as the image of God, are called to carry out the unified set of responsibilities God has given. Since both share in the same responsibilities, both must seek to be unified in the accomplishment of them.

Surely this is implied in the narrative of Genesis 2. When it is discovered that there is no helper suitable for the man, God puts the man to sleep, takes a rib from his side, and creates the woman who is to help him shoulder his load. Man responds by saying of her that she is bone of his bones and flesh of his flesh, and the inspired commentary says of their joining that they are now "one flesh" (Gen. 2:22-24). The implication is clear: As one flesh, she now joined to him, they seek to carry out together what God had previously called the man to do. The helper suitable for Adam is now here, so that the common work of fulfilling God's purposes can be advanced together.

Second, since our functioning as the image of God (representing God) is a reflection and extension of our natures (as representations of God), it follows that where our natures are misshapened, so our functioning likewise will be misdirected. True functioning as the image of God must give priority to the reshaping of our lives. Only as we seek, by God's grace, to be more like Christ in our *inner* lives will we increasingly live *outwardly* in a manner that is more reflective of Him. Dallas Willard is surely right when in his *The Spirit of the Disciplines* he argues that we can only live like Jesus when we have disciplined ourselves to think and feel and value like Jesus.[21] We can only live like Him to the extent that we are remade to be like Him. Male/female functioning as the image of God, a functioning that must exhibit a unity of vision and commonality of effort, must then be based on men and women seeking with earnestness that God would work to remake us incrementally and increasingly into Christ's image, that we may reflect that image in our carrying out of our common God-given work.

Third, the full essential and human equality of male and female in the image of God means there can never rightly be a disparaging of women by men or of men by women. Concepts of inferiority or superiority have no place in the God-ordained nature of male and female in the image of God. As mentioned earlier, 1 Peter 3:7 makes this point in relation to the believing husband's attitude toward his believing wife. He is to grant her honor as a fellow heir of the grace of life. And as the verse concludes, God feels so strongly about a husband's honoring of his wife as a fully equal and fellow inheritor of Christ's riches that He warns that any husband who violates this principle will not be heard by Him in prayer. Nowhere in Scripture is the differentiation between male and female a basis for the male's supposed superiority in value or importance, or for female exploitation. All such attitudes and actions are sinful violations of the very nature of our common humanity as males and females fully and equally created in the image of God.

Fourth, while unified in our essential human equality and our common responsibility to do the will of God, the temporal priority of the image of God in the man, through whom the woman is formed as a human bearer of God's image, supports the principle of male headship in functioning as the image-of-God persons that both men and women are. This is precisely Paul's point in 1 Corinthians 11. The reason he is concerned about head coverings is that he knows that God has designed women and men to function so that each respects the other's God-ordained roles. Women are to honor and men are to embrace the special responsibility that God has given men in the spiritual leadership in the home and in the believing community. Where male headship is not acknowledged, our functioning as the image of God is hampered and

---

[21]Dallas Willard, *The Spirit of the Disciplines* (San Francisco: Harper & Row, 1988).

diminished. This puts Paul's instruction in Ephesians 5 in a new light. What we realize is that when wives submit to their husbands as the church submits to Christ (5:22-24), and when husbands love their wives as Christ loves the church (5:25-27), they exhibit their God-ordained roles as bearers of the image of God. It is not only in their equality that they are the image of God. They also bear and express God's image as they function in a manner that acknowledges the headship of the male in the bestowing of the image of God (1 Cor. 11:7-9).

Fifth, how does this complementarian vision of male and female in the image of God relate to singles? As a preface to this question, let us be clear about one thing: While Scripture commends marriage as ordained of God and good (1 Tim. 4:3-5), it also commends singleness as a life of extraordinary purpose and contribution, never speaking of any fundamental loss but only extolling the potential gain of the single life devoted to God (1 Cor. 7:25-35). Since human marriage is the shadow of the reality of the union of Christ and the church (Eph. 5:32), no believing single will miss out on the *reality* of marriage even if God calls him or her to live without the *shadow*.

With this realization that God commends singleness and that some of the Bible's most honored individuals were single (Jesus, John the Baptist, Paul), how can male and female singles function as the image of God? First, let's start with the fundamental notion that the image of God is, at heart, God's making us His representations (images of God) in order that we might represent Him (imaging God) in carrying out His will. At this level, singles and married people have really only one common task. All of us need to seek to become more like Christ so that we will better be able to fulfill the responsibilities God gives each of us to do. This is part of what it means to be created and to live as images of God. To be what (by God's grace) we should *be* in order to do what (by God's grace) we should *do* is God's task for all of us, married and single, and this reflects our being made in the image of God.

But second, recall that we are to live out our responsibilities in relationship with God and others. For those who are married, there is a covenant relationship that forms the context for much of the living out of the image of God in a union that looks to the man for leadership and direction. What about singles? I find great help here in looking at the examples of Jesus and Paul for their vision of living out their calling to be representations of God who represent Him in carrying out their responsibilities. What we find as we look at these key individuals is that they both sought meaningful relationships as a source of strength and companionship in fulfilling their God-ordained tasks. For example, when Jesus was facing the reality of certain and imminent crucifixion, He went apart to pray. It is instructive that He asked His closest disciples to pray with Him for strength to face this calling. That His friends failed Him by falling asleep does not change the fact that Jesus expressed a true and deep need for others to come alongside and help in the completion of His mission. Or consider how often Paul speaks of the encouragement others have been in his preaching of the Gospel. The point is simple. God's call to be single is never a call to isolation. God created us to need one another and to help one another. The body-of-Christ principle makes this abundantly clear. Singles should seek to know and do God's will for their lives, and in seeking this they should also seek strength, help, comfort, encouragement, and resource from others so that in relationship with these they may seek to fulfill their calling.

There is one more question singles may rightly ask. How is the headship of the male who is created first in the image of God to be honored by single women and men? I begin with a comment on what the priority of the male does not mean. Biblical male headship does *not* entail the authority of *all men* over *all women*. Just a moment's thought will reveal that this is not true for married people either. Ephesians 5:22 says, "Wives, submit to *your husbands* as to the Lord." My wife is not under the authority of all men. She stands under the authority of me (her husband) and of the elders of our church. But this is a restricted sense of male headship, and it fits what Scripture clearly teaches.

So, in what sense is the headship of the male relevant for singles? I believe it means two things. First, it means that all single women and men need to be members of a local church where they may be involved in the authority structure of that church. Qualified male elders are responsible for the spiritual welfare of their membership, and so single women, in particular, may find a source of spiritual counsel and guidance from these male elders in the absence of a husband who might otherwise offer such help. (Note: Wives of unbelieving husbands might likewise avail themselves of the counsel of their male eldership to fill the spiritual void that is lacking in their married relationship.) Second, the temporal priority of the male in the image of God means that in general, within male-female relationships among singles, there should be a deference offered to the men by the women of the group, which acknowledges the woman's reception of her human nature in the image of God through the man, but which also stops short of a full and general submission of women to men. Deference, respect, and honor should be shown to men, but never should there be an expectation that all the women must submit to the men's wishes. And for single men, there should be a gentle and respectful leadership exerted within a mixed group, while this also falls short of the special authority that husbands and fathers have in their homes or that elders have in the assembly. Because all are in the image of God, and because women generally are the image of God through the man, some expression of this male headship principle ought to be exhibited generally among women and men, while reserving the particular full relationships of authority to those specified in Scripture—viz., in the home and the believing community.

CONCLUSION

That we are male and female in the image of God says much about God's purposes with us, His human creatures. We are created to reflect His own nature so that we may represent Him in our dealings with others and over the world He has made. Our goal is to fulfill His will and obey His word. Yet, to accomplish this He has established a framework of relationship. Male and female, while fully equal as the image of God, are nonetheless distinct in the manner of their possession of the image of God. The female's becoming the image of God through the male indicates a God-intended sense of her reliance upon him, as particularly manifest in the home and community of faith. And yet all of us should seek through our relationships to work together in accomplishing the purposes God gives us to do. We face in this doctrine the dual truths that we are called to *be* both individually and in relationship what God intends us to be, so that we may *do* what honors Him and fulfills His will. Divine representations who, in relationship with God and others, represent God and carry out their God-appointed responsibilities—this, in the end, is the vision that must be sought by male and female in the image of God if they are to fulfill their created purpose. May we see God's good and wise design of manhood and womanhood understood and lived out more fully, so that God's purposes in and through us, His created images, might be accomplished—for our good, by His grace, and for His glory.

3

The Surpassing Goal: Marriage Lived for the Glory of God

John Piper

————❧————

My topic for this chapter is "Marriage lived for the glory of God." The decisive word in that topic is the word "for." "Marriage lived *for* the glory of God." The topic is not: "The glory of God *for* the living of marriage." And not: "Marriage lived *by* the glory of God." But: "Marriage lived *for* the glory of God."

This little word means that there is an order of priority. There is an order of ultimacy. And the order is plain: God is ultimate and marriage is not. God is the most important Reality; marriage is less important—far less important, infinitely less important. Marriage exists to magnify the truth and worth and beauty and greatness of God; God does not exist to magnify marriage. Until this order is vivid and valued—until it is seen and savored—marriage will not be experienced as a revelation of God's glory but as a rival of God's glory.

I take my topic, "Marriage lived for the glory of God," to be an answer to the question: Why marriage? Why is there marriage? Why does marriage exist? Why do we live in marriages? This means that my topic is part of a larger question: Why does anything exist? Why do you exist? Why does sex exist? Why do earth and sun and moon and stars exist? Why do animals and plants and oceans and mountains and atoms and galaxies exist? The answer to all these questions, including the one about marriage is: All of them exist to and for the glory of God.

That is, they exist to magnify the truth and worth and beauty and greatness of God. Not the way a *microscope* magnifies, but the way a *telescope* magnifies. Microscopes magnify by making tiny things look bigger than they are. Telescopes magnify by making unimaginably big things look like what they really are. Microscopes move the appearance of size away from reality. Telescopes move the appearance of size toward reality. When I say that all things exist to magnify the truth and worth and beauty and greatness of God, I mean that all things—and marriage in particular—exist to move the appearance of God in people's minds toward Reality.

God is unimaginably great and infinitely valuable and unsurpassed in beauty. "Great is the LORD, and greatly to be praised, and his greatness is unsearchable" (Ps. 145:3). Everything that exists is meant to magnify that Reality. God cries out through the prophet Isaiah (43:6-7), "Bring my sons from afar and my daughters from the end of the earth, everyone who is called by my name, whom I created *for my glory.*" We have been created to display the glory of God. Paul concludes the first eleven chapters of his great letter to the Romans with the exaltation of God as the source and end of all things: "For from him and through him and *to him* are all things. To him be glory forever. Amen" (11:36). He makes it even clearer in Colossians 1:16, where he says, "By [Christ] all things were created, in heaven and on earth . . . all things were created through him and *for him.*"

And woe to us if we think that "for him" means "for His need," or "for His benefit, or "for His improvement." Paul made it crystal clear in Acts 17:25 that God is not "served by human hands, as though he needed anything, since he himself gives to all mankind life and breath and everything." No, the term "for His glory" and "for Him" means, "for the display of His glory," or "for the showing of His glory," or "for the magnifying of His glory."

We need to let this sink in. Once there was God, and only God. The universe is His creation. It is not co-eternal with God. It is not God. "In the beginning was the Word, and the Word was with God and the Word was God. . . . All things were made through him" (John 1:1-3). All things. All that is not God was made by God. So once there was only God.

Therefore God is absolute Reality. We are not. The universe is not.

Marriage is not. We are derivative. The universe is of secondary importance, not primary. The human race is not the ultimate reality, nor the ultimate value, nor the ultimate measuring rod of what is good or what is true or what is beautiful. God is. God is the one ultimate absolute in existence. Everything else is from Him and through Him and for Him.

That is the starting place for understanding marriage. If we get this wrong, everything goes wrong. And if we get it right—really right, in our heads and in our hearts—then marriage will be transformed by it. Marriage will become what it was created by God to be—a display of the truth and worth and beauty and greatness of God.

This leads to a very simple conclusion—so simple and yet so far-reaching. If we want to see marriage have the place in the world and in the church that it is supposed to have—that is, if we want marriage to glorify the truth and worth and beauty and greatness of God—we must teach and preach less about marriage and more about God.

Most young people today do not bring to their courtship and marriage a great vision of God—who He is, what He is like, how He acts. In the world there is almost no vision of God. He is not even on the list to be invited. He is simply and breathtakingly omitted. And in the church the view of God that young couples bring to their relationship is so small instead of huge, and so marginal instead of central, and so vague instead of clear, and so impotent instead of all-determining, and so uninspiring instead of ravishing, that when they marry, the thought of living marriage to the glory of God is without meaning and without content.

What would the "glory of God" mean to a young wife or husband who gives almost no time and no thought to knowing the glory of God, or the glory of Jesus Christ, His divine Son . . .

• the glory of His *eternality* that makes the mind want to explode with the infinite thought that God never had a beginning, but simply always was;

• the glory of His *knowledge* that makes the Library of Congress look like a matchbox and quantum physics like a first grade reader;

• the glory of His *wisdom* that has never been and can never be counseled by men;

• the glory of His *authority* over heaven and earth and hell, without whose permission no man and no demon can move one inch;

• the glory of His *providence* without which not one bird falls to the ground or a single hair turns gray;

• the glory of His *word* that upholds the universe and keeps all the atoms and molecules together;

• the glory of His *power* to walk on water, cleanse lepers, heal the lame, open the eyes of the blind, cause the deaf to hear, still storms with a word, and raise the dead;

• the glory of His *purity* never to sin, or to have a two-second bad attitude or evil thought;

• the glory of His *trustworthiness* never to break His word or let one promise fall to the ground;

• the glory of His *justice* to render all moral accounts in the universe settled either on the cross or in hell;

• the glory of His *patience* to endure our dullness for decade after decade;

• the glory of His sovereign, slave-like *obedience* to embrace the excruciating pain of the cross willingly;

• the glory of His *wrath* that will one day cause people to call out for the rocks and the mountains to fall on them;

• the glory of His *grace* that justifies the ungodly; and

• the glory of His *love* that dies for us even while we were sinners?

How are people going to live their lives so that their marriages display the truth and worth and beauty and greatness of this glory, when they devote almost no energy or time to knowing and cherishing this glory?

Perhaps you can see why over the last twenty years of pastoral ministry I have come to see my life-mission and the mission of our church in some very basic terms: namely, I exist—we exist—to spread a passion for the supremacy of God in all things for the joy of all peoples. That's our assessment of the need. Until there is a passion for the supremacy and the glory of God in the hearts of married people, marriage will not be lived for the glory of God.

And there will not be a passion for the supremacy and the glory of God in the hearts of married people until God Himself, in His manifold glories, is known. And He will not be known in His manifold glories until pastors and teachers speak of Him tirelessly and constantly and deeply and biblically and faithfully and distinctly and thoroughly and passionately. Marriage lived for the glory of God will be the fruit of churches permeated with the glory of God.

So I say again, if we want marriage to glorify the truth and worth and beauty and greatness of God, we must teach and preach less about marriage and more about God. Not that we preach too much on marriage, but that we preach too little on God. God is simply not magnificently central in the lives of most of our people. He is not the sun around which all the planets of our daily lives are held in orbit and find their proper, God-appointed place. He is more like the moon, which waxes and wanes, and you can go for nights and never think about Him.

For most of our people, God is marginal and a hundred good things usurp His place. To think that their marriages could be lived for His glory by teaching on the dynamics of relationships, when the glory of God is so peripheral, is like expecting the human eye to glorify the stars when we don't stare at the night sky and have never bought a telescope.

So knowing God and cherishing God and valuing the glory of God above all things, including your spouse, is the key to living marriage to the glory of God. It's true in marriage, as in every other relationship: God is most glorified in us when we are most satisfied in Him.

Here is a key that unlocks a thousand doors. Superior satisfaction in God above all earthly things, including your spouse and your health and your own life (Psalm 63:3, "your steadfast love is better than life") is the source of great long-suffering without which husbands cannot love like Christ, and wives cannot follow like the bride of Christ, the church. Ephesians 5:22-25 makes plain that husbands take their cues of leadership and love from Christ, and wives take their cues of submission and love from the devotion of the church for whom He died. And both of those complementary acts of love—to lead, and to submit—are unsustainable for the glory of God without a superior satisfaction in all that God is for us in Christ.

Let me say it another way. There are two levels at which the glory of God may shine forth from a Christian marriage:

One is at the structural level when both spouses fulfill the roles God intended for them—the man as leader like Christ, the wife as advocate and follower of that leadership. When those roles are lived out, the glory of God's love and wisdom in Christ is displayed to the world.

But there is another deeper, more foundational level where the glory of God must shine if these roles are to be sustained as God designed. The power and impulse to carry through the self-denial and daily, monthly, yearly dying that will be required in loving an imperfect wife and loving an imperfect husband must come from a hope-giving, soul-sustaining, superior satisfaction in God. I don't think that our love for our wives or theirs for us will glorify God until it flows from a heart that delights in God more than marriage. Marriage will be preserved for the glory of God and shaped for the glory of God when the glory of God is more precious to us than marriage.

When we can say with the apostle Paul (in Philippians 3:8), "I count all things to be loss in view of the surpassing value of knowing Christ Jesus my Lord" (NASB)—when we can say that about marriage—about our husband or wife—then that marriage will be lived to the glory of God.

I close by trying to say this one more way, namely, with a poem that I wrote for my son on his wedding day.

LOVE HER MORE AND LOVE HER LESS

For Karsten Luke Piper
At His Wedding to
Rochelle Ann Orvis
May 29, 1995

The God whom we have loved, and in
Whom we have lived, and who has been
Our Rock these twenty-two good years
With you, now bids us, with sweet tears,
To let you go: "A man shall leave
His father and his mother, cleave
Henceforth unto his wife, and be
One unashaméd flesh and free."
This is the word of God today,
And we are happy to obey.
For God has given you a bride
Who answers every prayer we've cried
For over twenty years, our claim
For you, before we knew her name.

And now you ask that I should write
A poem—a risky thing, in light
Of what you know: that I am more
The preacher than the poet or
The artist. I am honored by
Your bravery, and I comply.
I do not grudge these sweet confines

Of rhyming pairs and metered lines.
They are old friends. They like it when
I bid them help me once again
To gather feelings into form
And keep them durable and warm.

And so we met in recent days,
And made the flood of love and praise
And counsel from a father's heart
To flow within the banks of art.
Here is a portion of the stream,
My son: a sermon poem. Its theme:
A double rule of love that shocks;
A doctrine in a paradox:

If you now aim your wife to bless,
Then love her more and love her less.

If in the coming years, by some
Strange providence of God, you come
To have the riches of this age,
And, painless, stride across the stage
Beside your wife, be sure in health
To love her, love her more than wealth.

And if your life is woven in
A hundred friendships, and you spin
A festal fabric out of all
Your sweet affections, great and small,
Be sure, no matter how it rends,
To love her, love her more than friends.

And if there comes a point when you
Are tired, and pity whispers, "Do
Yourself a favor. Come, be free;
Embrace the comforts here with me."
Know this! Your wife surpasses these:
So love her, love her more than ease.

And when your marriage bed is pure,
And there is not the slightest lure
Of lust for any but your wife,

And all is ecstasy in life,
A secret all of this protects:
Go love her, love her more than sex.

And if your taste becomes refined,
And you are moved by what the mind
Of man can make, and dazzled by
His craft, remember that the "why"
Of all this work is in the heart;
So love her, love her more than art.

And if your own should someday be
The craft that critics all agree
Is worthy of a great esteem,
And sales exceed your wildest dream,
Beware the dangers of a name.
And love her, love her more than fame.

And if, to your surprise, not mine,
God calls you by some strange design
To risk your life for some great cause,
Let neither fear nor love give pause,
And when you face the gate of death,
Then love her, love her more than breath.

Yes, love her, love her, more than life;
Oh, love the woman called your wife.
Go love her as your earthly best.
Beyond this venture not. But, lest
Your love become a fool's facade,
Be sure to love her less than God.

It is not wise or kind to call
An idol by sweet names, and fall,
As in humility, before
A likeness of your God. Adore
Above your best beloved on earth
The God alone who gives her worth.
And she will know in second place
That your great love is also grace,
And that your high affections now
Are flowing freely from a vow

Beneath these promises, first made
To you by God. Nor will they fade
For being rooted by the stream
Of Heaven's Joy, which you esteem
And cherish more than breath and life,
That you may give it to your wife.

The greatest gift you give your wife
Is loving God above her life.
And thus I bid you now to bless:
Go love her more by loving less.

III

RESOLVING THE
DISPUTED
QUESTIONS

4

DOES GALATIANS 3:28 NEGATE GENDER-SPECIFIC ROLES?

Richard Hove

⸻⸺

The debate over gender roles inevitably involves the use (or misuse!) of a variety of biblical texts. Doubtless the prize for the most oft-mentioned biblical text in this dispute would be awarded to 1 Timothy 2:12ff. But a runner-up award in this contest could easily be presented to Galatians 3:28:

> *There is neither Jew nor Greek, slave nor free, male nor female, for you are all one in Christ Jesus.*

Does this text negate gender-specific roles in marriage and the church? Or, put more positively, what was Paul's intent in this statement? This is the question before us.

For those of the egalitarian[1] persuasion, Galatians 3:28 is a critically important verse. In fact, virtually all egalitarian scholars appeal to this verse to substantiate their position. Rebecca Groothuis, in her book *Good News for Women: A Biblical Picture of Gender Equality*, states, "Of all the texts that support biblical equality, Galatians 3:26-28 is probably the *most* important."[2] In her estimation this verse, above thousands of others, is the ultimate statement of equality in the Scriptures. The organi-

---

[1] *Egalitarian* is a label commonly used for those who believe that the Scripture teaches the equality of men and women in a way that minimizes or denies gender-specific roles in marriage or the church.

[2] Rebecca Groothuis, *Good News for Women: A Biblical Picture of Gender Equality* (Grand Rapids, MI: Zondervan, 1997), 25. Italics mine.

zation Christians for Biblical Equality (CBE) makes Galatians 3:28 its hallmark verse: "Christians for Biblical Equality is an organization of Christians who believe the Bible, properly interpreted, teaches the fundamental equality of men and women of all racial and ethnic groups, all economic classes, and all age groups, based on biblical teachings summarized in Galatians 3:28."[3] A multitude of other examples could be provided, but these suffice to illustrate that for some in the evangelical camp, Galatians 3:28 is more than a key text in the debate over men's and women's roles in the home and church; rather, it is the fundamental or most important statement in the New Testament on this issue.

There are others, however, who don't find Galatians 3:28 to be anything of the sort. Complementarians[4] believe Galatians 3:28, when interpreted in its context, says little to nothing about gender roles. In fact, they argue, the use of this verse in a discussion of gender roles is a *misuse* of Paul's writings. John Piper and Wayne Grudem comment:

> The context of Galatians 3:28 makes abundantly clear the sense in which men and women are equal in Christ: they are equally justified by faith (v. 24), equally free from the bondage of legalism (v. 25), equally children of God (v. 26), equally clothed with Christ (v. 27), equally possessed by Christ (v. 29). . . . Galatians 3:28 does not abolish gender-based roles established by God and redeemed by Christ.[5]

Andreas Köstenberger joins in agreement:

> Of course, some insist Paul's statements in Galatians 3:28 *imply* a change in human relationships. But whether a change in human relationship is implied in Galatians 3:28 or not, this does not appear to be the point Paul actually intended to make. The interpreter should take care to distinguish between authorial intention and possible implications. Moreover, it seems questionable to focus on the implications of Paul's statements to the extent that the point Paul actually intended to make all but retreats into the background.[6]

---

[3] Brochure advertising a CBE meeting in Deerfield, Illinois.

[4] *Complementarian* is a label commonly used for those who believe that the Scriptures teach that men and women are equal in Christ but have different, complementary roles in marriage and the church.

[5] John Piper and Wayne Grudem, "An Overview of Central Concerns: Questions and Answers," in *Recovering Biblical Manhood and Womanhood*, eds. John Piper and Wayne Grudem (Wheaton, IL: Crossway Books, 1991), 71-72.

[6] Andreas Köstenberger, "Gender Passages in the NT: Hermeneutical Fallacies Critiqued," *Westminster Theological Journal* 56 (1994), 277.

For all their differences, complementarians and egalitarians share this in common: Both agree that the issue of gender roles is critically important, and both appeal to the Scriptures to settle this matter. Galatians 3:28 has become a vitally important, hotly debated text at the center of an often bitter struggle over the roles of men and women in marriage and the church.

This chapter will first examine the context of Galatians 3:28, beginning with an overview of Paul's sustained argument through the middle portion of Galatians and then concluding with a more detailed examination of the specific argument as contained in Galatians 3:26-29. This will be followed by a detailed look at the content of Galatians 3:28, focusing on the structure of the verse, the importance of the phrase "for you are all one in Christ Jesus," and the meaning of the negations "there is neither Jew nor Greek, slave nor free, male nor female." I will then offer and defend four propositions regarding the meaning and significance of Galatians 3:28 that, in my estimation, capture Paul's intent. Finally I will respond to two of the most common egalitarian claims regarding Galatians 3:28.

This chapter is a brief summary of sections of my book-length treatment of this verse found in *Equality in Christ? Galatians 3:28 and the Gender Dispute*.[7] Readers desiring more details or additional resources should consult that book, as the space limitations of this chapter necessarily limit the discussion of many important issues.

THE CONTEXT OF GALATIANS 3:28

Context is crucial for determining the meaning of virtually any message, whether it be written or communicated through another medium.[8] If, for example, an audience views a scene in a movie that shows an elderly man embracing and kissing an attractive younger woman, they will interpret this action completely differently if they are first aware that 1) the two were finally able to get married after five

---

[7]Richard W. Hove, *Equality in Christ? Galatians 3:28 and the Gender Dispute* (Wheaton, IL: Crossway Books, 1999).

[8]A discussion on context, meaning, and texts is well beyond the scope of this chapter. A helpful summary of the hermeneutical shift that has occurred in recent years can be found in D. A. Carson, *The Gagging of God: Christianity Confronts Pluralism* (Grand Rapids, MI: Zondervan, 1996). Previously meaning was located in the text, and context was thus critical to the interpretive process. Now many locate meaning in the reader, thus minimizing the need to understand context. Kevin Vanhoozer has made an excellent contribution to this topic, arguing that meaning is anchored to an author and a text: Vanhoozer, *Is There a Meaning in This Text?* (Grand Rapids, MI: Zondervan, 1998).

years of long-distance romance, or 2) the elderly man is cheating on his invalid wife, or 3) the younger woman is really the daughter of the elderly man. The action is the same, but the meaning radically changes based on the context.[9]

Biblical texts are no exception. Paul's statement in Galatians 3:28 that "there is neither . . . male nor female, for you are all one in Christ Jesus," if taken out of its context, could mean 1) in Christ there will be genderless people, or 2) there should be no Christian marriage because in Christ there is no male or female, or 3) since there is no male or female in Christ, Christians should utilize single-sex bathrooms. Hopefully these options strike the reader as less than sensible, but they are possibilities if one extracts Galatians 3:28 out of its context. Paul's intent (and God's intent) will only be clear if this statement is interpreted in its context.

So we begin by looking at the broader context of Galatians 3—4.

The Broad Context

Galatians 3—4 is an extended response to Galatians 2:11-14, where Paul records his rebuke of Peter for his "hypocrisy" in the way in which he related to Gentiles. Peter evidently had table fellowship with Gentiles until certain Jewish individuals appeared, at which point he abruptly ceased fellowship with those Gentiles. The episode ends with Paul's terse words to Peter: "You are a Jew, yet you live like a Gentile and not like a Jew. How is it, then, that you force Gentiles to follow Jewish customs?" (v. 14).

The *presenting* problem that precipitated this exchange was one of table etiquette: Was it proper for Jews to dine with Gentiles? Paul, however, understood that the *fundamental* problem was in fact much deeper. Peter, by his behavior, was not "acting in line with the truth of the gospel" (v. 14). By treating Gentiles in the same manner that a Jew would have treated Gentiles *before* the arrival of Christ, Peter was in essence, through his behavior, denying the reality of the Gospel.

Peter's inconsistent table manners are perhaps predictable. Given the Jewish root of the Gospel—the inheritance promised through Abraham, the Law, and now the arrival of a Jewish Messiah—how should Jewish Christians treat Gentile believers? Do Gentile Galatians need to become Jewish or become affiliated with the law-covenant in

---

[9]I heard John Mansfield use this illustration in a class on biblical interpretation.

order to become part of God's people? Do Gentile believers in the new covenant need to uphold various Jewish laws and traditions regarding table etiquette? If the locus of God's salvific activity in years past was the nation Israel, with her God-given promises and law, what has changed, both for the Jew and Gentile, now that the new covenant and the Spirit have arrived and the focus of God's salvific activity is no longer tribally based? Though these questions are somewhat moot for us today, they were critical questions for the early church.

Paul's chief concern was not Peter's table manners, as is evident from his extended response in Galatians 3—4. Paul realized that the *presenting* problem of who will eat with whom is answered only when one can answer the *fundamental* question of *what has changed with the arrival of Christ*. At least three different lines of evidence demonstrate that Paul was concerned with the fundamental problem.

First, note the number of times Paul mentions the progress of salvation-history[10] in his response to Peter's table fellowship problems:

> *3:8: The Scripture* foresaw *that God would justify the Gentiles by faith, and announced the gospel* in advance *to Abraham.*

> *3:17: The law,* introduced 430 years later, *does not set aside the covenant* previously established *by God.*

> *3:19: It [the law] was added because of transgressions* until *the Seed to whom the promise referred had come.*

> *3:22: The whole world is a prisoner of sin, so that what was promised* . . . might be given *to those who believe."*

> *3:23:* Before *this faith came, we were held prisoners by the law, locked up* until faith should be revealed.

> *3:25: Now that faith* has come, *we are no longer under the supervision of the law.*

---

[10]The term *salvation-history* or *redemptive-history* has been used differently by various biblical scholars. I use the term to denote *the progression of historical events and persons through which God reveals and accomplishes His redemptive activity.* According to this view, there is no radical distinction between history and salvation. On the contrary, the Scriptures themselves, both Old Testament and New Testament, point to real events and people as the means by which God reveals and accomplishes redemption. Salvation-history is portrayed as progressive; one event builds upon another, and past events are further clarified and illumined by more recent events.

4:2: He is subject to guardians and trustees until the time *set by his father.*

4:3-4: We were *in slavery. . . . But* when the time had fully come, *God sent his Son, born of a woman, born under the law.*

Second, Paul references several events predicted in the Old Testament, such as the arrival of the promised Spirit, as *now* being fulfilled. He alludes to at least three promised events that were linked to the arrival of the new covenant. a) In Joel 2:28ff. God promises to "pour out my Spirit on all people." In Galatians 4:4ff. Paul declares that this time has now come. b) Throughout the Old Testament it is clear that the Gentiles will one day be included as part of God's people (e.g., Gen. 12:3). Now Paul states that both Jews *and* Gentiles are heirs of Abraham through Christ (Gal. 3:26-29). God's people are no longer primarily a nation, but they are known, both Jew and Gentile, by virtue of being in Christ. c) A long anticipated event (Jer. 12:14-15; Isa. 58:13-14) is the reception of the promised inheritance. Paul states that now, through Christ, those who belong to Him can actually receive the promise (Gal. 3:29; 4:7).

Third, Paul presents Christ's death as a *means* to something new. In other words, the arrival of Christ, and His death and resurrection, have ushered in something new. This is clearly seen by examining two purpose clauses in Galatians 3—4. Note:

3:14: He [Christ] redeemed us in order that *the blessing given to Abraham might come to the Gentiles . . . so that by faith we might receive the promise of the Spirit.*

4:4-5: God sent his son . . . to redeem those under law . . . that *we might receive the full rights of sons.*

Paul describes Christ's death as the *means* by which the Gentiles received the blessings of Abraham, the promised Spirit was given, and the status of full sonship was procured. In other words, the life, death, and resurrection of Christ ushered in something new, but these changes were promised long ago.

In summary, Paul's argument throughout Galatians 3—4 is predicated upon changes in redemptive-history brought about by the arrival of Christ. It is necessary to highlight the significance of salvation-history in Paul's argument in Galatians 3—4, for without an appreciation of this foundation it is not possible to understand that Galatians 3:28, far from being an isolated saying regarding oneness or male/female relationships, occurs at a climactic point in Paul's extended description of changes brought about by the progress of salvation-history.

The Immediate Context

The immediate context of Galatians 3:28 is the paragraph found in Galatians 3:26-29. This paragraph functions as a hinge, tying Paul's discussion on Abraham, the promise, and the relationship of the Law to the promise (3:15-25) with the new sonship status of those who are now, with the arrival of Christ, full heirs of the promise (4:1-7). This section of text, 3:26-29, is intricately tied to what precedes (3:23-25) and follows (4:1-7); yet these verses comprise a unit, as evidenced by the following: 1) There is a shift in pronouns to the second person. The preceding section (3:23-25) is in the first person, and the following section (4:1-7) is in the third person. 2) Two phrases frame this section: "you are all sons . . . then you are Abraham's seed" (verses 26, 29). 3) The structure of 3:26-29 reveals a self-contained argument.[11] 4) Galatians 4:1 begins with "What I am saying is . . . ," which is a transition to an elaboration of the implications of verse 29.

Galatians 3:26-29 can be diagrammed:

26   *You are all sons of God*
               through faith in Christ Jesus,
27   *for all of you who were baptized into Christ*
          have been clothed with Christ.
28   *There is neither Jew nor Greek,*
                     slave nor free,
                     male nor female,
               for you are all one
                        in Christ Jesus.
29   *If you belong to Christ,*
    then you are Abraham's seed,
      and heirs according to the promise.

It is noteworthy that the oft-cited verse 28 is, in context, not an isolated saying but rather an integral part of a larger argument that ties

---

[11]This is clearer in the Greek, as the NIV has smoothed over some of the Greek prepositions. A literal translation of the Greek would be "*for* you are all sons, *for* you are all baptized into Christ, *for* you are all one in Christ . . . *therefore* you are Abraham's seed, heirs of the promise."

sonship (v. 26) and belonging to Christ (v. 29) to Abraham and the promise made to him (v. 29).

THE CONTENT OF GALATIANS 3:28

Verse 28 can now be unpacked in light of its context. We will first examine the structure of this verse and then turn our attention to the crucial phrase "for you are all one in Christ Jesus." This is the linchpin of Paul's argument, for it is the reason he himself offers for why "there is neither . . . male nor female." Finally we will examine the meaning of the negations and synthesize our findings.

The Structure

The structure of Galatians 3:28 is straightforward. The verse consists of three couplets and a final clause that provides the reason for the negation of the three couplets.

> *There is neither*
> > *Jew nor Greek,*
> > *slave nor free,*
> > *male nor female,*
> *for you are all one in Christ Jesus.*

The argument of verse 28 is in the form of "not this . . . *because* of this."[12] Each couplet is negated in light of the reason given in 28d, "for you are all one in Christ Jesus." Put another way: The reason there is no male or female is because "you are all one in Christ Jesus." The couplets are parallel except for a change from the same conjunction in the first two couplets to another in the third (in the original Greek).[13] Though they are parallel, there are differences between the couplets. The male/female couplet, for example, is the result of creation, while the slave/free couplet is the result of the Fall.[14] While the syntax of verse 28 is simple enough, the meaning and significance of it are ardently contested.

---

[12]Ben Witherington III, "Rite and Rights for Women," *New Testament Studies* 27 (1981), 596. Italics mine.

[13]The first two couplets are joined by the conjunction *oude*, which is often translated "or." The third couplet is joined by the conjunction *kai*, which is commonly translated "and." The significance of this change in pronouns is discussed in my book *Equality in Christ?*, pp. 66-69. Though the third conjunction varies from the first two, given the parallel structure of all three couplets, virtually all Bible translations translate the couplets in the same manner as the NIV: "there is neither Jew *nor* Greek, slave *nor* free, male *nor* female."

[14]For more on these couplets see my book. Ibid., 93-95.

The Meaning of "For You Are All One"

The final clause of verse 28, "for you are all one in Christ Jesus," is the crux of the verse; whatever Paul meant by the preceding negated couplets he bases upon this truth. The word "for" (Greek *gar*) introduces the grounds for what has gone before: There is no Jew or Greek, slave or free, male or female *because* "you are all one in Christ Jesus." It is interesting that this concept of oneness is also apparent in the so-called parallels found in 1 Corinthians 12:13 and Colossians 3:11.[15]

Paul delineates six different groups of people who are said to be "one" in Christ: Jews, Greeks, slaves, free individuals, males, and females. All individuals who are in Christ are one, regardless of their religious/ethnic heritage, legal status, or sexual identity. Questions, nevertheless, remain about this expression. What does it mean for a diverse plurality to be "one"? If, for example, a plurality is one, what does this imply about the relationship between the parts? If Jews and Greeks are one in Christ, how might this change how Jews and Greeks relate to one another?

What did Paul mean by the expression, "for you are all one"? In order to answer this question we will first examine the lexical possibilities for the word "one" (Greek *heis, mia, hen*). When Paul says "you are all one," what are some possible meanings of this word "one"? Second, a study will be made of other parallel Greek expressions where a plurality of objects or people are said to be "one."[16] This search is possible utilizing a database of all known Greek writings.[17] What other plurality of objects or people were said to be "one," and what can we learn about Galatians 3:28 from other uses of nearly parallel expressions?

Lexical options for "one": The standard Greek lexicon for the New Testament period is BAGD.[18] It lists the following lexical options for the Greek word translated "one" in Galatians 3:28.[19] It will be convenient to present them in outline form.

---

[15]First Corinthians 12:13: "For we were all baptized by one Spirit into *one body*—whether Jews or Greeks, slave or free." Colossians 3:15: "Let the peace of Christ rule in your hearts, since as members of *one body* you were called to peace." Italics mine.

[16]Specifically, a search was made for plural forms of the Greek verb *eimi* used with a nominative form of *heis, mia*, or *hen*.

[17]This database is called Thesaurus Linguae Graecae (TLG). It is an ancient Greek database consisting of texts between Homer and 600 A.D. The database is exhaustive, containing "virtually all authors represented by text, whether in independent editions or in quoted form."

[18]*Greek-English Lexicon of the New Testament and Early Christian Literature* by Walter Bauer, William Arndt, F. Wilbur Gingrich, and Frederick W. Danker (BAGD) (Chicago: University of Chicago Press, 1979).

[19]BAGD, 230-232. The revised edition (2000) does not differ from this list of meanings in any significant way (291-293).

1. Literal Uses
   A. In contrast to more than one.
      i.   as an adjective: "one baptism," ex. Ephesians 4:5.
      ii. as a noun with a partitive genitive: "one of these," ex. Matthew 6:29.
   B. In contrast to the parts, of which a whole is made: "we, though many, form one body," Romans 12:5.
   C. With a negative following: "not one of them will fall," Matthew 10:29.
2. Emphatic Uses
   A. One and the same: "one and the same loaf," 1 Corinthians 10:17.
   B. Single, only one: "he had an only son," Mark 12:6.
   C. Alone: "who can forgive sins but God alone?" Mark 2:7.
3. Indefinite Uses
   A. Someone, anyone: "one of the days," Luke 5:17.
   B. As an indefinite article: "a scribe," Matthew 8:19.
   C. Used with *tis* [an indefinite pronoun]: "a certain young man," Mark 14:51.
4. Perhaps as a Hebraism: "on the first day of the week," 1 Corinthians 16:2.
5. Different special combinations.

The term "one" in Galatians 3:28, then, can have many different uses in the New Testament. BAGD lists Galatians 3:28 as an example of 1.B., where "one" emphasizes the whole in contrast to the parts. Paul is highlighting the whole—"you are all *one* in Christ Jesus"—in contrast to the parts (Jew/Greek, slave/free, male/female).

Likewise, in a major dictionary article on this word for "one," Stauffer notes the variety of ways it is used in the New Testament: "Only rarely is *heis* ["one"] used as a digit in the NT (e.g., 2 Pt 3:8). It usually means 'single,' 'once-for-all,' 'unique' or 'only,' or 'unitary,' 'unanimous,' or 'one of two or many,' only one."[20] Here in Galatians 3:28, according to Stauffer, Paul is emphasizing the unity of the people of God. Stauffer notes that just as the destiny of the human race was decided in Adam, so, in Christ, the "destiny of the new humanity is determined."[21] In other words, "you are . . . one" means that all Galatian believers are united in Christ.

---

[20]E. Stauffer, "*heis,*" *TDNT,* 2:434.
[21]Ibid., 439.

So the lexical possibilities for "one" are many, but both Stauffer and BAGD agree that this term, as used in Galatians 3:28, denotes a unity, the whole in contrast to the parts. It is important at this point simply to note that the lexical possibilities for this word do not include "equal." Correspondingly, the *lexical* options for "you are . . . one" do not include "you are equal." The idea of equality and Galatians 3:28 will be discussed below.

Parallel uses in Greek literature: In an effort to understand the expression "you [plural] are . . . one," a search was made for other similar uses of this phrase in Greek, where a plural form of the Greek verb used in Galatians 3:28, *eimi*, was coupled with a form of the word "one" (Greek *heis, mia, hen*). All known Greek literature written in the three centuries around the New Testament (2 B.C.—A.D. 1) was searched using the TLG Greek database. Forty-five searches were run, looking for parallel expressions.[22] In that day what other things or people were said to be "one"?

In the three hundred years surrounding the writing of the New Testament, sixteen Greek expressions quite similar to Galatians 3:28 were found. These examples are helpful toward understanding Paul's use in Galatians 3:28 and are listed below. Because this search was done in Greek, the Greek text is listed first, followed by the English translation. The results are easy to follow even if you don't know Greek. A summary table is found after the specific citations.

Occurrences of ἐσμέν with ἕν ("We are one.")
1. John 10:30
   ἐγὼ καὶ ὁ πατὴρ *ἕν ἐσμεν*
   "I and the Father are one."
2. Romans 12:5
   οὕτως οἱ πολλοὶ *ἓν σῶμά ἐσμεν* ἐν Χριστῷ
   ". . . so we, who are many, are one body in Christ." (NASB)
3. 1 Corinthians 10:17
   ὅτι εἷς ἄρτος, *ἓν σῶμα* οἱ πολλοί *ἐσμεν*
   "Since there is one bread, we who are many are one body." (NASB)

---

[22]The search was for uses of a plural form of ἐμί coupled with a nominative form of εἷς, μία, or ἕν. I looked for only nominative forms of εἷς, μία, and ἕν in light of their use with a copulative verb. TLG searched for plural forms of ἐμί within six words of a nominative form εἷς, μία, or ἕν. These were the plural forms searched: present indicatives ἐσμέν, ἐστέ, εἰσίν, εἰσί; future indicatives ἐσόμεθα, ἔσεσθε, ἔσονται; imperfect indicatives ἦμεν, ἤμεθα, ἦτε, ἦσαν; and subjunctives ὦμεν, ἦτε, ὦσιν, ὦσι. I sought matches within six words for any of these forms with either of the three nominatives for "one." For complete results of this search, see the appendix in my book.

4. Ignatius, *Epistulae interpolatae et epistulae suppositiciae* 11.4.2.5[23]

ἵνα, ὡς ἐγὼ καὶ σὺ ἕν ἐσμεν, καὶ αὐτοὶ ἐν ἡμῖν ἓν ὦσιν

"so that as you and I are one, also they may be one in us."

Occurrences of ἐστε with εἷς ("You are one.")

5. Galatians 3:28

πάντες γὰρ ὑμεῖς εἷς ἐστε ἐν Χριστῷ Ἰησοῦ

". . . for you are all one in Christ Jesus."

6. Dio Chrysostom, *Orationes* 41.10.7

καὶ σχεδὸν εἷς ἐστε δῆμος καὶ μία πόλις ἐν οὐ πολλῷ διαστήματι

"You are almost one community, one city only slightly divided."

Occurrences of εἰσίν with εἷς ("They are one.")

7. Philo, *De Mutatione Nominum* 200.2

οἱ δὲ πρὸς ἄμυναν εὐτρεπεῖς τῶν οὕτως βεβήλων καὶ ἀκαθάρτων τρόπων δύο μέν εἰσιν ἀριθμῷ, Συμεὼν καὶ Λευί, γνώμῃ δὲ εἷς

". . . and the champions who stand ready to repel such profane and impure ways of thinking are two in number, Simeon and Levi, but they are one in will."

Occurrences of εἰσί with εἷς ("They are one.")

8. Philo, *Legum Allergoriarum* 3.105.4

ὁρᾷς ὅτι κακῶν εἰσὶ θησαυροί · καὶ ὁ μὲν τῶν ἀγαθῶν εἷς—ἐπεὶ γὰρ ὁ θεὸς εἷς, καὶ ἀγαθῶν θησαυρὸς «εἷς»

"You see that there are treasuries of evil things. And the treasury of good things is one, for since God is One, there is likewise one treasury of good things."

Occurrences of εἰσίν with μία ("They are one.")

9. Matthew 19:6

ὥστε οὐκέτι εἰσὶν δύο ἀλλὰ σὰρξ μία

"So they are no longer two, but one."

10. Mark 10:8

ὥστε οὐκέτι εἰσὶν δύο ἀλλὰ μία σάρξ

"So they are no longer two, but one."

Occurrences of εἰσίν with ἕν ("They are one.")

11. 1 Corinthians 3:8

ὁ φυτεύων δὲ καὶ ὁ ποτίζων ἕν εἰσιν

"Now he who plants and he who waters are one" (NASB).

---

[23]This portion of Ignatius' Epistle to the Ephesians is missing from most manuscripts, including the volume *The Apostolic Fathers* in the Loeb Classical Library. This text is from the TLG database, which gives its source as *Patres Apostolici,* eds. F. X. Funk and F. Diekamp, Vol. 2, 3rd ed. (Tübingen: Laupp, 1913), 234-258. Translation is mine.

12. 1 John 5:8

τὸ πνεῦμα καὶ τὸ ὕδωρ καὶ τὸ αἷμα, καὶ οἱ τρεῖς εἰς τὸ ἕν εἰσιν

". . . the Spirit, the water and the blood; and the three are in agreement."

Occurrences of ὦσιν with ἕν ("They may be one.")

13. John 17:11

ἵνα ὦσιν ἕν καθὼς ἡμεῖς

". . . so that they may be one as we are one."

14. John 17:21

ἵνα πάντες ἕν ὦσιν

". . . that all of them may be one."

15. John 17:22

ἵνα ὦσιν ἕν

". . . that they may be one."

16. John 17:22

καθὼς ἡμεῖς ἕν

". . . as we are one."

17. John 17:23

ἵνα ὦσιν τετελειωμένοι εἰς ἕν

". . . that they may be perfected in unity" (NASB).

The sixteen occurrences (other than Galatians 3:28) fall into several categories. It is helpful to summarize these as follows:

Different Elements	*One _____?*
Jesus/Father (John 10:30; 17:11, 21, 22 [2x], 23; *Epistulae* 11.4.2.5)	one nature?
Husband/wife (Matt. 19:6; Mark 10:8)	one flesh
Different believers (Rom. 12:5; 1 Cor. 10:17)	one body
Planter/waterer (1 Cor. 3:8)	one purpose?
Spirit, water, blood (1 John 5:8)	one witness
2 cities	one community
2 people, Simeon and Levi (*De Mutatione Nominum* 200.2)	one will
Many good things (*Legum Allergoriarum* 3.105.4)	one treasury/ one God

Several observations can be drawn from this data that will be helpful in understanding Galatians 3:28.

1) Diverse people and objects are said to be "one." For example, the

one who plants is different from the one who waters; each has a distinct role and reward, though both are said to be one (1 Cor. 3:8). Members of the body of Christ have different gifts and functions, but together they are said to form "one body" (Rom. 12:5). Two cities, though separated geographically, are said to be almost one community. The expression "we/you/they are one" is used to unify *diverse and distinct* people and objects.

2) While the expression "we/you/they are one" unifies different people and objects, it is used because the separate elements have something in common. In nearly half the occurrences this is clearly stated by the author—e.g., one *flesh*, one *will*, one *community*. In the remaining cases, however, the referent is not clearly stated, although it is usually easily discernible. For example, the one who plants and the one who waters are one (no referent is given, but one purpose is assumed). Likewise, the Father and the Son are one (again, no referent given, but one essence or nature seems correct); yet here, too, They are different persons with different roles.

3) The expression "we/you/they are one" fails to provide specific details about the individual elements except that the individuals are "one" in some aspect. The reader is informed as to what the different elements have *in common*, not how each element compares to or relates with the other. For example, Philo notes that Simeon and Levi are one in will and purpose, but beyond that it is not possible to know, for example, if Levi is brighter than Simeon, if Simeon resents Levi, or if Simeon is Levi's boss (which seems doubtful from the context). Likewise, a husband and a wife become one flesh, but this expression, in itself, doesn't inform the reader how husbands and wives should relate to one another. It simply informs the reader that two individuals are now one flesh. Doubtless there are ramifications to becoming one flesh, but the expression doesn't provide the details; instead it emphasizes that the husband and wife are one flesh.

In sum, our study of the parallel uses of the expression "you are all one" and the lexical options for "one" both point to the same conclusion: *The expression "you are all one" is used of diverse objects to state that these different objects share something in common.* It does not provide specifics regarding the relationship between the parts. Rather, the expression simply states that diverse parts share something in common; they are united in some aspect, in contrast to their diversity. Most helpful for our study are the parallels with Paul, especially

1 Corinthians 3:8 and Romans 12:5. In 1 Corinthians 3:8 Paul clearly states that the one who plants and the one who waters have different tasks and different rewards, and yet they are one (likely in purpose). Similarly, in Romans 12:5 Paul states that the members of the body are different, with different tasks, but they, too, are "one." This pattern is true of all seventeen of the examples; a diverse plurality is said to be one because they share something in common, not because they are similar or the same. The evidence gathered from the use of the phrase "you are all one" in the three hundred years around the New Testament is decidedly against those who would argue Paul's phrase "you are all one" means "you are all equal" or "you are all similar" or "you are all the same."

Lexically we've seen that the word "one" can be used many ways, but it is not used to denote equality. In Galatians 3:28 this word is used to express unity in distinction to a plurality; Jews/Greeks, slaves/free, males/females, by virtue of each sharing in one Christ, are one.

The Meaning of the Negations

What, then, is the meaning of the negation "there is neither . . . male nor female"? The reason for the negations is clear: It is because all the Galatians are "one in Christ Jesus." Clearly the concept of being "in Christ" is crucial to Paul's argument here. Now *in Christ*, all—regardless of ethnicity, economic status, or gender—are heirs of the promise made to Abraham. Precisely what Paul had in mind with these negations, however, is not so self-evident.

The couplets are in the form "there is no x or y."[24] It is clear that Paul did not intend this expression literally to mean "x and y do not exist." No one believes Paul denied the existence of Jews, Greeks, slaves, free persons, males, or females. This expression must be a figure of speech meant to communicate something other than the nonexistence of these categories.

Most of the proposals for the meaning of "there is no Jew/Greek, slave/free, male/female" have suggested that Paul's use of this expression is intended to negate some particular distinction between these groups. Paul cannot be denying all distinctions between these groups, as he later, for example, addresses Jews and Gentiles. So what exactly

---

[24]It has already been acknowledged that the third couplet is slightly different than the first two. It is of the form "there is no x *and* y." For more on this, see the discussion in my book, *Equality in Christ?*, 66-69.

is the meaning of "there is no x or y"? Unfortunately, none of the other uses of this Greek phrase in the three hundred years surrounding the New Testament[25] is used in a similar manner ("there is no x or y"). So it is necessary to determine the meaning of this expression by examining its immediate context, as well as its broader, biblical context. At least four different evidences may be presented to argue that the phrase "there is no x or y" is another way of saying "there is no distinction between x and y in this sense—*all* believers, regardless of their ethnic, religious, sexual, or economic state, are one in Christ."

First, within Galatians 3:26-29 there is a clear emphasis on the *universal* nature of the benefits brought about by the advent of Christ: "you are *all* sons" (3:26), "for *all of you* who were baptized into Christ have clothed yourselves with Christ" (3:27), "for you are *all* one in Christ Jesus" (3:28). *All* who belong to Christ are sons and heirs. If all people share in something, say the quality R, then there is no distinction between these people insofar as they share in R.

Second, Galatians 3:28 is part of a larger salvation-historical argument, and the Old Testament clearly anticipated that the new covenant would be universal, for all people. Paul writes that the Galatians are no longer minors but full sons because the fullness of time has arrived (cf. 4:1-7). The new covenant age has appeared, and Gentiles and Jews are now heirs of the promise made to Abraham. This event, as predicted by the Old Testament prophets Jeremiah and Joel, included the universal blessing of God on those who believe, whatever their place in life. Here are the words of Jeremiah:

> *"This is the covenant I will make with the house of Israel after that time," declares the LORD. "I will put my law in their minds and write it on their hearts. I will be their God, and they will be my people. No longer will a man teach his neighbor, or a man his brother, saying, 'Know the LORD,' because they will* all *know me, from the least of them to the greatest," declares the LORD.*
> — JER. 31:33-34A (EMPHASIS MINE)

Jeremiah points to the universal nature of the new covenant; everyone, from the least to the greatest, will be able to know the Lord. Joel's prophetic description of the arrival of this day includes the same element:

---

[25]The fifteen other occurrences of this phrase are found in my book. Ibid., 62-64.

"And afterward I will pour out my Spirit on all *people. Your* sons and
daughters *will prophesy, your old men will dream dreams, your young
men will see visions. Even on my servants, both* men and women, *I
will pour out my Spirit in those days."*
—JOEL 2:28-29 (EMPHASIS MINE)

Joel, like Paul in Galatians 3:28, uses couplets of opposites to deline-
ate "all people": "I will pour out my Spirit on *all* people . . . both *men*
and *women*." He describes all people by contrasting sons/daughters,
old/young, men/women; *all* people will receive God's Spirit.

Jeremiah 31 and Joel 2 are important Old Testament descriptions
of the arrival of the new covenant, the fulfillment of which is described
in Galatians 3—4. These two Old Testament passages stress the universality of the new covenant by using couplets of opposites, much like
the couplets found in Galatians 3:28. It is clear that phrases such as
"from the least of them to the greatest" and "even on my servants, both
men and women" are meant to include everybody, without distinction.
It is important to note, however, that the mere presence of universal
language here in Galatians 3:26-29 does not, by itself, insure a direct
link from Galatians 3:28 to the Old Testament passages noted above.
Likewise, there is no evidence that Paul was citing these Old Testament
authors or that his expression "there is no x or y" is directly tied to
Jeremiah's somewhat different phrase "from the least to the greatest"
("from x *to* y").

What is argued here is that: 1) the anticipated new covenant blessing was universal, promised to all individuals who believed, without
distinction: "*whoever* calls on the name of the LORD will be delivered"
(Joel 2:32, NASB). Furthermore, the promise to Abraham, which is
clearly in view in Galatians 3—4, had a universal scope: "I will bless
those who bless you, and *whoever* curses you I will curse; and *all* peoples on earth will be blessed through you" (Gen. 12:3; cf. Gen. 17:5).
2) Galatians 3:28 describes the new covenant people of God who are
recipients of the promise made to Abraham. 3) Since the Old
Testament prophecies (Jer. 31; Joel 2) and the promise made to
Abraham (Gen. 12) emphasized that God's blessings in the new
covenant would be available to all without distinction, and since
Galatians 3:28 describes the people of the new covenant, it is reasonable to conclude that the formula "there is no x or y" has the same
intent as what was predicted in the Old Testament. That is, everybody

is included, without distinction, from the least to the greatest (Jer. 31), men and women (Joel 2), old and young (Joel 2).

Third, the New Testament often uses pairs of opposites as a literary device to express the concept of "universal." This figure of speech is a "merism." For example, the expression "I searched high and low for you" does not mean that I literally searched the high places and then the low places. Rather, the opposites high/low are used to denote high, low, and everything in between: I searched *everywhere* for you. Granted, in places in the New Testament pairs of opposites may have other functions (e.g., life/death, light/darkness); but when the opposites consist of groups of people, these figures of speech frequently denote *all* people. For example, 1 Corinthians 12:13: "For we were *all* baptized by one Spirit into one body—whether Jews or Greeks, slave or free—and we were all given the one Spirit to drink." Here two pairs of opposites—Jew/Greek and slave/free—function in apposition to "all"; the pairs Jew/Greek and slave/free are another way of denoting all people. Further examples of this include Revelation 19:18: "so that you may eat the flesh of kings, generals, and mighty men, of horses and their riders, and the flesh of *all people*, free and slave, small and great" and Ephesians 6:8: "because you know that the Lord will reward *everyone* for whatever good he does, whether he is slave or free." Also note Romans 10:11-12; 1 Corinthians 10:32; Colossians 3:11; Revelation 6:15.

Modern examples of this are not difficult to find. Consider, for example, Martin Luther King, Jr.'s famous "I Have a Dream" speech, delivered in front of the Lincoln Memorial in August 1963:

> I have a dream my four little children will one day live in a nation where they will not be judged by the color of their skin but by [the] content of their character. . . . This will be the day when all God's children will be able to sing with new meaning—"my country 'tis of thee; sweet land of liberty; of thee I sing; land where my fathers died, land of the pilgrim's pride; from every mountainside, let freedom ring"—and if America is to be a great nation, this must become true. So let freedom ring. . . .
>
> And when we allow freedom to ring, when we let it ring from every village and hamlet, from every state and city, we will be able to speed up the day when *all* of God's children—*black men and white men, Jews and Gentiles, Catholics and Protestants*—will be able to join hands and sing the words of the old Negro spiritual,

"Free at last, free at last; thank God Almighty, we are free at last."
(italics mine)[26]

Dr. King longed for the day when freedom would ring everywhere, when *every* person would celebrate the emancipation of people
of color from racial discrimination. He chose pairs of opposites—
black/white, Jew/Gentile, Catholic/Protestant—to convey the universality of his dream.

Fourth, other Pauline passages that are similar in many ways
specifically confirm this proposal. Compare these two passages in
Romans with Galatians 3:26-28 (emphasis mine):

> *But now apart from the Law the righteousness of God has been man-
> ifested, being witnessed by the Law and the Prophets, even the righ-
> teousness of God through faith in Jesus Christ for all those who believe;
> for there is* no distinction.
>
> —ROM. 3:21-22 (NASB)

> *For the Scripture says, "Whoever believes in Him will not be disap-
> pointed." For there is* no distinction *between Jew and Greek; for the
> same Lord is Lord of* all, *abounding in riches for* all *who call on Him,
> for "Whoever will call on the name of the LORD will be saved."*
>
> —ROM. 10:11-13 (NASB)

> *For you are* all *sons of God through faith in Christ Jesus. For all of you
> who were baptized into Christ have clothed yourselves with Christ.
> There is neither Jew nor Greek, there is neither slave nor free man, there
> is neither male nor female; for you are* all *one in Christ Jesus.*
>
> —GAL. 3:26-28 (NASB)

Several common themes are repeated in all three of these passages.
1) All three passages occur in a salvation-historical context. 2) There is
an unmistakable universal emphasis; the blessings of God are available
to *all* who are in His Son, regardless of human distinctions. 3) Each passage refers to the inclusion of the Gentiles. Although Romans 3:21-22,
quoted above, contains no mention of the Gentiles, just after these

---

[26]Martin Luther King, Jr., "I Have a Dream" (speech given in Washington, D.C., August 28,
1963), in *A Testament of Hope: The Essential Writings of Martin Luther King, Jr.*, ed. James Melvin
Washington (San Francisco: Harper & Row, 1986), 219-220.

verses, in the same thought unit, Paul writes: "Is God the God of Jews only? Is he not the God of Gentiles too? Yes, of Gentiles too, since there is only one God, who will justify the circumcised by faith and the uncircumcised through that same faith" (vv. 29-30). 4) Though many different expressions are used, there is a repeated emphasis upon believing in Christ: "through faith in Christ to all who believe" (Rom. 3:22), "whoever believes," "all who call on Him" (Rom. 10:11-12, NASB), "in Christ Jesus" (Gal. 3:28). 5) The Jew/Greek couplet used in Galatians 3:28 is used in much the same manner as in Romans 10:12. Of even greater interest is that Romans 10:13 directly cites Joel 2:28-32.

In Romans Paul's intent is not clouded by the ambiguous "there is no x or y" as in Galatians 3:28, but his use of this couplet here is clear: There is *no distinction* between Jew and Greek with regard to salvation— all who call upon Him will be saved. If Galatians 3:28 is tied to Joel 2:28-32, which seems likely, then given the use of the Jew/Greek couplet in Romans 10:12, the meaning of "there is no x or y" in Galatians 3:28 is, "there is no distinction between x or y in this respect: all believers, without distinction, are one in Christ and are heirs of the new covenant blessings that He brings."

The negations in verse 28 function as "merisms" to denote that *all* believers, without distinction, regardless of their racial status (Jew, Gentile), economic status (slave, free), or gender (male, female), are recipients of what was first promised to Abraham's one Seed and is now, in the fullness of time, delivered to all who are united to Christ.

Galatians 3:26-29 is the climax of Paul's argument that began with the Antioch incident (2:11-14). Failing to understand the changes that resulted from the arrival of Christ, the Gentile Galatians were susceptible to the false teaching that they must somehow be related to the ways of Abraham and the law-covenant in order to be a true heir. Their confusion is understandable. Since the Old Testament tied the promise and its blessings to being of the seed of Abraham, the Gentile Galatians, lacking a connection to Abraham, could easily conclude it would be impossible for them to become heirs without doing something to be tied to Abraham. Now, however, in contrast to this God has made sonship and the inheritance available to all who are in Christ.

The inheritance is still dependent upon being related to Abraham. What has changed, however, is that now one becomes a seed of Abraham by being related to *the* Seed of Abraham, Christ, through faith. So the inheritance is now available to Jew and Greek alike.

Christians are the seed of Abraham because they are 'one in Christ' (Gal 3.28b) who is the true seed of Abraham. All those who are in Christ are the seed of Abraham whether they be Jew or Gentile. For Paul, as well as for the rest of the New Testament, the concept of Inheritance is Christocentric. Christ is the true Seed from whom the rest of the spiritual descendants of the Promise spring.[27]

Sandwiched between verse 26 and verse 29, Galatians 3:28 describes God's people in the new covenant. These people have fully associated with Christ; they have been baptized into Him and have been clothed with Him. By nature of their incorporation into Him, they have become the rightful heirs of the blessing promised to Abraham and to sons of God. As predicted by the Old Testament, the new covenant is now known by its universal call; *all* are invited, whether Jew or Greek, slave or free, male or female. There is no distinction among God's people; no race, nation, class, or gender has favored status with God. As the old revival preachers used to say, "The ground is level at the foot of the cross." Every member of God's household enters the same way, by being related to God's Son. And because all of God's family shares in His one Son, there is now a new unity among God's people.

THE MEANING AND SIGNIFICANCE OF GALATIANS 3:28

In light of the exegetical, lexical, and syntactical data already presented, I will now put forth and defend four statements about Galatians 3:28 that I believe capture Paul's intent.

Galatians 3:28 Describes the New People of God

Complementarians have sometimes tended to ignore the salvation-historical implications of Galatians 3—4. Klyne Snodgrass is right when he states, "Whatever else is done with the other texts concerning women, justice must be done to the *newness* proclaimed in Galatians 3:28" (italics mine).[28] Though the term *new* is found nowhere in Galatians 3:26-29, these verses are preceded by 3:23-25 and are followed by 4:1-7; any interpretation of Galatians 3:28 must address the

---

[27]James D. Hester, *Paul's Concept of Inheritance: A Contribution to the Understanding of Heilsgeschichte*, Scottish Journal of Theology Occasional Papers, No. 14 (Edinburgh: Oliver and Boyd, 1968), 51.
[28]Klyne Snodgrass, "Galatians 3:28: Conundrum or Solution?" *Women, Authority, and the Bible* (Downers Grove, IL: InterVarsity Press, 1986), 178.

question, "What is new here?" If the meaning of Galatians 3:28 is simply that Jew/Greeks, slaves/free, men/women are all God's people, it is difficult to see how such an interpretation does justice to the new era brought about by the arrival of Christ.

What, then, is new about the people of God in the new covenant? It is beyond the scope of this chapter to fully flesh this out, but I will list a couple of changes that are representative of the types of changes I believe Paul had in mind.

First, there was a corporate flavor to salvation under the law-covenant. W. D. Davies comments, "The religion of the Torah was essentially a national religion. To accept the Torah meant not merely initiation into a religion . . . but incorporation into a nation."[29] Generally speaking, since it was necessary to be tied to Abraham to inherit the promised blessings, and since Abraham was intricately linked to the Jewish nation, then naturally salvation became associated with the Jewish nation.[30] With the arrival of Christ and the new covenant this nationalistic/ethnological emphasis has vanished. In the old system one outside of Judaism and the Jewish nation could feel excluded, but now, as Galatians 3:28 clearly proclaims, this is no longer true. All people can come to Christ. "The locus of the people of God is no longer national and tribal; it is international, transracial, transcultural."[31]

Second, the new era brings a time when God's Spirit is poured out on *all* believers. In Old Testament times the Spirit was primarily poured out upon individuals with distinctive roles—prophets, priests, and kings. These leaders guided the nation, teaching, leading, and protecting the people. They represented God to the people, and their Spirit-empowered roles were primarily mediatorial. But though the prophets "tended to focus on the corporate results, the restoration of the nation . . . they also anticipated a transformation of individual 'hearts'—no longer hearts of stone but hearts that hunger to do God's will."[32] They looked forward to the new, when God promised that He would "pour out [His] Spirit on all people" (Joel 2:28) and give each of His people "a new heart" and "a new spirit" to follow His decrees (Ezek. 36:24-27). Galatians 3:26-29

---

[29]W. D. Davies, *Paul and Rabbinic Judaism* (London: SPCK, 1962), 67.

[30]There are exceptions to the nationalistic flavor of salvation in the Old Testament, such as the Ninevites, who repented after hearing Jonah's preaching. It is probably more precise, then, to say there was a "corporate" or "tribal" flavor to salvation under the law-covenant.

[31]D. A. Carson, *The Gagging of God*, 254.

[32]D. A. Carson, *The Gospel According to John* (Grand Rapids, MI: Eerdmans, 1991), 195.

highlights the fact that *all* God's people now are sons and hence heirs. Each believer is an heir, and as a result each receives the promised Spirit (Gal. 3:14; 4:6-7). God's people no longer look to specific mediatorial leaders, empowered by the Spirit to show them God's ways. Now *all* God's people have the promised inheritance, His Spirit.

Galatians 3:28 definitely describes a new, important, and exciting change. It is not difficult to imagine Paul's enthusiasm as he proclaimed the truths in Galatians 3:26-29: "You are ALL sons of God. You have ALL put on Christ. You ALL are fully heirs. You ALL have God's Spirit and call out *Abba*, Father." The new age has brought about an era when God's Spirit indwells each believer and each of God's people may know and respond to Him personally. It is a new time, a time of *Abba*, Father, when God Himself dwells with each of His people (cf. Ezek. 37:26-27).

In sum, it is important to recognize the newness of the proclamation of Galatians 3:26-29. Complementarians and egalitarians differ regarding the specifics of what is new, but any responsible interpretation of Galatians 3:28 must acknowledge the arrival of the new covenant and the accompanying changes in the people of God.

Oneness in Galatians 3:28 Does Not Imply Unqualified Equality

Egalitarians have misinterpreted the phrase "you are all one in Christ Jesus." To say a plurality of groups of people are one does *not* mean that each group is equal in every sense, or even in most senses. To label two groups who are equal in one aspect equal without clarification is to invite confusion and misunderstanding.

The importance of the phrase "for you are all one in Christ Jesus" has already been noted. There are two substantive reasons why "you are all one" does not mean "you are all equal." The first reason is the lexical range of the word "one" (Greek *heis, mia, hen*). Lexically this word cannot mean "equal." An overview of BAGD will confirm this, as there is no known example of it being used this way.

The second reason "you are all one" does not mean "you are all equal" is the meaning of this phrase. As was previously demonstrated, a study of every parallel use of the phrase "we/you/they are one" in the three hundred years surrounding the New Testament reveals that this expression fails to express the concept of unqualified equality. In fact, "you are all one" is used of diverse objects; it is not used of similar objects to denote they are similar. This is confirmed by Paul's similar expressions in 1 Corinthians 3:8 and Romans 12:5. The expression "you are one" is an expression that denotes what *different* people, with *different* tasks or gifts, have in common—viz., one body in Christ. The use is the same with the Father and Son (John 10:30) and the husband and wife (Mark 10:8). In every case the expression "you are one" highlights an element that diverse objects share in common. In the case of the Godhead, the Father and the Son, though different in person and role, share the same nature. In marriage the husband and wife, though different in creation, fall, and roles,[33] share one flesh.

Perhaps a contemporary example will help. If the expression "you are all one" was used today in a manner similar to the way in which Paul used it, we would read something like "The Republicans and the Democrats are one in their resolve to fight terrorism." This statement links two disparate entities by delineating something they share in common. We would not expect to find this expression used in this manner: "The twins are one in appearance," as this links two nearly identical objects.

In summary, then, the lexical evidence as well as the meaning of "you are all one" are decidedly against any interpretation that attempts to read unconstrained equality into this expression. When Paul states that Jew/Greek, slave/free, male/female are one, he is saying that these widely diverse people share something in common. The expression "you are one" does not mean "you have so much in common" or that the plurality of pieces are interchangeable, but the opposite.

The expression "you are all one" does, however, contain *some* notion of equality. If, for example, two objects share in R, they are equal in that they both share in R. So if Jew/Greek, slave/free, male/female share in Christ, then they are equal in this regard—they all share in Christ. *In this sense* egalitarians are correct when they assert "men and women are equal in Christ." But simply because x and y share something in common—they are equal in this one respect—it does not follow that x and y are equal (i.e., the same) in other respects. It is important at this point to take a brief look at the concept of equality.

---

[33]This is not a case of assuming what I am trying to prove. What is meant here is that, taken at face value, the New Testament gives husbands and wives different roles (cf. Eph. 5; Col. 3; 1 Pet. 3; Titus 2). Even if one argues these roles were the result of Paul accommodating the church to the demands of culture and hence are no longer valid, at the time Mark 10:8 and Matthew 19:6 were written, the husband and the wife would have been perceived as having different, noninterchangeable roles.

Excursus on Equality

The concept of equality has become central in the debate over Galatians 3:28, even though Paul never uses the *hisos* (Greek word for "equal") word group in this verse. Though this chapter has focused on the exegetical and contextual details of Galatians 3:28, it is nevertheless important to say something about the link between Galatians 3:28 and the notion of equality, for virtually every egalitarian treatment of this verse ties Galatians 3:28 to equality.

What does it mean for two entities to be equal? If a seven-year-old, for example, asks his father, "Does a cup of sugar equal a cup of flour?" the father faces a dilemma. If by the son's question he means, "Is a cup of one granular material the same volume as a cup of another material?" the answer is "Yes." If, on the other hand, he is asking, "Can I put a cup of sugar in this recipe instead of a cup of flour since they are equal?" the answer is "No." A cup of sugar and a cup of flour are equal in one aspect, but not in all. The statement, "A cup of sugar and flour are equal" is valid and true, provided one understands the manner in which they are equal.

Consider the Declaration of Independence. It states: "We hold these truths to be self-evident, that all Men are created *equal . . .*" (italics mine). This statement is both true and false, depending on what one means by "equal." Surely all people aren't equal in many ways: All people do not write like Shakespeare or jump like Michael Jordan, all people are not given the same educational or vocational opportunities, and all people are certainly given different starts in life due to their family situation. But all people do equally have certain unalienable rights given to them by God. The writers of the Declaration recognized the possible confusion and clarified what they intended by the term "equal" by using a series of dependent clauses: "that they are endowed by their Creator with certain unalienable Rights, that among these are Life, Liberty, and the Pursuit of Happiness . . ." "All Men are created equal" is a profound statement, provided one rightly understands what is intended by "equal."

Both examples discussed above show that the claim "x and y are equal" really means "x and y are equal in some defined aspect."

Peter Westen, in his work *Speaking of Equality: An Analysis of the Rhetorical Force of 'Equality' in Moral and Legal Discourse*, provides some basic parameters that are helpful when considering the concept of equality. His basic definition of descriptive equality helps provide clarity in the discussion regarding the equality of men and women:

> Descriptive equality is the relationship that obtains among two or more distinct things that have been jointly measured by a common standard and found to be indistinguishable, or identical, as measured by that standard. Things that are equal by one standard of comparison are inevitably unequal by other standards, and vice versa. It therefore follows that the things of this world that we are capable of measuring are not *either* equal *or* unequal. They are *both* equal *and* unequal.[34]

Westen points out that in order to call two things "equal" one must at least have 1) two distinct entities, 2) a means of measurement, and 3) a common standard. If the common standard in the cup of sugar/flour illustration was volume, the two cups were equal. If, on the other hand, the common standard was substance, they were unequal. Likewise, if the common standard in the Declaration of Independence is artistic ability, all people are not created equal. If, however, the common standard is certain rights before God, then all people are created equal. Westen correctly notes that it is *crucial* to clarify the common standard of comparison, for "things that are equal by one standard of comparison are inevitably unequal by other standards."[35] Even two distinct dollar bills are equal by one standard of comparison (worth) and unequal in other standards (age, color, location, etc.). Inevitably, as Westen notes, things in life are not equal *or* unequal, but both equal *and* unequal, depending upon the standard of comparison. So it is confusing at best to call two things equal without clearly delineating the standard of comparison.[36]

Proponents of both the egalitarian and complementarian sides, though perhaps failing to understand Westen's basic parameters, have intuitively recognized the need to qualify the term *equal*, for it is obvious to virtually everybody that men and women aren't completely equal. Men and women, for example, assuredly do not have equal (i.e., the same) bodies. Thus, consider how some egalitarians have modified the term *equal*: "They [men and women] are equally *members of his*

---

[34]Peter Westen, *Speaking of Equality: An Analysis of the Rhetorical Force of 'Equality' in Moral and Legal Discourse* (Princeton, NJ: Princeton University Press, 1990), 41. Italics his.
[35]Ibid.
[36]Ibid.

body";[37] Paul sought to equalize "the *status* of male and female in Christ";[38] "we err greatly if we do not insist on equal *standing* for women with men in Christ";[39] "[t]hey still remain male and female, but such distinctions become immaterial to their equal *participation in the life of the church.*"[40]

And complementarians have likewise modified the term *equal*. Werner Neuer comments, "Galatians 3:28 means, therefore, that *as far as eternal salvation is concerned,* all, *whether male or female*, are equal before God and that each one may enjoy divine sonship through faith in Jesus (cf. Galatians 3:29)" (italics original).[41] John Jefferson Davis, while acknowledging that both men and women are equally entrusted with the joint exercises of dominion and image-bearing in Genesis 1:26-28, comments that it would be erroneous to conclude "that equality in *some* respects entails equality in *all* respects" (italics original).[42]

Both egalitarians and complementarians claim equality but fail to clearly specify the means of measurement (2 above) or the standard of comparison (3 above). Great confusion results. Note that both groups will heartily own the statement, "Men and women are equal in Christ." Both groups will gladly embrace the statement, "Men and women have equal roles in Christ."[43] In these two affirmations, however, both sides mean something substantially different by the statement. In sum, the nature of the concept of equal demands careful qualification—a means of measurement (2 above) and a clear standard of comparison (3 above).[44]

There is nothing inherently wrong with the concept of equality; properly clarified, it is a biblical concept. The crux of the issue is this: What is the standard of comparison when someone asserts "Galatians

---

[37]C. Boomsma, *Male and Female, One in Christ: New Testament Teaching on Women in Office* (Grand Rapids, MI: Baker, 1993), 38.

[38]F. F. Bruce, *The Epistle to the Galatians*, New International Greek Testament Commentary (Grand Rapids, MI: Eerdmans, 1982), 190.

[39]Klyne Snodgrass, "Galatians 3:28," 178.

[40]Gilbert Bilezikian, *Beyond Sex Roles* (Grand Rapids, MI: Baker, 1985), 128.

[41]Werner Neuer, *Man and Woman in Christian Perspective*, trans. Gordon Wenham (Wheaton, IL: Crossway, 1991), 108.

[42]John Jefferson Davis, "Some Reflections on Galatians 3:28, Sexual Roles, and Biblical Hermeneutics," *Journal of the Evangelical Theological Society* 19 (1976), 204.

[43]Complementarians will say, "Sure, men and women have equal roles—equally *valid* and equally *important*." Egalitarians will understand the statement that men and women have equal roles to mean men and women have the *same* roles.

[44]Note: Complementarians can agree with three of the four egalitarians quoted in the paragraph above, depending upon what is meant by the term *equal*: 1) men and women are equally members of Christ's body; 2) men and women have equal status in Christ; and 3) men and women have equal standing in Christ.

3:28 teaches the 'equality' of men and women"? Equal in what sense? Equal value? Equal abilities? Equal roles? Equal callings? Equal inheritance in Christ? And how is this equality to be measured?

With this background on the concept of equality in mind, it is now necessary to make some concluding remarks regarding the central affirmation of this section: Oneness in Galatians 3:28 does not imply unqualified equality. Lexically the term "one" (Greek *heis, mia, hen*) cannot mean "equal." And though the expression "you are all one" *implies* some notion of equality—Jews/Gentiles, slave/free, male/female share in one Christ—it does not follow that men and women are equal in an unqualified sense. Any meaningful statement on the relationship between equality and Galatians 3:28 must clearly state a common standard of comparison. Hence, unqualified statements like "Galatians 3:28 teaches the equality of men and women" are both dangerously imprecise and potentially misleading.

Galatians 3:28 Does Not Primarily Address the Issue of Sexual Roles

While rightly pointing to the need to consider the social implications of Galatians 3:28, egalitarians are mistaken when they consider the "primary" focus of this verse as being horizontal relationships within the Christian community.[45] To be fair, most egalitarians rightly say the primary focus is theological and the social implications are only secondary. Anyone who has extensively read egalitarian studies on Galatians 3:28, however, will readily notice that the ostensibly "secondary" becomes the primary. The very reason Galatians 3:28 has become a lightning rod in the contemporary debate over the roles of men and women is because egalitarians have trumpeted that this verse teaches that men and women have interchangeable roles in the home and church. Does Galatians 3:28 address the question of the roles of men and women? Three contextual and structural considerations reveal that Paul's primary concern was *not* with the roles of each of these groups.

The flow of Paul's argument: First, the entire flow of Paul's argument from 2:15 through 3:29 and beyond is salvation-historical. He is concerned with issues such as the purpose and relevancy of the Law, the fulfillment of the promise, and changes brought about by the arrival of Christ. The major story line is the progression from Abraham and the heirs-to-be of the promise made to him up to the fulfillment of this

---

[45]C. Boomsma, *Male and Female*, 35.

promise in Christ and the consequent blessing of all who are in Him. The concepts of the "one" and the "many" are critical. The many were in the one, Abraham. He was their representative head, and as a result the blessings of the promise came only through him, the one. In the same way Christ is the one Sëed; only through Him can the promised inheritance be received. The many are blessed through their relationship to the One.

When the flow of Galatians 3—4 is considered, it is evident that Paul's concern was not with how the many relate to one another or behave in the church or home. His main emphasis was that the many, because of their tie to the One, are now heirs of the blessings promised to Abraham. All believing individuals, regardless of their tribal or family connection, financial condition, or gender, are heirs of the inheritance.

The logic of Galatians 3:26-29: A second reason it is likely Galatians 3:28 has little specifically to say about the roles of men and women is because Galatians 3:28 is framed by verse 26 and verse 29. These statements reveal the heart of the paragraph Galatians 3:26-29: "you are all sons . . . then you are Abraham's seed, and heirs according to the promise." Paul's purpose is to describe how sonship, which is now available to all through God's Son, also results in one becoming an heir of the promises made to Abraham. Since 1) Galatians 3:26-29 describes the fulfillment of the promise made to Abraham, and 2) the promise made to Abraham highlighted the universal nature of this inheritance ("*all* peoples on earth will be blessed through you," Gen. 12:3, italics added), then it is highly likely that 3) the purpose of the three negated couplets in Galatians 3:28 is to express the universality of the new people of God: *all* people are included.

The two phrases in verse 26 and verse 29 provide the context for verse 28. If Paul's purpose is to teach about the *universal availability* of the inheritance, as predicted in the Old Testament, it is difficult to understand how the respective roles of Jew/Greek, slave/free, male/female fit into his argument. No doubt there may be *implications* for the roles of men and women, but the structure of the passage clearly shows Paul's intent was the universal nature of the new inheritance, not the respective roles of those who receive it.

The implication of "you are one": A third reason Paul likely did not have equality (sameness) of roles in mind in Galatians 3:28 stems from the critical expression "you are all one." As has already been noted, this expression is used to show what diverse objects have in common. If Paul's intent was to show that men and women have the same roles—

that is, their roles in the church, home, and society are interchangeable—it is doubtful he would have used this expression. But the expression "you are all one," while specifying a shared element between two entities, nevertheless implicitly points to *differences* between the two elements. The expression, when it is used in the New Testament of people, clearly presumes distinctions between the two entities. The New Testament examples of "we/you/they are one," where a plurality of people are called one, are the planter/waterer (1 Cor. 3:8), Father/Son (John 10:30; 17:11, 21, 22 [twice], 23), husband/wife (Matt. 19:6; Mark 10:8), and different believers with different gifts (Rom. 12:5, 1 Cor. 10:17). In *every* instance the groups of people in these four pairs have different roles. Given these expressions, which formally and directly parallel Galatians 3:28, it is very difficult to see how the meaning of "you are all one" can be "there are no distinctions of role between you."

Is it not possible, then, that even though Paul's intent was not to address the roles of men and women *directly*, there are still some important *implications* of the truth of Galatians 3:28 for men's and women's roles? This seems more in line with Paul's thought.

The advent of the new as described in Galatians 3:28 inevitably meant changes in the roles of Jews/Greeks, slaves/free, males/females. Masters are told to treat their slaves well, and slaves are told to obey their masters with sincerity of heart (Eph. 6:5ff.). Though this concept wasn't totally new—the Old Testament had provisions to protect slaves (Exod. 21:2; Lev. 25:47-55)[46]—these roles are now different because both masters and slaves are one in Christ. Similarly, Jews could no longer gloat over their national identity to the exclusion of the Gentiles (Rom. 2:17ff.). God's people, now Jew and Gentile, should relate to one another in a new manner (Eph. 2:14ff.) because they both are now one in Christ. And in the new era the husband is told to love his wife as his own body and to offer himself up for her as Christ did for the church, and the wife is told to submit to her husband and respect him (Eph. 5:22ff.). Again, though this teaching is not a decisive break from the Old Testament,[47] the new era does bring about something new:

---

[46]Grant Osborne, *The Hermeneutical Spiral: A Comprehensive Introduction to Biblical Interpretation* (Downers Grove, IL: InterVarsity Press, 1991), 12.

[47]The Old Testament speaks highly of the godly wife (Gen. 1:26-27; Prov. 12:4; 31) and encourages the husband to be committed to his wife (Gen. 2:24; Mal. 2:14ff.). In the Old Testament God Himself is said to be a "husband" to His people (Jer. 31:32), indicating that the concept of a husband in the Old Testament did not have demeaning implications.

Now we are told of the wonderful and mysterious parallel between Christ and the church and between the husband and wife. The husband is now told to love and cherish his bride *as* Christ did the church. And while it is doubtful Paul had this in mind as he penned Galatians 3:28, it is certain that some aspects of the roles of both men and women would have changed under the new covenant as a result of changes in the sacrificial and purification system (cf. Lev. 15).

In sum, it would be foolish to insist that the roles of these six groups didn't change when "the fullness of the time" (Gal. 4:4, NASB) arrived. Paul is fully aware that since all believers are now "in Christ Jesus," relationships between them will be transformed. This is implied by Galatians 3:28 and confirmed by the rest of the Pauline corpus. The acknowledgment of this reality, however, is a far cry from the egalitarian position that believes Galatians 3:28 is the most socially explosive verse in the whole Bible. This verse cannot be the most socially explosive verse in the whole Bible because Paul's primary intent was not sociological. The flow of Galatians 3—4 confirms this, as does the structure of Galatians 3:26-29 and the implications of the expression "you are all one." Ward Gasque is mistaken when he writes, "[Paul] is focusing on the new social reality created by our baptism into Christ."[48] Paul is *not* focusing on the new social reality, which is precisely why a fair interpretation of Galatians 3:28 must not make social roles the primary focus of this verse. There is great danger in focusing on possible implications of a passage to the exclusion of its central intent.

Those who see the primary focus of Galatians 3:28 as addressing sexual roles in the family and church err. Even though rightly insisting upon changes in God's people in the new era, they specify these changes by speculatively reading role relations into a passage that does not directly address roles. The new age did bring about sociological and relational changes, at least in some aspects; but these changes should be defined by passages that directly address this issue, not by Galatians 3:28.

Galatians 3:28 Has Social Implications

If men and women are one in Christ, what are some of the implications for the body of Christ today? Complementarians have sometimes

---

[48]W. Ward Gasque, "Response," in *Women, Authority, and the Bible,* ed. Alvera Mickelsen (Downers Grove, IL: InterVarsity Press, 1986), 189.

minimalized the social implications of Galatians 3:28. How can God's people daily reflect this truth?

One must proceed carefully when seeking to derive specific social applications from the theological truths contained in Galatians 3:28, as societal roles were not Paul's primary focus in the passage. Nevertheless, the principles Paul has provided have behavioral ramifications. At least three principles, which seem clear from the text, can serve to guide specific applications. First, all God's people are in Christ. Second, all God's people, by virtue of being in Christ, are one. Third, the great mercies and blessings of God are given to all God's people without distinction, regardless of one's gender, race, or social/financial background. Though doubtless many, many implications could be drawn from these three principles, the following applications seem both fair to the text and pertinent for our culture and church today.

1) Since all God's people share in Christ, there is no room for boasting or comparison for any reason, and certainly not on the basis of race, sex, or social standing. Feelings of superiority and feelings of inferiority both stem from an erroneous view of God's people in the new age.

2) Since God's people are one, the family of God should be characterized by unity. In Galatians 3—4, "one" is used first in the sense of incorporation (the many in the one) and then, derivatively, for unity. Unity is a prevalent New Testament theme (e.g., Eph. 4:3ff.; 1 Cor. 12:14ff.), as it is an important public demonstration of the reality that all believers share in one Christ. Many churches and Christian groups, however, often don't have united hearts and minds. Self-centeredness, racism, and sexism all contribute to the fracture of God's people. Galatians 3:28 implies that every effort should be made to create and maintain unity among God's diverse people.

3) God's people are diverse, yet stand equally before Him. Those who are racially, sexually, and socially different than us should be cherished and valued. There is no room for outcasts in the church, whether the discrimination be overt or subtle. All believers, regardless of race, sex, or social status, are clearly members of God's family. When there are problems in this area, God's people should be proactive to remedy the issue. Racial reconciliation efforts such as those of Promise Keepers are excellent applications of the truth of Galatians 3:28.

4) The universal emphasis in Galatians 3:28—that people from all nations and walks of life comprise God's people—should serve to challenge us to think more broadly about God's mission. As missiologists

have observed, people are ethnocentric: They naturally view the world through their own cultural perspective and intrinsically value what is important to them. Galatians 3:28 reveals God's universal heart for people; He is not ethnocentric, and we need to begin to think beyond our own culturally limited perspective. Those who love God the Redeemer will progressively love what He loves—people from all walks of life.

Surely other applications could be offered. The important issue, however, is to tie these applications as closely as possible to Paul's intent in the passage.

In summary, these four statements regarding the meaning and significance of Galatians 3:28 fit the specifics of the text and the context quite well. The three couplets function as "merisms" to describe the universal nature of the new covenant—*all* people are included. Though there are differences between the couplets, Paul uses them in a parallel fashion: Regardless of racial status, economic status, or gender, all in Christ are "one" and are heirs of the promises to Abraham. God's people are now known by being "in Christ Jesus," not by any nationalistic or tribal affiliation. Paul argues that labels such as Jew/Greek, slave/free, male/female, though important in their own right, are irrelevant when it comes to becoming heirs of the promise. This interpretation fits the overall flow of Galatians 3—4, as well as the microstructure of the unit of thought contained in Galatians 3:26-29 and the exegetical details of verse 28. The promise to Abraham was universal. Now, in its fulfillment, it is, as predicted, universally available to all, whether Jew or Greek, slave or free, male or female.

RESPONSES TO TWO EGALITARIAN USES OF GALATIANS 3:28

In closing I will reference the preceding exegetical material to reply succinctly to two claims egalitarians frequently make regarding Galatians 3:28.[49]

Claim 1: Galatians 3:28 Gives New Status to the "Have-Nots" of the Old Testament

It is common to find egalitarians arguing that Galatians 3:28 ushers in a new era where women, slaves, and Gentiles are no longer "second-class" citizens in God's kingdom. For example, Rebecca Groothuis writes:

---

[49]In my book I briefly address another common egalitarian assertion: Galatians 3:28 is somehow more cross-culturally applicable than texts such as 1 Timothy 2 or Ephesians 5. Richard Hove, *Equality in Christ?*, 129-130, 140-141.

The idea of a religious pecking order along lines of race, class, or gender is alien to the new order in Christ. Special spiritual prerogatives no longer belong only to males (or Jews, or freeborn citizens). No particular ethnic, sexual, or social class of believers has the intrinsic right to exercise spiritual authority over or assume spiritual responsibility for believers outside the privileged class. All are equal members and full participants. . . . Free Jewish male believers no longer have special religious status and privilege. . . . The most plausible, straightforward reading of Galatians 3:26-28 is that it is an acknowledgement of the fundamental spiritual equality of all categories of people, and a denial of the relevance of gender, race, or social class to the assignment of spiritual roles and privileges.[50]

In this quote Groothuis asserts that in the past (in the Old Testament?) "special spiritual prerogatives" belonged only to males and that Galatians 3:28 teaches that "free Jewish male believers no longer have special religious status and privilege." So Galatians 3:28 ushers in a new period when the "have-nots" of the Old Testament have new status. She states elsewhere:

The old order, in which religious life was almost exclusively in the hands of free Jewish men, had given way to a new order, in which there should no longer be any distinction in spiritual roles or privileges between Jew and Gentile, slave or free, male or female. Under the old covenant, Jesus chose free Jewish males for his apostles. Under the new covenant, women were the first to be commissioned to preach the gospel message.[51]

It is agreed that Galatians 3:28 describes the people of God in the new covenant. Is it accurate, however, to portray the old covenant as one that gave privileged status almost exclusively to freeborn Jewish males in contrast to the new, which provides equality to all? Does Galatians, particularly Galatians 3—4, present the arrival of Christ and the inauguration of the new covenant in terms of the arrival of new roles, status, and privileges for the "have-nots" of the Old Testament— women, slaves, and Gentiles? Groothuis's attempt to define the old/new contrast as those who "have not" in distinction to those who

---

[50]Rebecca Groothuis, *Good News*, 35-36.
[51]Ibid., 193.

"have" misinterprets Galatians 3:28 and ignores, or at least minimizes, the contrast(s) Paul himself makes between the new covenant and the old. Several observations are pertinent regarding changes resulting from the inauguration of the new covenant.

First, Galatians 3:28 doubtless teaches that *now* all who are in Christ, without distinction, are heirs and sons of God. Likewise, each believer now has the promised, greatly anticipated Spirit.

Second, though there are changes in the new covenant presented in Galatians 3—4, there is no specific mention of have/have-not class distinctions in Galatians. Some, such as David Scholer, see Galatians 2:11-14 as providing the perfect example of class distinctions. He states, "I would be tempted to say that Galatians 2:11-14 alone is almost enough evidence to make the whole case for [egalitarianism]."[52] It has already been argued, however, that the real issue in Galatians 2:11-14 is a salvation-historical problem: How are Jews and Gentiles to relate given the arrival of the new covenant? The *presenting* problem was food regulations; the *fundamental* problem was theological. This is clear from the arguments that follow after Galatians 2:11-14 and continue throughout most of the book. Paul does not go from 2:11-14 to talk about roles or inequities. He talks about the Law and the old covenant and the arrival of the new. It is reductionistic to view Galatians 2:11-14 as a description of the haves and have-nots. The Jew/Gentile distinction gets specific attention in Galatians 2 because of its salvation-historical significance, not because it is a convenient test case for social inequities. If the focus of the new covenant was rectifying the injustices of the old class distinctions, one would expect this to be mentioned, or at least alluded to, somewhere in Galatians.

Third, the contrasts provided in Galatians 3—4 are different than Groothuis's have/have not paradigm. In the old covenant, for example, God's people are called "children . . . in slavery under the basic principles of the world," but under the new covenant His people "receive the full rights of sons" (4:3, 5). Those Jews who through faith were blessed by sharing in the blessings of the promise made to Abraham (3:9) now see the promise come to the Gentiles (3:14). And those who could only long for the inheritance now can celebrate its arrival and subsequent blessings (4:7). There are, then, legitimate contrasts between the old and new as described in Galatians 3—4, but Paul himself does not pre-

---

[52]David M. Scholer, "Galatians 3:28 and the Ministry of Women in the Church," in *Theology, News and Notes* (Pasadena, CA: Fuller Theological Seminary, June 1998), 22.

sent the new covenant as a time that does away with "special religious status and privilege"[53] for Jews, free people, and men.

Fourth, any have/have not theme in Galatians 3—4 is not tied to class distinctions such as gender, race, or economic status, but to changes in salvation-history that are relevant to all groups of people. Note that it was primarily the *Jews* who were described as slaves awaiting the proper time to become full sons. Freeborn Jewish males were the "have-nots" in Galatians 3—4! *All* Old Testament saints, whether Jew/Gentile, slave/free, or male/female, eagerly awaited the promised inheritance. Galatians does not describe the new covenant as one that brings status and privilege for certain classes of second-class people under the old covenant. Rather, a fair reading of Galatians 3—4 shows that Paul's emphasis in these chapters is upon the arrival of new blessings for *all* who were held prisoner "until faith should be revealed" (3:23), and not upon the arrival of new privileges for particular classes of unequal Old Testament saints.[54]

Groothuis has taken a truth that is rightly found in the text and illegitimately added something that is not in the text. She correctly affirms an old/new contrast in Galatians 3:28 but then defines this contrast in ways foreign to Galatians 3—4 (have/have-nots based on gender, race, and social class).

Claim 2: Galatians 3:28 Is the Most Important Verse in the Bible on Equality

Egalitarians commonly argue like this: "You are all one" means "you are all equal." And "you are all equal" means "there are no gender-specific role distinctions in the home and church." Both of these moves—from oneness to equality and from equality to no gender-specific roles—are illegitimate. We have already seen that "you are all one" does not mean "you are all equal" (in an unqualified sense). And even if there is a notion of equality found in Galatians 3:28, it does not follow from this notion of equality that there are no gender-specific roles. The nature of equality is that things or people are *both* equal and unequal, depending upon the standard of comparison. That Jew/Gentile, slave/free, male/female equally share in Christ does not

---

[53]Rebecca Groothuis, *Good News*, 35.

[54]This is not to deny that the arrival of the new covenant means unique changes for different groups of people. Jews, for example, experience changes with the arrival of the new covenant, such as the end of ritual sacrifices, that are not experienced by Gentile believers.

mean that they are equal or interchangeable in other respects. So how does one respond to egalitarian claims that Galatians 3:28 is the most important verse on equality?

First, Galatians 3:28 itself makes no mention of equality. As has already been noted, Paul argues that there is no male/female, Jew/Gentile, slave/free because all are now "one in Christ Jesus." He affirms oneness in Christ, not equality. While not desiring to dismiss the reality of a notion of equality in Galatians 3:28, the absence of any direct mention of equality should give one cause to wonder whether this verse really is the most important verse in the Bible about equality.

Second, it is difficult to determine what is meant by the statement that "Galatians 3:28 is about 'equality.'" What precisely does Galatians 3:28 have to say about equality? Rebecca Groothuis notes that two persons, or groups of persons, can be equal in many ways:

> (1) equal human worth, (2) equal ability, (3) equal maturity, (4) equal rights and opportunities, (5) equal status, (6) equal social value, (7) equal identity (being the same, thus interchangeable in any role).[55]

This author agrees that Galatians 3:28, at least by implication, is relevant to the question of the equality of human worth of Jew/Greek, slave/free, male/female (1) and possibly equality of opportunity (4), status (5), and social value (6), depending upon how one defines these terms. It does not seem possible that Galatians 3:28 addresses questions of equality of abilities (2) or maturity (3), and it is not clear whether Groothuis believes this is the case.

Does Galatians 3:28 teach "equal identity"—that is, interchangeable roles between men and women (7)? It seems Groothuis believes this is true when *spiritual roles* are at stake:

> The most plausible, straightforward reading of Galatians 3:26-28 is that it is an acknowledgment of the fundamental spiritual equality of all categories of people, and a denial of the relevance of gender, race or social class to the assignment of *spiritual roles* and privileges.[56]

---

[55]Rebecca Groothuis, *Good News*, 45.

[56]Ibid., 36. Italics mine.

But in other places she is careful to point out that the roles of men and women are not always interchangeable.[57] The bottom line is that without a specified standard of comparison, it is impossible to understand fully what one might mean by "men and women are spiritually equal."

Third, it should be noted that when egalitarians fail to specify a clear standard of comparison for equality, that creates confusion, though it does provide a distinct rhetorical advantage. Galatians 3:28 *does*, after all, have something to say about the equality of men and women. By using Galatians 3:28 to claim that men and women are equal, and by failing to specify a standard of comparison for this equality claim, egalitarians are able to imply that Galatians 3:28 teaches that men and women are equal in a host of other ways as well. This plea for equality is powerful. Who, after all, wants to argue someone is *un*equal? And who wants to oppose "gender equality," the subtitle of Rebecca Groothuis's book? By carrying the banner of equality, albeit undefined, egalitarians are in the best position to promote egalitarianism.

Consider Westen's comments on Abraham Lincoln's rhetorical use of "equality" in the famous Lincoln-Douglas presidential debates:

> Rhetorically, however, Lincoln used "equality" to his advantage by exploiting two of its persuasive features. He was able to demand equality without having to specify the precise rules by which such equality would be measured. Lincoln's racial views, in fact, were rather complicated. On the one hand, he did not believe that blacks should be granted citizenship or that they should be allowed to vote, sit on juries, hold public office, or intermarry with whites. On the other hand, he did believe that they should be free from the bondage of chattel slavery, at least in the new territories in which slavery had not yet taken hold. By expressing his racial views in the elliptical language of equality, however, he could appeal to people possessing a range of racial views without alerting them to their potential differences. . . . More importantly, Lincoln exploited the favorable connotations of "equality" and the pejorative connotations of "inequality" by making himself the champion of equality and Douglas the defender of inequality.[58]

So egalitarians' claim that Galatians 3:28 "is the most important verse in the Bible on equality" is nearly impossible to evaluate owing

---

[57]Ibid., 49-50.
[58]Peter Westen, *Speaking of Equality*, 281-282.

to the unspecified standard of comparison. And yet, precisely for that reason, this claim is rhetorically powerful.

Is Galatians 3:28 the most important verse in the Bible on equality, as egalitarians argue? Yes and no, depending on the standard of comparison. Is it the most important verse describing how all groups of people, regardless of race, gender, or social status, may equally, without distinction, become sons of God and inherit the blessings of salvation promised from the beginning but now made available with the arrival of God's Son? Yes. Is it the most important verse teaching the equality of men and women in such a way that it negates gender-specific roles in the home and church? No. It has already been argued that the lexical data (the possible meanings for "one"), syntax (the meaning of "you are all one"), and context (the flow of Galatians 3—4 and the structure of the thought unit contained in 3:26-29) all fail to support the conclusion that oneness in Galatians 3:28 in some way negates unique men's and women's roles that are taught elsewhere in Scripture.

5

THE MEANING OF κεφαλή ("HEAD"): AN EVALUATION OF NEW EVIDENCE, REAL AND ALLEGED[1]

Wayne Grudem

᠃᠃᠃

The purpose of this article is to examine recent treatments of the meaning of the word κεφαλή ("head") as it pertains to certain passages in the New Testament,[2] focusing especially on new evidence cited by Catherine Kroeger in her article "Head" in the widely used *Dictionary of Paul and His Letters*.[3] Concerns will be raised about the level of care and accuracy with which evidence has been quoted in this reference book. In addition, some new patristic evidence on κεφαλή will be presented. Finally, the article will also cite new evaluations of the entry on κεφαλή in the Liddell-Scott lexicon from the editor of the *Supplement* to this lexicon and from another lexicographer who worked on this *Supplement*.

---

[1]This chapter is identical to the article by the same title that I published in *JETS* 44/1 (March 2001), 25-65, with the exception of the added interaction with Anthony Thiselton's recent commentary on 1 Corinthians in section VIII below (pp. 194-199).

[2]The meaning of κεφαλή has attracted much interest because of its use in Ephesians 5:23, "The husband is the *head* (κεφαλή) of the wife even as Christ is the head of the church," and in 1 Corinthians 11:3, "the *head* of every man is Christ, the *head* of a wife is her husband, and the *head* of Christ is God." I previously wrote about the meaning of κεφαλή in 1985 and 1990: Wayne Grudem, "Does *kephalē* ("Head") Mean "Source" or "Authority over" in Greek Literature? A Survey of 2,336 Examples" (*Trinity Journal* 6 NS [1985], 38-59), and then, answering objections and arguing this in more detail, "The Meaning of *kephalē*: A Response to Recent Studies" (*Trinity Journal* 11 NS [1990], 3-72; reprinted as an appendix to *Recovering Biblical Manhood and Womanhood*, eds. John Piper and Wayne Grudem [Wheaton, IL: Crossway Books, 1991], 425-468). The 1990 article has references to several other studies of this word, and significant studies published after 1990 are mentioned near the end of this present article.

[3]Edited by Gerald F. Hawthorne, Ralph P. Martin, and Daniel G. Reid (Downers Grove, IL and Leicester, England: InterVarsity, 1993), 375-377.

I. THE STRIKING QUOTATION FROM CHRYSOSTOM

When Dr. Kroeger's article appeared in 1993, it offered citations of a number of new references for the term κεφαλή and argued from these that κεφαλή primarily meant "source," not "authority over," and that it had that meaning not only at the time of the New Testament but also in the preceding classical period and in the subsequent patristic period in Greek literature. The most striking quotation in Dr. Kroeger's article was a statement from John Chrysostom (A.D. 344/354-407) that, if accurate, would appear to settle any dispute over whether κεφαλή meant "source" or "authority over," at least in the Christian world of the fourth century. Kroeger writes:

> In view of Scripture ascribing coequality of Christ with the Father (Jn. 1:1-3; 10:30; 14:9, 11; 16:15; 17:11, 21), John Chrysostom declared that only a heretic would understand Paul's use of "head" to mean "chief" or "authority over." Rather one should understand the term as implying "absolute oneness and cause and primal source" (PG 61.214, 216). (p. 377)

But is this what Chrysostom said? Kroeger claims (1) that Chrysostom is making a statement about the meaning of κεφαλή, (2) that Chrysostom denies that κεφαλή can mean "chief" or "authority over," and (3) that Chrysostom says that only a heretic would understand the word in that way.

Here is the quotation from Chrysostom:

> "But the head of the woman is the man; and the head of Christ is God." Here the heretics rush upon us with a certain declaration of inferiority, which out of these words they contrive against the Son. But they stumble against themselves. For if "the man be the head of the woman," and the head be of the same substance with the body, and "the head of Christ is God," the Son is of the same substance with the Father.[4] (Κεφαλὴ δὲ γυναικὸς ὁ ἀνήρ· κεφαλὴ δὲ Χριστοῦ ὁ Θεός. Ἐνταῦθα ἐπιπηδῶσιν ἡμῖν οἱ αἱρετικοὶ

---

[4]Chrysostom, Homily 26 on 1 Corinthians (NPNF series 1, Vol. 12, p. 150.) The Greek text is from TLG Work 156, 61.214.18 to 61.214.23.

Where available, English quotations in this article have been taken from the *Ante-Nicene Fathers* series (ANF) and the *Nicene and Post-Nicene Fathers* series (NPNF) (reprint edition, Grand Rapids, MI: Eerdmans, 1969). Where no English translation was available, the English translations are mine, as indicated in each case. Greek citations have been taken from the Thesaurus Linguae Graecae (TLG), Disk E, except where no TLG reference is given, in which case I have cited the source of the Greek citation at each point.

ἐλάττωσίν τινα ἐκ των εἰρημένων ἐπινοοῦντες τῷ Υἱῷ· ἀλλ᾽
ἑαυτοῖς περιπίπτουσιν. Εἰ γὰρ κεφαλὴ γυναικὸς ὁ ἀνὴρ,
ὁμοούσιος δὲ ἡ κεφαλὴ τῷ σώματι, κεφαλὴ δὲ τοῦ Χριστοῦ
ὁ Θεός, ὁμοούσιος ὁ Υἱὸς τῷ Πατρί.)

This is not a statement about the meaning of κεφαλή. Chrysostom
is opposing the views of the Arians, who denied the deity of Christ.
They did this by pointing to the statement, "the head of Christ is God"
(in 1 Cor. 11:3) and saying that therefore the Son is a lesser being, not
fully divine and not equal to the Father in essence. Chrysostom coun-
ters their claim, but in doing so he does not say anything about the
meaning of the word κεφαλή or say that only a "heretic" would take it
to mean "chief" or "authority over" as Kroeger claims. Rather, from the
idea that a head is "of the same substance (ὁμοούσιος) with the body,"
he affirms that the Son is "of the same substance (ὁμοούσιος) with the
Father." There is no statement here saying that he disagrees with the
Arians over the meaning of κεφαλή.

What comes next? In the following lines, Chrysostom says the
"heretics" will counter by saying that the Son is subject to the Father
and is therefore a lesser being:

> "Nay," say they, "it is not His being of another substance which
> we intend to show from hence, but that He is under subjection."
> (᾽Αλλ᾽ οὐ τὸ ἑτεροούσιον ἐντεῦθεν ἀποδεῖξαι βουλόμεθα;
> ἀλλ᾽ ὅτι ἄρχεται, φησί.)[5]

If Chrysostom had ever wanted to say that "head" could not mean
"one in authority," here was the perfect opportunity. He could have
answered these "heretics" by saying, as Dr. Kroeger apparently would
like him to say, that κεφαλή did not mean "one in authority" and that
"only a heretic" would understand Paul's use of "head" to mean "chief"
or "authority over." But he does not say this at all. Rather, he assumes
that κεφαλή *does* mean "authority over," because he *agrees* that the Son
is obedient to the Father, and then he goes on to show that His obedience is not servile, like a slave, but free, like that of a wife who is equal
in honor. Here are his words:

---

[5]Ibid., lines 23-25.

For what if the wife be under subjection (ὑποτάσσω) to us? It is as a wife, as free, as equal in honor. And the Son also, though He did become obedient to the Father, it was as the Son of God, it was as God. For as the obedience of the Son to the Father is greater than we find in men towards the authors of their being, so also his liberty is greater . . . we ought to admire the Father also, that He begat such a son, not as a slave under command, but as free, yielding obedience and giving counsel. For the counselor is no slave. . . . For with us indeed the woman is reasonably subjected (ὑποτάσσω) to the man.[6]

So is there any statement here about the meaning of κεφαλή? No, except the implication in the context that the Father is the "head" of the Son, and the Son is obedient to the Father. Chrysostom here does not deny that "head" means "one in authority" but assumes that "head" *does* mean this and explains what kind of authority that is with respect to the husband and with respect to God the Father.

Does Chrysostom differ with "the heretics" over the meaning of κεφαλή? No, he agrees with them. But they were saying that "the *head* of Christ is God" (1 Cor. 11:3) implied that the Son was a lesser being than the Father, that He was not equal in deity. Chrysostom says that the Son is *equal* in deity and is *also subject to* the Father.

Interestingly, "the heretics" in this passage were reasoning in the same way that egalitarians such as Dr. Kroeger reason today— they were saying that subordination to authority *necessarily implies* inferiority in a person's very being. They were saying that it is impossible for the Son to be equal to the Father in being (that is, equal in deity) and also subordinate in role. They used this reasoning as an argument to deny the deity of the Son. Egalitarians today use it as an argument to deny the unique, eternal subordination of the Son to the Father. But in both cases the fundamental assumption is that the Son cannot be *both* equal in deity and subordinate in role.

Chrysostom replies, however, that *both* are true. The Son is *equal* in deity (he, the "body," is ὁμοούσιος, of the same substance, as the "head"), and He also is *subordinate* to the authority of the

---

[6]English translation from NPNF, Series 1, Vol. 12, p. 150. Greek text in TLG, Chrysostom, *Homilies on 1 Corinthians*, Work 156, 61.214.56 to 61.215.18.

head, and yet His submission is not forced (as a slave) but is voluntary, as a Son, and is similar to the submission of a wife to her husband.

Is there in this entire context any statement by Chrysostom that only heretics understand κεφαλή to mean "chief" or "authority over"? No. The quotation does not exist.[7] In this entire section Chrysostom himself understands κεφαλή to mean "chief"[8] or "authority over."[9]

II. OTHER EVIDENCE FROM CHRYSOSTOM ON THE MEANING OF κεφαλή ("HEAD")

Further evidence that Chrysostom did not in fact use κεφαλή to mean "source" and did not say that only heretics would use it to mean "authority over" is seen in the way he uses κεφαλή to mean "authority over" or "ruler" in the following examples:

1. *Homily 26 on 1 Corinthians (NPNF series 1, Vol. 12, p. 156; TLG Work 156, 61.222.49 to 61.222.54): Husband as head and ruler.*

---

[7]I thought perhaps this reference in *Dictionary of Paul and His Letters* was a mistake. So I wrote to Dr. Kroeger saying that I could not find her quotation in that section of Chrysostom. She replied by sending me a printout (in Greek) of the exact passage that I cited at the beginning of this section. But the statement about only heretics using "head" to mean "chief" or "authority over" simply is not there. Chrysostom in fact said no such thing.

[8]I myself would prefer not to translate κεφαλή as "chief," which too narrowly implies tribal relationships, but I am here using Kroeger's terminology.

[9]It would have been nearly impossible for most readers of *Dictionary of Paul and His Letters* to discover that the striking quotation from Chrysostom did not exist. The only indication of the source of the quotation that Dr. Kroeger gave was "PG 61.214." This indicates a location in Migne, *Patrologia Graeca,* which took a considerable amount of time to locate and coordinate with an existing English translation (the standard English translation has a different numbering system). It is doubtful whether even 1 percent of the readers of *Dictionary of Paul and His Letters* would have enough ability to read patristic Greek to be able to find and understand this paragraph from Chrysostom. (Only very specialized research libraries have a complete set of the Migne collection of Greek and Latin texts of the writings of the church fathers. The set was published by Jacques Paul Migne in France in the mid-nineteenth century. *Patrologia Latina* (PL) was published in 221 volumes in Latin (1844-1864), and *Patrologia Graeca* (PG) was published in 162 volumes in Greek with Latin translation (1857-1866).)

Of course, if no published English translation had existed, citing Migne alone would have been the only thing that could be done. But this material from Chrysostom exists in English translation in the *Nicene and Post-Nicene Fathers* series, which is widely available (the whole set is now in the public domain and is frequently reprinted). It is not clear to me why Dr. Kroeger did not give the reference for the English translation of this passage. If the citation had been given as "Chrysostom, *Homily 26 on 1 Corinthians* (NPNF 1:12, 150); Greek text in PG 61.214," it would have taken only a few minutes for a reader to locate it in almost any library. In a reference work intended for a general as well as an academic audience (as this volume is), it would seem appropriate to cite references in a way that enables others to look them up and evaluate them. Several other references in the article were much more difficult to locate than this one (see below).

Consider nevertheless that she is a woman, the weaker vessel, whereas *thou art a man. For therefore wert thou ordained to be ruler; and wert assigned to her in place of a head*[10] (Διὰ γὰρ τοῦτο καὶ ἄρχων ἐχειροτονήθης, καὶ ἐν τάξει κεφαλῆς ἐδόθης), that thou mightest bear with the weakness of her that is set under thee. Make then thy rule glorious. And glorious it will be when the subject of it meets with no dishonor from thee.

2. Homily 5 on 1—2 Thessalonians (NPNF series 1, Vol. 13, p. 397; TLG Work 163, 62.499.34 to 62.500.14): Husband as head to rule the rest of the body.

For how is it not absurd, in other things to think thyself worthy of the preeminence, and *to occupy the place of the head* (τὴν τῆς κεφαλῆς χώραν ἐπέχειν), but in teaching to quit thy station. The ruler ought not to excel the ruled in honors, so much as in virtues. For this is the duty of a ruler, for the other is the part of the ruled, but this is the achievement of the ruler himself. If thou enjoyest much honor, it is nothing to thee, for thou receivedst it from others. If thou shinest in much virtue, this is all thine own.

Thou art the head of the woman, let then the head regulate the rest of the body (Κεφαλὴ τῆς γυναικὸς εἶ· οὐκοῦν ῥυθμιζέτω τὸ σῶμα τὸ λοιπὸν ἡ κεφαλή). Dost thou not see that it is not so much above the rest of the body in situation, as in forethought, directing like a steersman the whole of it? For in the head are the eyes both of the body, and of the soul. Hence flows to them both the faculty of seeing, and the power of directing. *And the rest of the body is appointed for service, but this is set to command* (Καὶ τὸ μὲν λοιπὸν τάττεται εἰς διακονίαν, αὐτὴ δὲ εἰς τὸ ἐπιτάττειν κεῖται). All the senses have thence their origin and their source (Πᾶσαι αἱ αἰσθήσεις ἐκεῖθεν ἔχουσι τὴν ἀρχὴν καὶ τὴν πηγήν·).[11] Thence are sent

---

[10]In this and several subsequent citations from ancient literature, I have added italics to enable readers to see more quickly the relevant section of the quotation.

Many of these patristic quotes contain expressions about the husband being "ruler" over his wife. I wish to make it clear that I am citing but not endorsing these statements. While many statements in the church fathers exhibit wonderful respect for women, at other points their language fails to show full understanding of the biblical teaching of men's and women's equality in value before God. Thus, rather than seeing the husband's authority as exhibiting itself in godly, loving leadership, they speak in harsher terms of "ruling" over one's wife. But my goal in this article is to report their language accurately, not to evaluate it.

[11]It is significant here that when Chrysostom does want to speak of a "source," he does not use the word κεφαλή, "head," nor does he use the term ἀρχή, "beginning, origin," but he rather uses the ordinary Greek word for "source," namely, πηγή. If Chrysostom or any other writer had wanted to say clearly, "head, which is source," he could easily have used πηγή to do so. But I did not find any place in Chrysostom or any other author where κεφαλή is defined as meaning πηγή, "source."

forth the organs of speech, the power of seeing, and of smelling, and all touch. For thence is derived the root of the nerves and of the bones. Seest thou not that it is superior in forethought more than in honor? So let us rule the women; let us surpass them, not by seeking greater honor from them, but by their being more benefited by us.

3. *Homily 3 on Ephesians (NPNF series 1, Vol. 13, p. 62; TLG Work 159, 62.26.22 to 62.26.46): Christ as head of the body, ruling over it, and head of all things.*

"Which is His Body." In order then that when you hear of the *Head* you may not conceive the notion of *supremacy* (ἀρχή)[12] only, but also of consolidation, and that you may behold Him not as *supreme Ruler* only, but as Head of a body. "The fulness of Him that filleth all in all" he says.... Let us reverence our Head, let us reflect of what a Head we are the body, —a Head, *to whom all things are put in subjection* (ᾗ πάντα ὑποτέτακται).

4. *Homily 13 on Ephesians (NPNF series 1, Vol. 13, p. 116; TLG Work 159, 62.99.22 to 62.99.29): Husbands as head ordained to rule over wives.*

But now it is the very contrary; women outstrip and eclipse us [that is, in virtue]. How contemptible! What a shame is this! *We hold the place of the head, and are surpassed by the body. We are ordained to rule over them*; not merely that we may rule, but that we may rule in goodness also (Ἄρχειν αὐτῶν ἐτάχθημεν, οὐχ ἵνα μόνον ἄρχωμεν, ἀλλ᾽ ἵνα καὶ ἐν ἀρετῇ ἄρχωμεν); for he that ruleth, ought especially to rule in this respect, by excelling in virtue; whereas if he is surpassed, he is no longer ruler.

5. *Homily 20 on Ephesians (NPNF series 1, Vol. 13, p. 144; TLG Work 159, 62.136.33 to 62.136.51): Husband as head with authority; wife as body with submission.*

Let us take as our fundamental position then, that *the husband occupies the place of the "head," and the wife the place of the "body."* Ver. 23, 24. Then, he proceeds with arguments and says that "the husband

---

[12]Note here the word ἀρχή used in Chrysostom not to mean "source" but "supremacy," understood by the NPNF translator to imply rulership, since he translates the cognate term ἄρχων (ἄρχοντα) as "supreme Ruler" in the parallel expression in the next clause.

is the head of the wife, as Christ also is the head of the Church, being Himself the Saviour of the body. But as the Church is subject to Christ, so let the wives be to their husbands in everything." Then after saying, "The husband is the head of the wife, as Christ also is of the Church," he further adds, "and He is the Saviour of the body." For indeed the head is the saving health of the body. He had already laid down beforehand for man and wife, the ground and provision of their love, *assigning to each their proper place, to the one that of authority and forethought, to the other that of submission* (ἑκάστῳ τὴν προσήκουσαν ἀπονέμων χώραν, τούτῳ μὲν τὴν ἀρχικὴν καὶ προνοητικὴν, ἐκείνῃ δὲ τὴν ὑποτακτικήν). As then "the Church," that is, both husbands and wives, "is subject unto Christ, so also ye wives submit yourselves to your husbands, as unto God."

6. *Homily 20 on Ephesians (NPNF series 1, Vol. 13, pp. 146-147; TLG Work 159, 62.140.51 to 62.141.13): Wife as body is subject to husband as head.*

The wife is a second authority (Ἀρχὴ δευτέρα ἐστὶν ἡ γυνή);[13] let not her then demand equality, for *she is under the head*; nor let him despise her as being in subjection, for she is the body; and if the head despise the body, it will itself also perish. But let him bring in love on his part as a counterpoise to obedience on her part. . . . Hence *he places the one in subjection, and the other in authority, that there may be peace; for where there is equal authority there can never be peace*; neither where a house is a democracy, nor where all are rulers; but the *ruling power* [14] must of necessity be one. And this is universally the case with matters referring to the body, inasmuch as when men are spiritual, there will be peace.

7. *Homily 20 on Ephesians (NPNF series 1, Vol. 13, p. 149; Greek portion in TLG Work 159, 62.144.45 to 62.144.47): Wife as body is to obey the husband as head.*

Neither let a wife say to her husband, "Unmanly coward that thou art, full of sluggishness and dullness, and fast asleep! here is such a one, a low man, and of low parentage, who runs his risks, and

---

[13]Note here the use of the term ἀρχή in Chrysostom to mean "authority, person in authority," not "source." With respect to governance of the household, Chrysostom says the wife is a second authority, under the authority of her husband.

[14]Here also Chrysostom uses ἀρχή in the sense of "ruling power, authority."

makes his voyages, and has made a good fortune; and his wife wears her jewels, and goes out with her pair of milk-white mules; she rides about everywhere, she has troops of slaves, and a swarm of eunuchs, but thou hast cowered down and livest to no purpose." Let not a wife say these things, nor anything like them. *For she is the body, not to dictate to the head, but to submit herself and obey* (σῶμα γάρ ἐστιν, οὐχ ἵνα διατάττῃ τῇ κεφαλῇ, ἀλλ᾽ ἵνα πείθηται καὶ ὑπακούῃ).

8. *Homily 6 on Ephesians (NPNF series 1, Vol. 13, p. 78; TLG Work 159, 62.47.55 to 62.47.59): Church rulers as head of church.* In this passage, the "rulers" in the church are called the "head" of the church.

(for hear what he says writing to Timothy, (I Tim. 5:20) "Them that sin, reprove in the sight of all;") it is that the *rulers* are in a sickly state; for if the *head* (κεφαλή) be not sound, how can the rest of the body maintain its vigor? But mark how great is the present disorder.

9. *Homily 15 on Ephesians (NPNF series 1, Vol. 13, p. 124; Greek portion in TLG Work 159, 62.110.21 to 62.110.25): A woman as head of her maidservant.* This is the only passage I found in Chrysostom—in fact, the only passage I have ever seen—where a woman is called the "head." This instance gives strong confirmation to the meaning "authority over, ruler," for here Chrysostom says that a woman is "head" of her maidservant, over whom she has authority.

"But," say ye, "the whole tribe of slaves is intolerable if it meet with indulgence." True, I know it myself. But then, as I was saying, correct them in some other way, not by the scourge only, and by terror, but even by flattering them, and by acts of kindness. If she is a believer, she is thy sister. Consider that thou art her mistress, and that she ministers unto thee. If she be intemperate, cut off the occasions of drunkenness; call thy husband, and admonish her. . . . Yea, be she drunkard, or railer, or gossip, or evil-eyed, or extravagant, and a squanderer of thy substance, thou hast her for the partner of thy life. Train and restrain her. Necessity is upon thee. *It is for this thou art the head. Regulate her therefore*, do thy own part (διὰ τοῦτο κεφαλὴ εἶ σύ. Οὐκοῦν ῥύθμιζε, τὸ σαυτοῦ ποίει). Yea, and if she remain incorrigible, yea, though she steal, take care of thy goods, and do not punish her so much.

10. *The claim that* ἀρχή *means "source" in Chrysostom's Homily 26 on 1 Corinthians (NPNF series 1, Vol. 12, p. 151; TLG Work 156, 61.216.1 to 61.216.10).*

There is one more sentence to consider in Kroeger's claims about Chrysostom. Here again is the quotation from *Dictionary of Paul and His Letters* with which we began:

> In view of Scripture ascribing coequality of Christ with the Father (Jn. 1:1-3; 10:30; 14:9, 11; 16:15; 17:11, 21), John Chrysostom declared that only a heretic would understand Paul's use of "head" to mean "chief" or "authority over." Rather one should understand the term as implying "absolute oneness and cause and primal source" (PG 61.214, 216).[15]

In the last sentence, Kroeger claims that Chrysostom said we should understand κεφαλή as implying "absolute oneness and cause and primal source." She bases this idea on the second reference, PG 61.216, which reads as follows in the NPNF translation:

> Christ is called "the Head of the Church" . . . We should . . . accept the notion of a perfect union and the *first principle*, and not even these ideas absolutely, but here also we must form a notion . . . of that which is too high for us and suitable to the Godhead: for both the union is surer and the beginning more honorable. (NPNF Series 1, Vol. 12, p. 151)
>
> κεφαλὴ τῆς Ἐκκλησίας ὁ Χριστός· . . . .᾽Ἀφεῖναι μὲν ταῦτα ἃ εἶπον, λαβεῖν δὲ ἕνωσιν ἀκριβῆ, [καὶ αἰτίαν] καὶ ἀρχὴν τὴν πρώτην· καὶ οὐδὲ ταῦτα ἁπλῶς, ἀλλὰ καὶ ἐνταῦθα τὸ μεῖζον οἴκοθεν ἐπινοεῖν καὶ Θεῷ πρέπον· καὶ γὰρ ἡ ἕνωσις ἀσφαλεστέρα, καὶ ἡ ἀρχὴ τιμιωτέρα.[16]

The expression that the NPNF translator rendered "perfect union" Kroeger translated "absolute oneness," which is similar in meaning. Next Kroeger says "and cause," which accurately repre-

---

[15]Kroeger, "Head," 377.

[16]TLG, Chrysostom, *Homilies on 1 Corinthians*, Work 156, 61.216.1 to 61.216.10. I have added the brackets to show the textual variant that is not translated by the NPNF translator.

sents the words καὶ αἰτίαν, a textual variant that was not translated in the NPNF edition. But then where did she get the phrase "and primal source"? This was her translation of καὶ ἀρχὴν τὴν πρώτην, which was translated "first principle" in the NPNF translation (with no idea of "source"). Later in the same sentence the NPNF translation renders the word ἀρχή as "beginning," and the context shows that this refers back to the same word earlier in the sentence.

What Kroeger has done here (as elsewhere) is take one possible sense of ἀρχή—namely, the sense "source"—and not tell her readers that other senses of ἀρχή are possible. Nor has she mentioned that the commonly used English translation in the NPNF series translates this example not as "source" but as "principle" and then "beginning."

It is true that Lampe's *Patristic Greek Lexicon* lists "origin, source" as one of several possible senses for ἀρχή.[17] But the meanings "beginning," "principle," "foundation," "cause," "First Cause," and "Creator" are also listed, as well as "rule, authority," "rulers, magistrates," "ecclesiastical authority," and "spiritual powers."[18]

It is difficult to understand why Kroeger took *one possible sense* of ἀρχή, one that the lexicons do not specifically use to apply to Christ, and did not tell the reader that this was a disputed translation unique to herself. Her writing sounds as if Chrysostom had defined κεφαλή as "source," whereas he had only used the term ἀρχή to explain how the head-body metaphor could apply both to the Father and the Son, and also to Christ and the church. He said it applied in a sense "suitable to the Godhead," in which the metaphor implied both the "perfect union" between the Father and Son and also that the Father is the

---

[17]P. 234. Note here, however, that we are now talking about ἀρχή, not about κεφαλή, for which the meaning "source" is not given in Lampe. As commonly happens with two different words, some of the senses of ἀρχή are shared with κεφαλή, and some are not.

An example from English may clarify this. I might say, "George Washington was the first head (that is, the first ruler) of the United States." Here "ruler" means "one who governs." But the term "ruler" has another meaning in American English, namely, "a straight-edged strip, as of wood or metal, for drawing straight lines and measuring lengths." The word "head" does not share that sense of "ruler" (I would not say, "I measured the margins of the page with my wooden head"). Similarly, the word "head" refers to a part of the human body, and the word "ruler" does not share that sense (I would not say, "I bumped my ruler on the door this morning").

Kroeger is making a methodological error to think that she can import all the senses of ἀρχή into the meaning of κεφαλή. Those specific meanings that she claims need first to be demonstrated for κεφαλή with clear evidence from lexicons and supported by persuasive citations from ancient literature where such meanings are required.

[18]Lampe, 234-236.

"first principle" in the Trinity.[19] Chrysostom did not say that the Father was the "primal source" of the Son, and if he had said so he could be accused of Arianism, the heresy that said the Son was created by the Father. As with many other examples of Chrysostom's use of κεφαλή, no example of the metaphor "head" meaning "source" can be found here.

11. *Conclusion on Chrysostom's use of* κεφαλή.

Chrysostom uses κεφαλή to say that one person is the "head" of another in at least six different relationships: (1) God is the "head" of Christ; (2) Christ is the "head" of the church; (3) the husband is the "head" of the wife; (4) Christ is the "head" of all things; (5) church leaders are the "head" of the church; and (6) a woman is the "head" of her maidservant. In all six cases he uses language of rulership and authority to explain the role of the "head" and uses language of submission and obedience to describe the role of the "body."[20] Far from claiming that "only a heretic" would use κεφαλή to mean "authority over," Chrysostom repeatedly uses it that way himself.

I admit, of course, that fourth-century usage of a word by Chrysostom does not prove that word had the same sense in the first century; so this is not conclusive evidence for New Testament meanings. But since Dr. Kroeger appealed to patristic usage to argue for "source," it seemed appropriate to investigate this patristic evidence directly. This material is certainly of some value for New Testament studies, because the meanings of many words continued to be understood quite precisely by the church fathers, especially by those whose first language was Greek. If their date is clearly indicated, these new examples of κεφαλή in the sense "authority over" may be added to the more than forty examples cited in my 1990 article,[21] and they do show

---

[19]The meaning "authority" is also legitimate for ἀρχή; so this passage could also be translated, "the notion of a perfect union, and the *first authority*." In fact, in light of Chrysostom's calling the wife a "second authority" elsewhere (see citation 6 above from his "Homily 20 on Ephesians," for example), the meaning "first authority" would be appropriate here, and the parallel would be that the Son is a "second authority" after the Father. Moreover, this is in the same sermon as the very first quotation from Chrysostom that I listed in this article (NPNF 1:12, p. 150; TLG 156, 61.214), where he sees the husband's role as "head" implying that the wife is "reasonably subjected" to him, and where he sees the Father's role as "head" as one in which the Son freely yields obedience to him.

[20]This usage is so frequent in the passages I examined in Chrysostom, and receives so much emphasis, that I expect further examples could be found if one were to do an exhaustive examination of all his uses of κεφαλή, which I did not attempt.

[21]Grudem, "Meaning of *kephalē*" (see footnote 1 above).

that the sense "authority over" continued to attach to κεφαλή at least until the end of the fourth century. But they also show an absence of the meaning "source" in this one church father, for Chrysostom does not use κεφαλή to mean "source" in any of the texts I found.

What then shall we make of Kroeger's statement that "John Chrysostom declared that only a heretic would understand Paul's use of 'head' to mean 'chief' or 'authority over'"? It is simply false.

III. KROEGER'S CITATIONS FROM OTHER CHURCH FATHERS

1. *Nine other patristic references.* Chrysostom is not the only church father whom Kroeger cites. In attempting to establish that the sense "chief" or "master" was "rarely" the sense "of the Greek *kephalē* in NT times," she writes:

> The contemporary desire to find in 1 Corinthians 11:3 a basis for the subordination of the Son to the Father has ancient roots. In response to such subordinationism, church fathers argued vehemently that for Paul *head* had meant "source." Athanasius (*Syn. Armin.* 26.3.35; *Anathema* 26. Migne PG 26, 740B), Cyril of Alexandria (*De Recte Fide ad Pulch.* 2.3, 268; *De Recte Fide ad Arcadiam* 1.1.5.5(2).63.), Basil (PG 30.80.23), Theodore of Mopsuestia, *Eccl. Theol.* 1.11.2-3; 2.7.1) and even Eusebius, *Eccl. Theol.* 1.11.2-3; 2.7.1) were quick to recognize the danger of an interpretation of 1 Corinthians 11:3 which could place Christ in a subordinate position relative to the Father.[22]

The first thing to note about this statement is the inaccurate equation of "the subordination of the Son to the Father" with "subordinationism" (which, in this context, Kroeger uses as a reference to a heresy the church rejected). The heresy commonly called "subordination*ism*" (emphasis added) is a denial that Christ is fully divine, a denial that He is "of the same substance" as the Father. The Arians whom Chrysostom was opposing in the citations quoted above would hold to subordinationism. But this is not the same as to say that 1 Corinthians 11:3 teaches the "subordination of the Son to the Father," for that language is an orthodox description of how the Son relates to the Father—He is *subject to* the Father, who creates the world *through* Him and sends Him into the world to die for our sins. To say that the Son is *subject to* the Father,

---

[22]Kroeger, "Head," 377.

or that He is *subordinate* in His relationship to the Father, has been orthodox teaching according to Roman Catholic, Eastern Orthodox, and
Protestant theology through the whole history of the church at least
since the Council of Nicea in A.D. 325, and Kroeger is simply mistaken
to apply the name of the heresy "subordinationism" to it. But to say that
the Son is not fully divine and thus to deny the deity of Christ would
be subordinationism, and that the early fathers do not do.[23]

We can now examine these texts to see if they actually establish the
idea that "church fathers argued vehemently that for Paul *head* had
meant 'source,'" and if they show that these church fathers "were quick
to recognize the danger" of understanding 1 Corinthians 11:3 to mean
that Christ has a "subordinate position relative to the Father." The texts
are given by Kroeger as follows:

---

[23]Historian Philip Schaff, though he uses the term "subordinationism" in two senses, directly
contradicts Kroeger's statement when he says, "The Nicene fathers still teach, like their prede-
cessors, a certain *subordinationism*, which seems to conflict with the doctrine of consubstantial-
ity. But we must distinguish between a subordinationism of essence (οὐσία) and a
subordinationism of hypostasis, of order and dignity. The former was denied, the latter affirmed.",
History of the Christian Church (3rd edition; Grand Rapids, MI: Eerdmans, 1971-72, reprinted
from 1910 edition), Vol. 3, 680-681.
    Several evangelical theologians speak of the subordination of the Son to the Father. For
example, Charles Hodge says, "Notwithstanding that the Father, Son, and Spirit are the same
in substance, and equal in power and glory, it is no less true, according to the Scriptures, (a)
That the Father is first, the Son second, and the Spirit third. (b.) The Son is of the Father (ἐκ
θεοῦ, the λόγος, εἰκὼν, ἀπαύγασμα τοῦ θεοῦ); and the Spirit is of the Father and of the Son.
(c.) The Father sends, and the Father and Son send the Spirit. (d.) The Father operates through
the Son, and the Father and Son operate through the Spirit. *The converse of these statements is never
found. The Son is never said to send the Father, nor to operate through Him; nor is the Spirit ever said to
send the Father, or the Son, or to operate through Them.* The facts contained in this paragraph are
summed up in the proposition: *In the Holy Trinity there is a subordination of the Persons as to the mode
of subsistence and operation.*" Charles Hodge, *Systematic Theology* (three volumes; reprint edition;
Grand Rapids, MI: Eerdmans, 1970; first published 1871-73), Vol. 1, 444-445. (Italics for
emphasis added in this and the other quotations in this footnote.)
    Hodge continues later: "On this subject the Nicene doctrine includes, —1. The principle
of *the subordination of the Son to the Father*, and of the Spirit to the Father and the Son. *But this
subordination does not imply inferiority*" (ibid., 460). "The creeds [Nicea and Constantinople] are
nothing more than a well-ordered arrangement of the facts of Scripture which concern the
doctrine of the Trinity. They assert the distinct personality of the Father, Son, and Spirit; their
mutual relation as expressed by those terms; their absolute unity as to substance or essence,
and their consequent perfect equality; and *the subordination of the Son to the Father, and of the Spirit
to the Father and the Son, as to the mode of subsistence and operation. These are Scriptural facts to which
the creeds in question add nothing; and it is in this sense they have been accepted by the Church universal*"
(ibid., 462).
    See also B. B. Warfield: "There is, of course, no question that in 'modes of operation,' . . .
the principle of subordination is clearly expressed" (*Works*, Vol. 2 [Grand Rapids. MI: Baker, 1991;
reprint of 1929 edition], 165); similarly, A. H. Strong, *Systematic Theology* (Valley Forge, PA:
Judson Press, 1907), 342, with references to other writers; also Louis Berkhof, *Systematic
Theology* (4th edition, Grand Rapids, MI: Eerdmans, 1939), 88-89.
    These statements, together with the patristic evidence cited in the following material, indi-
cate that Kroeger's claim that church fathers denied the subordination of the Son to the Father
is incorrect.

1. Athanasius, *Syn. Armin.* 26.3.35
2. Athanasius, *Anathema* 26, MPG 26, 740B
3. Cyril of Alexandria, *De Recte Fide ad Pulch.* 2.3, 268.
4. Cyril of Alexandria, *De Recte Fide ad Arcadiam* 1.1.5.5(2).63.
5. Basil, PG 30.80.23
6. Theodore of Mopsuestia, *Eccl. Theol.* 1.11.2-3
7. Theodore of Mopsuestia, *Eccl. Theol.* 2.7.1
8. Eusebius, *Eccl. Theol.* 1.11.2-3
9. Eusebius, *Eccl. Theol.* 2.7.1

2. *The ambiguity of quotations that explain* κεφαλή *as* ἀρχή. The first thing to notice is that five of these nine references (numbers 2, 3, 4, and apparently 6 and 7 when corrected)[24] are found in one paragraph on page 749 of Lampe's *Patristic Greek Lexicon*, II.B. 4, a paragraph that gives examples of κεφαλή used "as equivalent of ἀρχή." But ἀρχή is itself an ambiguous word and can mean "beginning" or "authority," as was indicated above, or in some cases "source."[25]

The distinction between the senses "source" and "beginning" is an important distinction because the beginning of something is not always the source of something. (For example, my oldest son is the "beginning" or "first" of my sons, but he is not the "source" of my other sons.) In the Bible itself we find several examples of ἀρχή used as "beginning" where the idea of "source" would not fit:

Genesis 1:1: In the beginning *(*ἀρχή*), God created the heavens and the earth.*

We could not say, "In the *source* God created the heavens and the earth."

Matthew 19:4: He answered, "Have you not read that he who created them from the beginning *(*ἀρχή*) made them male and female . . . ?"*

We could not say, "He who made them from the *source* made them male and female." The same reasoning applies to other examples:

---

[24]The references to Theodore of Mopsuestia are incorrect; see discussion below.

[25]Note that Lampe's *Lexicon* does not translate ἀρχή when it is used to explain κεφαλή in discussions of 1 Corinthians 11:3 but just says "as equivalent of ἀρχή." The difficulty of translation is partly due to the fact that both words can mean "ruler, authority," and both words can mean "beginning." But ἀρχή has several other possible meanings as well (see the above discussion in II.10, especially n.18 and 19).

Mark 1:1: The beginning *(ἀρχή) of the gospel of Jesus Christ, the Son of God.* Ἀρχὴ τοῦ εὐαγγελίου Ἰησοῦ Χριστοῦ [υἱοῦ θεοῦ].

This verse is not the "source" of the rest of Mark, but it is the starting point or "beginning" of Mark, the first in a series of many statements to follow.

John 1:1: In the beginning *(ἀρχή) was the Word, and the Word was with God, and the Word was God.*

John 2:11 This, the first *(ἀρχή) of his signs, Jesus did at Cana in Galilee, and manifested his glory. And his disciples believed in him.*

Colossians 1:18: He is the head of the body, the church. He is the beginning *(ἀρχή), the firstborn from the dead, that in everything he might be preeminent.*

Here Christ is said to be the "beginning" or "first in a series" of the people who would be raised from the dead. He is the first; others will follow.

Revelation 22:13: "I am the Alpha and the Omega, the first and the last, the beginning *(ἀρχή) and the end."*

The idea "source" would not fit any of these examples. Nor is it the correct meaning in any other New Testament example. The BAGD *Lexicon* (pp. 111-112) does not list "source" as a possible meaning for .ἀρχή in the New Testament or early Christian literature. It sometimes means "beginning." It sometimes means "authority" or "ruler," as in citations 3 and 6 from Chrysostom in the previous section of this paper. Therefore, to find examples of κεφαλή used as equivalent of ἀρχή does not prove that "church fathers argued vehemently that for Paul *head* had meant 'source.'" It would be just as legitimate on the basis of ἀρχή alone to say that they argued vehemently that for Paul *head* had meant "ruler" or *head* had meant "beginning."

IV. THE ACTUAL PATRISTIC CITATIONS

We can now look at these nine references cited by Kroeger, in which she says the church fathers "argued vehemently that for Paul *head* had meant 'source'" and denied that Christ is subordinate to the Father.

1. *Athanasius (ca. A.D. 296-373), Syn. Armin. 26.3.35.* This is not actually a statement by a church father. This quotation is from an Arian creed, the "Macrostich" or 5th Confession of A.D. 344, which Athanasius quotes, along with several other Arian creeds, in order to show that they cannot even agree among themselves on what they teach. It is surprising that Kroeger cites this as evidence of what the "church fathers" taught, for Arianism was rejected as a heresy by the orthodox church, and this Arian creed does not represent what the recognized church fathers taught.

The quotation is as follows:

> Yet we must not consider the Son to be co-unbegun and co-ingenerate with the Father. . . . But we acknowledge that the Father who alone is Unbegun and Ingenerate, hath generated inconceivably and incomprehensibly to all; and that the Son hath been generated before ages, and in no wise to be ingenerate Himself like the Father, but to have the Father who generated Him as His *beginning* (ἀρχή); for "the Head of Christ is God."[26]

Here ἀρχή is used in the sense "beginning," according to the NPNF translator. In any case, the quotation of an Arian creed, with no subsequent comment on this word or phrase by Athanasius himself, is not reliable evidence on which to decide anything about the way κεφαλή was understood by Athanasius or other church fathers, as Kroeger claims. Nor does it provide any evidence that church fathers argued against the subordination of the Son to the Father.

2. *Athanasius (ca. A.D. 296-373), Anathema 26, MPG 26, 740B.* This quotation is not actually from an orthodox church father either. It is from another Arian creed, which Athanasius also quotes to show how the Arians cannot agree among themselves.

> Whosoever shall say that the Son is without beginning and ingenerate, as if speaking of two unbegun and two ingenerate, and making two Gods, be he anathema. For the Son is the Head, namely the beginning (ἀρχή) of all: and God is the *Head*, namely the beginning (ἀρχή) of Christ; for thus to one unbegun begin-

[26]The Greek text is in TLG Athanasius, *De synodis Arimini*, Work 010, 26,3.3. The English translation is from NPNF, Second Series, Vol. 4, 463, with extensive notes on the Arian theology represented here.

ning (ἀρχή) of the universe do we religiously refer all things through the Son.[27]

Here again ἀρχή is used by the Arians in the sense of "beginning" to explain κεφαλή. But it does not show us how κεφαλή was understood by Athanasius or other church fathers, as Kroeger's article claimed.

In fact, Athanasius himself did not "argue vehemently" that for Paul, *head* meant "source," nor did he deny that κεφαλή could mean "authority over," for he refers to "the bishops of illustrious cities," for example, as "the *heads* of great churches" (κεφαλαὶ τοσούτων ἐκκλησιῶν).[28]

3. *Cyril of Alexandria (died A.D. 444), De Recte Fide ad Pulch. 2.3, 268.*

. . . the one of the earth and dust has become (γέγονεν) to us the first head of the race, that is ruler (ἀρχή) but since the second Adam has been named Christ, he was placed as head (κεφαλή), that is ruler (τουτέστιν ἀρχή) of those who through him are being transformed unto him into incorruption through sanctification by the Spirit. Therefore he on the one hand is our ruler (ἀρχή), that is head, in so far as he has appeared as a man; indeed, he, being by nature God, has a head, the Father in heaven. For, being by nature God the Word, he has been begotten from Him. But that the head signifies the ruler (ἀρχή), the fact that the husband is said to be the head of the wife confirms the sense for the truth of doubters: for she has been taken from him (ἐλήφθη γὰρ ἐξ αὐτοῦ). Therefore one Christ and Son and Lord, the one having as head the Father in heaven, being God by nature, became for us a "head" accordingly because of his kinship according to the flesh.[29]

In this quotation, κεφαλή is explained by ἀρχή, probably in the sense of "ruler," but the ambiguity of ἀρχή confronts us here, and the sense "beginning" or the sense "origin or source" for ἀρχή would also fit.

In 1990 I responded to Kroeger's citation of this passage[30] and said that even if the sense "source" were understood here, this is still not an

---

[27]The Greek text is in TLG, Athanasius, *De synodis Arimini*, Work 010, 27.3,26 to 27.3,27. The English translation is from NPNF, Second Series, Vol. 4, p. 465.

[28]The Greek text is in TLG, Athanasius, Work 005, 89.2.3. The English translation is in NPNF, Second Series, Vol. 4, p. 147. This text is also quoted by Joseph Fitzmyer, "*kephalē* in I Corinthians 11:3," *Interpretation* 47 (1993), 56, as evidence of the meaning "leader, ruler" for κεφαλή.

[29]The Greek text is found in Eduard Schwartz, ed., *Acta Conciliorum Oecumenicorum* (Berlin: de Gruyter, 1927), 1.1.5, p. 28. The English translation is mine.

[30]Grudem, "Meaning of *kephalē*, " 464-465.

instance of "source" apart from authority, for God and Christ and the husband are all in positions of authority.[31] Of course, if we took this passage in an isolated way, apart from its context in patristic writings and ancient Trinitarian controversies, and apart from previously established meanings for κεφαλή, there would be no strong objection to thinking that the meaning "source" would fit this passage as well, even though it would not be necessary for the sense of the passage. And it must also be recognized that it is an elementary fact of life that we receive our nourishment through our mouths, and thus in a sense through our heads, and this idea was plain to the ancient world as well; therefore, the idea that a metaphor would occur in which "head" meant "source" is not impossible.[32] But even if that sense were accepted here, it would scarcely be decisive for Pauline usage, since this passage comes four hundred years *after* Paul wrote.[33]

Yet several factors make me hesitate to jump to the meaning "source" here:

(1) First, a very similar connection between the man's headship and the woman's being taken from the man is made by an earlier Alexandrian writer, Clement of Alexandria (ca. A.D. 155-ca. 220), in *The Stromata* 4:8 (ANF 2, 420):

> "For I would have you know," says the apostle, "that the head of every man is Christ; and the head of the woman is the man: for the man is not of the woman, but the woman of the man (οὐ γὰρ ἔστιν ἀνὴρ ἐκ γυναικὸς, ἀλλὰ γυνὴ ἐξ ἀνδρός)."[34]

Such an explicit connection between man's headship and woman's being taken out of man might lead us to think that Clement of Alexandria would understand "head" to mean "source, origin" here,

---

[31]Gregory W. Dawes, *The Body in Question: Metaphor and Meaning in the Interpretation of Ephesians 5:21-33* (Leiden: Brill, 1998), says that in analyzing this passage from Cyril of Alexandria, Grudem "suggests (rightly) that even here the term κεφαλή retains the sense of authority, and that a passage like this needs to be read in its historical context (the Trinitarian controversies of the early church)" (p. 128). However, Dawes differs with my hesitancy to see the meaning "source" as the most likely one here, saying that "different (metaphorical) senses of a word are possible in different contexts." He thinks that authority is present in the passage, but that it may be related to the idea of origin.

[32]This is the point made by Dawes, as mentioned in the previous footnote.

[33]Note the caution that was expressed above about the merely moderate relevance of the quotations from Chrysostom, who wrote over three hundred years after Paul.

[34]The English translation in both quotations is that of the ANF series (2, 420). The Greek text is in the TLG, Clement of Alexandria, Work 4, 4.8.60.2.

just as we might in the statement from Cyril of Alexandria. But this is not so, for later on the same page Clement explains:

> The ruling power is therefore the head (κεφαλὴ τοίνυν τὸ ἡγεμονικόν). And if "the Lord is head of the man, and the man is head of the woman," the man, "being the image and glory of God, is lord of the woman." Wherefore also in the Epistle to the Ephesians it is written, "Subjecting yourselves one to another in the fear of God. Wives, submit yourselves to your own husbands, as to the Lord. For the husband is head of the wife. . . ."[35]

This means that Clement of Alexandria's first statement should be understood in the sense: the man has ruling authority over the woman *because* she was taken from him. Clement of Alexandria is simply connecting 1 Corinthians 11:3 with 1 Corinthians 11:8 and sees one as the reason supporting the other.

This means that a similar manner of reasoning would not be inappropriate for Cyril of Alexandria, writing later and coming from the same city: the man is the head of (that is, has ruling authority over) the woman *because* she was taken from him.

And there are several other factors that argue against the meaning "source" in Cyril of Alexandria, such as the following: (2) the way that a third writer, Theodore of Mopsuestia, who is contemporary with Cyril, so clearly connects the wife's obedience to her husband to the idea that she was taken from him in 1 Corinthians 11:7-8;[36] (3) the way other patristic writers so clearly understand κεφαλή to mean "authority over" in 1 Corinthians 11:3 and connect it to ἀρχή meaning "authority over";[37] (4) the fact that it says Adam "has become" (γέγονεν) first head of the race, which would be a strange notion for "source" (for a source is there from the beginning, and one does not later become a source, nor does one become a "first" source); and (5) the fact that "authority over" is a commonly under-

---

[35]ANF 2, 420; TLG, Work 4, 4.8.63.5 to 4.8.64.1.

[36]See the material from Theodore of Mopsuestia below, in patristic citation 7a (section III.3.7a).

[37]See the quotations from Chrysostom, above, and from Basil and Eusebius, below. For example, Joseph Fitzmyer speaks of "the many places in patristic literature where comments are made on I Corinthians 11:3. . . . In these places the sense of *kephalē* as 'leader, ruler, one having authority over' is clear" (*"kephalē* in I Corinthians 11:3").

stood and established meaning for κεφαλή, while "source" has yet to be demonstrated by anything other than ambiguous passages.

A factor related to (5) is (6) the absence of support from the lexicons for the meaning "source." This meaning is not given in Lampe's *Patristic Greek Lexicon*, the standard lexicon for this material, in the entry for κεφαλή, nor is it given in BAGD, the standard lexicon for New Testament Greek.[38] At this point sound lexicography should cause us to be cautious about adopting a new meaning for a word based on one difficult passage, or one passage where it "could" have that meaning. This point was emphasized by John Chadwick in reflecting on his many years of work on the editorial team for the Liddell-Scott *Lexicon*:

> A constant problem to guard against is the proliferation of meanings. . . . It is often tempting to create a new sense to accommodate a difficult example, but we must always ask first, if there is any other way of taking the word which would allow us to assign the example to an already established sense. . . . As I have remarked in several of my notes, there may be no reason why a proposed sense should not exist, but is there any reason why it must exist?[39]

For these reasons, it seems to me that the established sense, "ruler, authority," best fits this passage in Cyril of Alexandria. By weighing these considerations on this and other passages, readers will have to form their own conclusions.

Yet one more point needs to be made. Cyril of Alexandria clearly did not deny the subordination of the Son to the Father, nor does his material support Kroeger's claim that these writers "were quick to recognize the danger of an interpretation of 1 Corinthians 11:3 which could place Christ in a subordinate position relative to the Father," for no denial of the Father's authority over the Son is found here. In fact, in his *Dialogues on the Trinity* Cyril of Alexandria has an extensive discussion of the subordination of the Son to the Father, explaining that it is a voluntary submission, like that of Isaac to Abraham, or like that of Jesus to His earthly parents, and that it does not show Him to be a

---

[38]The meaning "source" in the way Kroeger understands it is not given in the Liddell-Scott Lexicon either; see the discussion in section E below.

[39]John Chadwick, *Lexicographica Graeca: Contributions to the Lexicography of Ancient Greek* (Oxford: Clarendon Press, 1996), 23-24.

lesser being but is consistent with His being of the same nature with His Father and thus fully God.[40]

4. *Cyril of Alexandria (died A.D. 444), De Recte Fide ad Arcadiam 1.1.5.5(2).63.*

> "But I want you to know that the head of every man is Christ, and the head of a woman is the man, and the head of Christ is God." The blessed Luke, composing for us the genealogy of Christ, begins (ἄρχεται) from Joseph, then he comes to Adam, soon speaking of God, placing as the beginning (ἀρχή) of man the God who made him. Thus we say Christ is the head of every man: for man was made through him and he was brought to birth, the Son not creating him in a servile way, but more divinely, as in the nature of a workman. "But the head of a woman is the man," for she was taken out of his flesh, and she has him even as (her) beginning (ἀρχή). And similarly, "the head of Christ is God," for he is from him according to nature: for the Word was begotten out of God the Father. Then how is Christ not God, the one of whom the Father, according to (his) nature, has been placed as head? Whenever I might say Christ appeared in the form of man, I understand the Word of God.[41]

This text gives an understanding of κεφαλή as ἀρχή, probably in the sense of "beginning," namely, the point from which something started. In both of these quotes from Cyril, someone might argue for the sense "source, origin," but the sense "authority" would fit as well (it seemed to be the sense in the earlier quote; however, here he could be making a different point). Yet "beginning" fits better than "source," because Cyril could have thought that "woman" had one man (Adam) as the starting point from which women began, but he would not have thought that any other women had subsequent men as their "source," for no woman since Eve has been taken out of a man. Cyril is tracing

---

[40]See Cyril of Alexandria, *Dialogues sur la Trinité*, ed. and trans. Georges Matthieu de Durand (Sources Chrétiennes 237; Paris: Cerf, 1977), 2:372-379 (with Greek text and French translation). Cyril's concern in this section is to show that submission does not negate the Son's deity, and so he emphasizes that, though the Son does submit to the Father, He remains equal with Him in "being" (οὐσία). He says it does not disturb the traits of the "substance" (τῆς οὐσίας) to give obedience "as a son to a father" (ὡς ἐξ υἱοῦ πρὸς πατέρα) (Durand, 374; 582.28-30). (I am grateful to my pastor Stephen E. Farish for saving me much time by quickly providing me with an English translation of many pages of the French translation of Cyril's intricate argumentation on the Trinity.)

[41]The Greek text is found in Schwartz, *Acta Conciliorum Oecumenicorum*, 1.1.5, p. 76. The English translation is mine.

back a genealogy to its starting point and comes to Adam. "Beginning, starting point" therefore seems to fit this context. But the ambiguity of ἀρχή makes it difficult to decide.

5. *Basil (the Great, of Caesarea, c. 329-379,) In Psalmum 28 (homilia 2), MPG 30:80 (TLG 53.30.80.23).*

> "And the beloved is as a son of unicorns" [LXX Ps. 28:6b]. After the opposing powers are raised up, then love for the Lord will appear plainly, and his strength will become evident, when no one casts a shadow over those in his presence. Therefore he says, after the [statement about] beating: "the beloved will be as the son of unicorns." But a unicorn is a *royal* (ἀρχικὸς, "royal, fit for rule") animal, *not made subject* to man, his strength *unconquerable* (ἀνυπό-τακτον ἀνθρώπῳ, τὴν ἰσχὺν ἀκαταμάχητον) always living in desert places, trusting in his one horn. Therefore the *unconquerable* nature of the Lord (ἡ ἀκαταγώνιστος τοῦ Κυρίου φύσις) is likened to a unicorn, both because of his *rule* (ἀρχή) upon every-thing, and because he has one *ruler* (ἀρχή) of himself, the Father: for "the head (κεφαλή) of Christ is God."[42]

This passage is significant, even though Basil's discussion is based on the Septuagint mistranslation of Psalm 28:6, "And the beloved is as a son of unicorns." But Basil uses this text as an opportunity to com-ment on the unconquerable nature of a unicorn and likens this to the supreme rule of Christ over everything. Then he adds that the Son has one ruler over himself, namely, God the Father. For our purposes, it is significant that for Basil "the head of Christ is God" meant "the ruler over Christ is God," and the word ἀρχή meant "ruler" when it was used as a synonym for κεφαλή.

6. *Theodore of Mopsuestia (ca. 350-428 AD), Eccl. Theol. 1.11.2-3,* and
7. *Theodore of Mopsuestia (ca. 350-428 AD), Eccl. Theol. 2.7.1.*

These two references do not exist.[43] The numbers were apparently copied by mistake from the Eusebius references below them (Eusebius, *Eccl. Theol.* 1.11.2-3 and 2.7.1). However, perhaps Kroeger intended to copy the reference to Theodore of Mopsuestia in the entry for κεφαλή in Lampe's *Lexicon*. That reference is as follows:

---

[42]The Greek text is in TLG Basil, *In Psalmum 28 (homilia 2)*, Work 053, 30.80.12 to 30.80.23. The English translation is mine.

[43]Theodore of Mopsuestia has no work with the title or abbreviation *Eccl. Theol.* (see Lampe, *Lexicon*, xli) .

7a. *Theodore of Mopsuestia, 1 Cor. 11:3 (p. 187.12ff; M.66.888c):*

This he wishes to say: that, on the one hand, we move forward from Christ to God (ἀπὸ μὲν τοῦ Χριστοῦ ἐπὶ τὸν Θεὸν χωροῦμεν), out of whom he is, but on the other hand from man to Christ (ἀπὸ δὲ τοῦ ἀνδρὸς ἐπὶ τὸν Χριστόν): for we are out of him according to the second form of existence. . . . For on the one hand, being subject to suffering, we consider Adam to be head (κεφαλή), from whom we have taken existence. But on the other hand, not being subject to suffering, we consider Christ to be head (κεφαλή), from whom we have an unsuffering existence. Similarly, he says, also from woman to man (καὶ ἀπὸ τῆς γυναικὸς ἐπὶ τὸν ἄνδρα), since she has taken existence from him.[44]

This text at first seems ambiguous regarding the meaning of κεφαλή, perhaps because Theodore's commentaries exist only in fragments, and we may not have all that he wrote on this verse. The idea of "head" as "leader, ruler" seems possible, especially since he says we "advance" or "move forward"(χωρέω ἀπὸ [person B] ἐπὶ [person A]), in each case to the one who is "head," suggesting higher rank. But the idea of "beginning" (that is, the first one to exist in the condition specified) is also possible.

But Theodore's subsequent comments seem to tip the issue toward κεφαλή meaning "leader, authority over." This is because in 1 Corinthians 11:3 he connects man's headship with woman's being created from man, an idea that Theodore then explains when he comments on 1 Corinthians 11:7-8. These verses read as follows in the New Testament:

For a man ought not to cover his head, since he is the image and glory of God; but woman is the glory of man. (For man was not made from woman, but woman from man.) (RSV)

When Theodore comments on this passage, he sees a woman's "glory" as consisting in her obedience to her husband:

He calls the woman "glory" but surely not "image," because it applied faintly, since "glory" looks at obedience (εἰς τὴν ὑπακοήν), but "image" looks at rulership (εἰς τὸ ἀρχικόν).[45]

---

[44]The Greek text is found in Karl Staab, ed., *Pauluskommentare aus der griechischen Kirche* (Münster: Aschendorff, 1933), 187. The English translation is mine.

[45]Greek text in Staab, *Pauluskommentare*, 188. The English translation is mine.

These subsequent remarks, coming just a few lines after his comment on 1 Corinthians 11:3, make the sense "authority over" most likely for κεφαλή in the 11:3 comment above. Theodore thinks that man is the authority over woman, since she was taken from him, and he says that this means she is his "glory" and should obey him, "since 'glory' looks at obedience, but 'image' looks at rulership."

8. *Eusebius (ca. A.D. 265-ca. 339) , Eccl. Theol. 1.11.2-3.*

And the great apostle teaches that the head of the Son himself is God, but (the head) of the church is the Son. How is he saying, on the one hand, "the head of Christ is God," but on the other hand saying concerning the Son, "and he gave him to be head over all things for the church, which is his body"? Is it not therefore that he may be *leader* (ἀρχηγός) and *head* (κεφαλή) of the church, but of him (the head) is the Father: Thus there is one God the Father of the only Son, and there is *one head*, even of Christ himself. But if there is one *ruler* (ἀρχή) and head, how then could there be two Gods? Is he not one alone, the one above whom no one is higher, neither does he claim any other cause of himself, but he has acquired the familial, unbegun, unbegotten deity from the *monarchial authority* (τῆς μοναρχικῆς ἐξουσίας),[46] and he has given to the Son his own divinity and life; who through him caused all things to exist, *who sends him, who appoints him, who commands, who teaches, who commits all things to him, who glorifies him, who exalts (him), who declares him king of all, who has committed all judgment to him. . . .* [47]

Far from demonstrating that the church fathers "were quick to recognize the danger of an interpretation of 1 Corinthians 11:3 which could place Christ in a subordinate position relative to the Father" (as Kroeger claims), this quotation from Eusebius shows that the Father as "head" has supreme authority, and that His authority over the Son is seen in many actions: He sends the Son, He appoints Him, He commands Him, He teaches Him, He commits all judgment to Him, and so forth. The Father's headship here means that He is the one in "authority over" the Son, and the Son's headship over the church means that He is the leader or ruler of the church.

9. *Eusebius (ca. A.D. 265-ca. 339), Eccl. Theol . 2.7.1.*

---

[46]The Father's deity is said to come from His own supreme authority, His "monarchial authority."

[47]The Greek text is found in TLG, Eusebius, *De ecclesiastica theologia*, Work 009, 1.11.2.4 to 1.11.3.11. The English translation is mine.

. . . but fear, O man, lest having confessed two substances, you would bring in two rulers (ἀρχή)[48] and would fall from the *monarchial* deity? Learn then thus, since there is one unbegun and unbegotten God, and since the Son has been begotten from him, there will be one ruler (ἀρχή), and one *monarchy and kingdom*, since even the Son himself claims his Father as ruler (ἀρχή). "For the head of Christ is God," according to the apostle.[49]

Again, Eusebius explains "the head of Christ is God" to imply that God the Father has supreme authority, and the Son is not another authority equal to Him.

Conclusion on patristic citations. Kroeger gave nine patristic references (in addition to the two from Chrysostom) to support her claims that "church fathers argued vehemently that for Paul *head* had meant 'source,'" and that they "were quick to recognize the danger" of understanding 1 Corinthians 11:3 to mean that Christ has a "subordinate position relative to the Father." Two of the citations (1, 2) were not statements of any church father but statements from heretical Arian creeds. Two more (6, 7) did not exist but may have been intended as a reference to Theodore of Mopsuestia in a commentary on 1 Corinthians 11 that relates the headship of the husband to his rulership and the wife's obedience. Three others (5, 8, 9) assumed that to be "head" of someone else implied having a position of authority or rule and thus supported the meaning "authority over." Two references from Cyril of Alexandria (3, 4) were ambiguous, due to ambiguity in the meaning of ἀρχή, since the meanings "authority," "beginning," or "origin" would all make sense in the contexts.

In none of the references did any church father "argue vehemently" that "for Paul *head* had meant 'source.'" And none of the references argued against an interpretation of 1 Corinthians 11:3 that placed Christ in a "subordinate position relative to the Father"; indeed, some of the references specify that Christ is obedient to the Father and that the Father rules over Him. In light of this evidence, it seems that Kroeger's assertion that church fathers "were quick to recognize the danger" of understanding 1 Corinthians 11:3 to

---

[48]Here I have translated ἀρχή as "ruler," which is consistent with the previous Eusebius quotation from this same document, where this sense seems necessary.
[49]The Greek text is found in TLG, Eusebius, *De ecclesiastica theologia*, Work 009, 2.7.1.1 to 2.7.2.1. The English translation is mine.

mean that Christ has a "subordinate position relative to the Father" is also false.[50]

A failure to mention the way Lampe defines and does not define κεφαλή. Kroeger's apparent use of page 749 of Lampe's *Patristic Greek Lexicon* to find four of her actual eight patristic references is puzzling for two other reasons. First, she fails to mention that the meaning "source," which she claims was "vehemently" defended by the church fathers, is nowhere mentioned as a meaning for κεφαλή in this standard lexicon for patristic Greek. If the meaning "source" was "vehemently" defended by the church fathers, it is surprising that the editorial team of this definitive lexicon did not discover this fact as they worked through the writings of the church fathers for fifty-five years, from 1906 to 1961 (see *Preface*, iii). And it is inexcusable in a popular reference work to claim that a meaning was "vehemently" defended by the church fathers and fail to mention that that meaning simply is not listed in the standard Greek lexicon of the church fathers.

Second, it is troubling to see that Kroeger claims a nonexistent quote from Chrysostom to *deny* the meaning "chief" or "authority over" for the patristic period, but she does not mention that this is the essential meaning of the first five metaphorical definitions for κεφαλή (as applied to persons) that are given on the same page in Lampe's *Lexicon* (p. 749) from which she took several of her examples:

B. of persons; **1.** *head* of the house, Herm.*sim.* 7.3; **2.** *chief, head-man* . . . **3.** religious *superior* . . . **4.** of bishops, κεφαλαὶ ἐκκλησιῶν [other examples include "of the bishop of the city of Rome, being head of all the churches"] . . . **5.** κεφαλὴ εἶναι c. genit. [to be head, with genitive] *take precedence of*

All five of these categories include leadership and authority attaching to the term κεφαλή. They show that κεφαλή meant "chief" and "authority over," according to the standard lexicon for patristic Greek. Since Kroeger's article depended so heavily on patristic evidence, and in fact (apparently) on this very page in this lexicon, these definitions from this standard patristic lexicon should have been mentioned. It is difficult to understand how she could claim that Chrysostom said that

---

[50]In direct contrast to Kroeger's claim, Joseph Fitzmyer mentions "the many places in patristic literature where comments are made on I Corinthians 11:3 or use of it is made. In these places the sense of *kephalē* as 'leader, ruler, one having authority over' is clear" (" *kephalē* in I Corinthians 11:3," 56).

"only a heretic" would use this meaning when the standard lexicon for patristic Greek lists five different categories with this meaning in their entry on κεφαλή.

V. EVIDENCE FROM CLASSICAL LITERATURE

One other section from Kroeger's article deserves comment. In a section called "The Classical View of Head as Source," Kroeger attempts to demonstrate that *kephalē* meant "source" because it was equated with *archē*, which meant "source." She writes:

> By the time of Plato, adherents of Orphic religion were using *kephalē* with *archē* ("source" or "beginning"). (p. 375).

For support she gives the following references (with no quotations, no dates, and no further information).

1. Kern, *Orph. Fr.* 2. nos. 21 a.2., 168
2. Plato, *Leg.* IV.715E and sch
3. Proclus, *In Tim.* II 95.48 (V.322)
4. Pseudo-Aristides *World* 7
5. Eusebius, *Praep. Ev.* 3.9
6. Deveni Papyrus, col. 13, line 12
7. Stobaeus, *Ecl.* 1.23
8. Plutarch, *Def. Orac.* 436D
9. Achilles Tatius, fr. 81.29
10. Isaiah 9:14-15 (LXX)
11. Irenaeus, PG 7.496.
12. Tertullian, *Marc.* 5.8
13. Philo, *Congr.* 61.
14. Photius, *Comm. 1 Cor. 11:3*, ed. Staab 567.1

This looks like an impressive set of references to demonstrate "the classical concept of head as source." In fact, one review of *Dictionary of Paul and His Letters* pointed to C. Kroeger's article on "head" as one of the outstanding articles in the volume because it has "excellent Graeco-Roman material," deals with "the classical view of head as source," and "cites many primary references."[51] But do these fourteen references

---

[51]Aida Besançon Spencer, review of *Dictionary of Paul and His Letters* in *Themelios* 20:2 (Jan.. 1995), 27-28. The review quotes as noteworthy Kroeger's quotation of John Chrysostom: "only a heretic would understand Paul's use of 'head' to mean 'chief' or 'authority over.'"

demonstrate that "head" meant "source," as Kroeger claims? Do they
show examples of κεφαλή used with ἀρχή as "source" or "beginning"
and so demonstrate the meaning "source" for κεφαλή? The first one is
familiar to anyone following the previous discussions of κεφαλή:

1. *Kern, Orph. Fr. 2.nos. 21 a.2., 168 (5th cent. B.C.).*

Zeus was first, Zeus is last with white, vivid lightning;
  Zeus the head (κεφαλή, but with ἀρχή as a variant reading) ,
Zeus the middle, Zeus from whom all things are perfected
  (Ζεὺς κεφαλή, Ζεὺς μέσσα, Διὸς δ᾽ ἐκ πάντα τέτυκται;
Orphic Fragments 21a).[52]

The sense "beginning, first one" seems most likely for either
κεφαλή or ἀρχή here, because of (1) the similarity to the idea of "first"
and "last" in the previous line, and (2) the contrast with "middle" and
the mention of perfection, giving the sense, "Zeus is the beginning,
Zeus is the middle, Zeus is the one who completes all things." The
Oxford Classical Dictionary, in discussing the basic tenets of Orphic religion, mentions a "common myth" in which "Zeus was praised as the
beginning, the middle, and the end of all"[53] and so supports the sense
"beginning" in this and similar texts. In any case, the meaning "source"
cannot be established for κεφαλή from this passage.

2. *Plato (ca. 429-347 B.C.), Leg. IV.715E and sch.*

O men, that God who, as old tradition tells, holds the *beginning*
(ἀρχή), the end, and the centre of all things that exist, completes
his circuit by nature's ordinance in straight, unswerving course.
(Plato, *Laws* IV.715E, LCL translation)

This text does not even contain κεφαλή; so it is not helpful for our
inquiry. The term ἀρχή is here translated as "beginning" (not "source")
by the LCL edition. It could not mean "source," because Plato would
not say that God "holds" the source of all things. The best meaning
would be "beginning," with the sense that God holds the beginning,
the end, and the middle of all things that exist.

---

[52]The Greek text is found in Otto Kern, *Orphicorum Fragmenta* (Berlin: Weidmannsche
Verlagsbuchhandlung, 1922), 91); TLG, Orphica, Work 010, 6.13-14. The English is my
translation.
[53]*Oxford Classical Dictionary*, 2nd edition, eds. N. G. L. Hammond and H. H. Scullard (Oxford:
Clarendon Press, 1970), 759.

Moreover, Kroeger claims that these texts show that κεφαλή was used *with* ἀρχή. But if κεφαλή does not even occur in this quotation, it cannot show that Plato was using κεφαλή *with* ἀρχή. In the absence of the term κεφαλή, this reference cannot be used as evidence for the meaning of that term.

3. *Proclus (A.D. 410-485), In Tim. II 95.48 (V.322).* This may be an incorrect reference, because Proclus *In Tim.* 2.95 ends at line 31, and line 48 does not exist.[54] Perhaps Kroeger meant to cite *In Tim.* 1.313.21, which has the same quote again about Zeus, this time in the form,

Zeus the head, Zeus the middle, Zeus from whom comes all that is
(Ζεὺς κεφαλή, Ζεὺς μέσσα, Διός δ' ἐκ πάντα τέτυκται).[55]

This reference gives no more support to the meaning "source" than the earlier passage in *Orphic Fragments*. It is difficult to understand why Kroeger includes this reference in a section on "The Classical View of Head as Source," since the classical period in Greek was prior to the time of the New Testament (the classical period in Greek literature is generally thought of as the period prior to 325 B.C.),[56] while Proclus was a Neoplatonist philosopher who lived from A.D. 410 to 485.

4. *Pseudo-Aristides World 7 (4ᵗʰ cent. B.C.?).* This is an incorrect reference, because there is no work called *World* written by Aristides or Pseudo-Aristides.[57]

However, the following quotation does appear in Aristotle (or Pseudo-Aristotle), *de Mundo* ("*On the Cosmos*" or "*On the World*"), section 7 (401a.29-30):[58]

Zeus is the head, Zeus the centre; from Zeus comes all that is
(Ζεὺς κεφαλή, Ζεὺς μέσσα, Διὸς δ' ἐκ πάντα τέτυκται).

Perhaps Kroeger found a reference to Ps-Arist., *World* 7 and understood Arist. to refer to Aristides rather than Aristotle. In any case, this

---

[54]However, it is possible that Dr. Kroeger is citing some edition of Proclus with a numbering system different from that used in the standard text in the TLG database.

[55]Proclus, *in Platonis Timaeum commentarii*, ed. E. Diehl, 3 vols, Leipzig (T.) 1903, 1904, 1906 (TLG, Proclus, *In Tim.* 1.313.21-22). The English is my translation in this and all subsequent citations of this sentence about Zeus, unless otherwise indicated.

[56]*The Oxford Companion to Classical Literature*, comp. Paul Harvey (Oxford and New York: Oxford University Press, 1937), 106.

[57]See LSJ, xix.

[58]The text is found in the Loeb Classical Library edition of Aristotle, Vol. 3, 406.

is another quotation of the same sentence and adds no new evidence for the meaning of κεφαλή.

5. Eusebius (ca. A.D. 265-ca. 339), Praep. Ev. 3.9.
This text quotes followers of Orphic religion as saying,

Zeus the head, Zeus the middle, Zeus from whom comes all that is

(Ζεὺς κεφαλή, Ζεὺς μέσσα, Διὸς δ᾽ ἐκ πάντα τέτυκται).[59]

This is a repetition of the same sentence again, with no additional evidence. Eusebius is also wrongly placed in this discussion of "The Classical Concept of Head," since he was a Christian historian who lived approximately A.D. 265-339.

6. Deveni Papyrus, col. 13, line 12 (4ᵗʰ cent. B.C.). This is a misspelled reference, and as a result it turned out to be very difficult to locate. It should read, *Derveni Papyrus*, col. 13, line 12.[60] It is from the late fourth century B.C. The text says:

Zeus the head, Zeus the middle, Zeus from whom comes all that is

(Ζεὺς κεφα[λή, Ζεὺς μέσσ]α, Διὸς δ᾽ ἐκ [π]άντα τέτ[υκται]).[61]

This is a repetition of the same sentence. It provides no additional evidence.

7. Stobaeus, Ecl. 1.23 (5th cent. A.D.).
This text also quotes followers of Orphic religion as saying,

Zeus the head, Zeus the middle, Zeus from whom comes (τέτυκται) all that is
(Ζεὺς κεφαλή, Ζεὺς μέσσα, Διὸς δ᾽ ἐκ πάντα τέτυκται).[62]

This is a repetition of the same sentence once again, with no additional evidence. Stobaeus is also wrongly placed in this discussion of "The Classical Concept of Head," since he lived in the fifth century A.D.

---

[59]TLG, Eusebius, *Praep. Evang.* 3.9.2.2.
[60]The text was published in *Zeitschrift für Papyrologie und Epigraphik* 47 (1982), appendix, 8. Because of the misspelling of the name, I was unable to locate this until I received help from David Chapman, who was (in 1997) a graduate student at the University of Cambridge.
[61]TLG, Orphica, *Fragmenta* (P. Derveni), Work 013, col 12.
[62]TLG Joannes Stobaeus Anthologus, Work 001, 1.1.23.2-6.

8. *Plutarch (ca. A.D. 46- ca. 120), Def. Orac. 436D.* This text says:

Zeus the beginning, Zeus the middle, Zeus from whom all things come about
(Ζεὺς ἀρχὴ Ζεὺς μέσσα, Διὸς δ' ἐκ πάντα πέλονται).[63]

This text does not use κεφαλή but uses ἀρχή and therefore is wrongly included in this list. Plutarch is also incorrectly placed in this discussion of "The Classical Concept of Head," since he lived approximately A.D. 46-120.

9. *Achilles Tatius, fr. 81.29 (3rd cent. A.D.).* This is an incomplete reference, and it turned out to be very difficult to locate. The Loeb Classical Library edition of Achilles Tatius has only eight chapters. No such document as "fr." (presumably "fragment") from Achilles Tatius is listed in the preface to Liddell and Scott.

However, this turns out to be a reference not to the better known Greek romantic writer Achilles Tatius (2nd century A.D.) found in the Loeb Classical Library series, but to another Achilles Tatius, a 3rd-century A.D. author with one surviving work, a commentary on the writings of Aratus. The citation of line 29 is not quite accurate, for the term κεφαλή does not occur in line 29. However, just three lines later, in lines 32-33, the text does contain ἀρχή in the following quotation:

Zeus the beginning, Zeus the middle, Zeus from whom all things are perfected
(Ζεὺς ἀρχή, Ζεὺς μέσσα, Διὸς δ' ἐκ πάντα τέτυκται).[64]

The word κεφαλή does not occur in this text; so it should not be included in this list. Nor is a third century A.D. author useful evidence for the "classical" period in Greek.

10. *Isaiah 9:14-15 (LXX verses 13-14) (2nd cent. B.C. Greek translation).*

So the LORD cut off from Israel *head* (κεφαλή) and tail, palm branch and reed in one day—the elder and honored man is the head (ἀρχή, "ruler"), and the prophet who teaches lies is the tail.

---

[63]TLG, Plutarch, Work 92, 436D.8-9.

[64]The text is found in Ernest Maass, *Commentariorum in Aratum reliquiae* (Berlin: Weidmann, 1898), 81, lines 32-33.

Far from establishing the meaning "source" for *kephalē*, this shows the sense "leader, one in authority," for it is the elder who is said to be "head."

11. *Irenaeus, PG 7.496 (ca. A.D. 175-ca. 195)*. In describing the teaching of the Gnostics, Irenaeus reports this:

> They go on to say that the Demiurge imagined that he created all these things of himself, while in reality he made them in conjunction with the productive power of Achamoth. . . . They further affirm that his mother originated this opinion in his mind, because she desired to bring him forth possessed of such a character that he should be the head and source of his own essence (κεφαλὴν μὲν καὶ ἀρχὴν τῆς ἰδίας οὐσίας), and the absolute ruler (κύριος) over every kind of operation [that was afterwards attempted]. This mother they call Ogdoad, Sophia, Terra. . . . (Irenaeus, *Against Heresies* 5.3 [ANF 1, 322-323])

Here the ambiguity about the meaning of ἀρχή confronts us again. The translator of the Ante-Nicene Fathers series rendered it "source," which is possible, but "ruler" or "beginning" are also possible. In any case, the text does not equate "head" with "source/ruler/beginning" but lists them as two items. So even if ἀρχή is translated "source," the phrase would still mean, "the head and source of his own being," with "head" in the sense of "ruler." The text is ambiguous and does not provide convincing evidence of "head" meaning "source." Since Irenaeus wrote between about A.D. 175 and 195, this text should not be counted as evidence of a classical understanding of κεφαλή.

12. *Tertullian, Marc. 5.8 (ca. A.D. 160- ca. 220)*.

> "The head of every man is Christ." What Christ, if he is not the author of man? The *head* here he has put for *authority*; now "authority" will accrue to none else than the "author." (*The Five Books Against Marcion*, book 5, chap. 8; ANF vol. 3, p. 445)

This text is translated from Latin, not Greek; so it is of little help in determining the meaning of *kephalē*, for the word does not occur here. If the text is counted as evidence, it supports not the idea of "source" but the idea of "head" as "ruler, one in authority." Since Tertullian lived ca. A.D. 160/170 to ca. 215/220 and wrote in Latin, this quotation is not from classical Greek but from patristic Latin.

13. *Philo (ca. 30 B.C. -A.D. 45), Congr. 61.* This quotation says:

And of all the members of the clan here described Esau is the progenitor, the head as it were of the whole creature. (LCL, Vol. 4, 489; κεφαλὴ δὲ ὡς ζῴου πάντων τῶν λεχθέντων μερῶν ὁ γενάρχης ἐστὶν Ἡσαῦ.)

Kroeger translates this "the progenitor" but fails to note that the ambiguity attaching to *archē* also attaches to *genarchēs*. The Liddell-Scott *Lexicon* gives two definitions for *genarchēs:* (1) "founder or first ancestor of a family," and (2) "ruler of created beings."[65] The quotation is ambiguous, and Philo, as is his custom, is constructing an allegory. In any case, it does not demonstrate any absence of the idea of authority from the "head," for Esau was surely the ruler of the clan descended from him.[66]

14. *Photius, Comm. 1 Cor. 11:3, ed. Staab 567.1 (9ᵗʰ cent. A.D.).* Finally, Kroeger adds a citation from Photius, not connecting κεφαλή with ἀρχή but saying "*kephalē* was considered by Photius to be a synonym for *procreator* or *progenitor* (Photius, *Comm. 1 Cor. 11:3,* ed. Staab 567.1)." This is the most egregious disregard of dating in all the citations that give the appearance of support for an early, "classical" view of head as source, because Photius is far from being a pre-New Testament writer. He died in A.D. 891. This also makes him a highly dubious source for determining the New Testament meaning for κεφαλή. But Kroeger gives readers no indication of dates for any of what she claims as "classical" sources, thus leading the vast majority of readers (who have never heard of the ninth century A.D. author

---

[65]LSJ, 342.

[66]This text is not new but has been considered previously in studies of κεφαλή. As I wrote in my 1990 article: "The sense of 'head' here is difficult to determine. Payne suggests the meaning 'source of life' for head, a specific kind of 'source' that has never before been given in any lexicon. Yet it is possible that Philo thought of the physical head of an animal as in some sense energizing or giving life to the animal—this would then be a simile in which Esau (a representative of stubborn disobedience in this context) gives life to a whole list of other sins that Philo has been describing as a 'family' in this allegory. On the other hand, the word translated above as progenitor (*genarchēs*) also can mean 'ruler of created beings' (LSJ, 342). In that case the text would read: 'And Esau is the ruler of all the clan here described, the head as of a living animal.' Here the meaning would be that Esau is the ruler over the rest of the sinful clan and head would mean 'ruler, authority over.' It seems impossible from the context that we have to decide clearly for one meaning or the other in this text" (Grudem, "Meaning of *kephalē*," 454-455).

Finally, Philo should not be cited as evidence for the "classical" view of a word, since he wrote in the first century A.D.

Photius) to think that she has given evidence of an established meaning for κεφαλή prior to the time of the New Testament.

In any case, we can examine the Photius quotation, which says:

> On the one hand, the head of us who believe is Christ, as we are members of the same body and fellow partakers with him, having been begotten through the fellowship of his body and blood: for through him we all, having been called "one body," have him as head. "But the head of Christ is God" even the Father, as a begetter and originator and one of the same nature as him.[67] "And the head of the woman is the man," for he also exists as her begetter and originator and one of the same nature as her. The analogy is suitable and fits together. But if you might understand the "of every man" [1 Cor. 11:3] also to mean over the unbelievers, according to the word of the creation this (meaning) only is allowed: For having yielded to the man[68] to *reign* over the others, *he allowed him to remain under his own unique authority and rule* (αὐτὸν ὑπὸ τὴν ἰδίαν μόνον εἴασε μένειν ἐχουσίαν καὶ ἀρχήν) not having established over him another ruler and supreme authority.[69]

Kroeger is correct to say that the ideas of "procreator" and "progenitor" are contained in this ninth century A.D. text, but it is not clear that these terms are used to *define* "head," any more than it would be to say that "head" *means* "of the same nature" (ὁμοούσιος), which is the third term used in this explanation. In all three terms (begetter, originator, of the same nature), Photius is using classical Trinitarian language to explain the Father's role as "head," saying it is "as" one who is begetter, originator, and of the same nature. This is standard Trinitarian language, and in dealing with 1 Corinthians 11:3, "the head of Christ is God," Photius maintains the orthodox definitions of the Father as the one who eternally begets the Son and eternally sends forth the Holy Spirit.

But this Trinitarian language does not establish Kroeger's claim in

---

[67]Photius is using language from prior Trinitarian controversies here. He says that the Father is "begetter and originator and of the same nature" as the Son. "Begetter" (γεννήτωρ) refers to the Father's eternal relationship to the Son, in what was called the "eternal generation of the Son." "Originator" (προβολεύς), according to Lampe's *Patristic Greek Lexicon*, was used in Trinitarian discussion particularly to refer to the Father's role with respect to the procession of the Holy Spirit (1140). And "of the same nature" (ὁμοούσιος) was the term used from the Nicene Creed onward to affirm the full deity of the Son.

[68]Here "the man" refers to Christ as man.

[69]The English translation is mine. The Greek text is from Karl Staab, *Pauluskommentare aus der griechischen Kirche* (Münster: Aschendorf, 1933), 567; TLG Photius, *Fragmenta in epistulam I ad Corinthias*, Work 15, 567.1-567.11.

this section that there was a "classical" meaning of "source" for κεφαλή. Instead, the passage once again indicates that Photius understands "head" to mean "authority over." This is evident from the last two sentences in the citation, where we see how he relates "the head of every man is Christ" to "the head of Christ is God." Photius explains "the head of every man is Christ" to mean that Christ is appointed by the Father "to reign" even over unbelievers. This is consistent with the idea that the head of Christ is God, since Christ remains under God the Father's "own unique authority and rule." Once again, to be "head" is seen to mean that one is in the role of "authority over" another.

In any case, this obscure text from the ninth century A.D. is hardly relevant for Kroeger's section, "The Classical View of Head as Source," and hardly relevant for understanding the New Testament meaning of κεφαλή, since it came 800 years later.

Conclusion on Kroeger's section on "The Classical View of Head as Source." Of the fourteen references given by Kroeger in her section on "The Classical View of Head as Source," four (2, 8, 9, 12) did not contain the term κεφαλή and are not relevant for understanding the meaning of the term. Of the remaining ten, only three (1, 4, 6) were from the pre-New Testament "classical" period in Greek. All three of those were repeating the same sentence about Zeus, which means that the fourteen references in this section boil down to one piece of evidence. In that sentence, the meaning "source" is not proven, for the sense "beginning" best fits the context and follows the translation of the *Oxford Classical Dictionary*. This means that of the fourteen references in this section, none turned out to support the idea that classical Greek had a meaning "source" for κεφαλή.

If examples from all dates are included, however, then of the ten that contained κεφαλή, two (10, 14) clearly use κεφαλή to mean "authority over," and two others (11, 13) are ambiguous, since both the meaning "beginning" and the meaning "authority over" are possible. The remaining six (1, 3, 4, 5, 6, 7) use κεφαλή in the sense "beginning," all in the same sentence about Zeus. Once again, not one of the fourteen references turned out to support the meaning "source" for κεφαλή.

One more characteristic of these references should be noted. Kroeger's goal is to show that "source" is often the sense of κεφαλή in the New Testament *instead of* the meaning "authority over." She says at one point, "By the Byzantine era *kephalē* had acquired the sense of 'chief ' or 'master' . . . this was rarely true of the Greek *kephalē* in NT times."[70] In order to appreciate Kroeger's statement, we must realize that the Byzantine Age in Greek literature lasted from A.D. 529 to 1453,[71] and Greek usage during that time is of very little relevance for New Testament study. Thus Kroeger is implying, if not asserting, that "source" was a common and well-established sense for κεφαλή at the time of the New Testament, while "authority over" was a rare sense until about five hundred years after the New Testament.

But do any of her references prove this? It is significant to notice what kind of persons are called "head" in these quotations, both from patristic texts and from others:

1. husband (head of wife)
2. God (head of Christ)
3. Christ (head of every man)
4. church leaders (head of church)
5. a woman (head of her maidservant)
6. Christ (head of the church)
7. Adam (head of human race)
8. Zeus (head of all things)
9. elders (head of Israel)
10. Gnostic Demiurge (head of his own being)
11. Esau (head of his clan)

In every case, ancient readers would have readily understood that the person called "head" was in a position of authority or rule over the person or group thought of as the "body" in the metaphor. Even in those cases where the sense "beginning" is appropriate, there is no idea of "beginning" without authority; rather, the person who is the "head" is always the one in authority. Therefore, it seems inevitable that the sense "authority" attaches to the metaphor when one person is called "head" (κεφαλή) of another person or group. The sense "authority over" for κεφαλή is firmly established.

---

[70]Kroeger, "Head," 377.
[71]*The Oxford Companion to Classical Literature*, comp. Paul Harvey (Oxford and New York: Oxford University Press, 1937), 83.

VI. DR. KROEGER'S RESPONSE

I read an earlier version of this article as a paper at the 1997 annual meeting of the Evangelical Theological Society in Santa Clara, California.[72] Then at the 1998 meeting of the ETS in Orlando, Dr. Kroeger read a four-page response to my paper, entitled "The Use of Classical Disciplines in Biblical Research." In this response, she makes the following points:

(1) Although Photius wrote in the ninth century A.D., his work as a lexicographer remains valuable to us, for he studied Greek literature from earlier centuries (p. 1).

(2) In the statements about "Zeus the head, Zeus the middle . . ." etc., the interchange of κεφαλή with ἀρχή as the quotation appears in various authors shows that "in the writers' minds they have the same semantic value and may be freely exchanged" (p. 2).

(3) Regarding erroneous citations in her article, she says, "Here my own effort to condenese [sic] the lengthy citations led to the scrambling of a couple of references, although the majority were accurate" (pp. 2-3).

(4) The citation that I had been unable to locate (Achilles Tatius, fr. 81.29) was not from the commonly known Achilles Tatius (second century A.D.) but from a lesser known Achilles Tatius (third century A.D.), fragments of whose commentary on Aratus are published in Maass, *Commentariorum in Aratum reliquiae* (1898, repr. 1958). Dr. Kroeger says that my difficulty in finding this was because I "failed to recognize that in classical antiquity more than one writer might bear the same name" (p. 3).

(5) With respect to my critique of her article, she says that I "failed to differentiate between *archōn*, meaning ruler or commander, and the cognate *archē* meaning beginning, first principle or source. To be sure, *archē* can also indicate authority, rule, realm or magistracy. Almost never, however, does *archē* denote the person ruling. That sense is supplied by the cognate, *archōn*" (p. 3).

(6) Chrysostom held to the "commonly held anatomical views of antiquity, that the head was the source of the body's existence," and this led Chrysostom to "conventional metaphorical uses" for κεφαλή (by this she means the metaphor of "head" as "source") (p. 3).

---

[72]The paper contained all the substantive points of this present article except the survey of commentaries and journal articles in the last section, and the paper was distributed to all interested attendees at the conference. Dr. Kroeger was present and also received a copy of the paper.

(7) In Chrysostom's view, "as applied to the Trinity, *kephalē* must imply 'perfect oneness and primal cause and source.'" She concludes, "Indubitably he viewed one of the meanings of 'head' to be 'source' or 'origin' and deemed it theologically important" (p. 4).

In response to these seven items, the following points may be made:

(1) *Photius*: I agree that Photius' ninth-century A.D. lexicon has some value for scholarly work, but the fact remains that citing his commentary on 1 Corinthians (not his lexicon) in a section on "The Classical View of Head as Source" without giving readers any indication that he wrote eight hundred years after the New Testament or that he uses κεφαλή to mean "authority over" is misleading.

(2) *Statements about Zeus*: The fact that κεφαλή is used in some of the statements about Zeus and ἀρχή in others does not show that the words "have the same semantic value and may be freely exchanged," but only that they shared the one sense that fits that context, namely, "beginning, first in a series." In fact, one word (κεφαλή) signifies this meaning by means of a metaphor (the "head" as the end point, furthest extremity), and the other word (ἀρχή) means it literally. Therefore these quotes still fail to provide proof that κεφαλή could mean source. They just show what everyone has recognized all along, that κεφαλή in a metaphorical sense could mean "beginning, first in a series, extremity, end-point."

(3) *Accuracy*: To say that she scrambled "a couple of references" is a rather low estimate. Of twenty-four key references to ancient literature, fourteen were accurate, but ten were not: Four did not contain κεφαλή, two had the wrong author listed, three had the wrong reference listed, and the one from Chrysostom did not exist at all. I agree with her that "the majority were accurate," since fourteen of twenty-four key references is more than half. But the standard of accuracy in scholarly works is not to get the "majority" of one's references right. They should all be right. This article fell far short of the standard of accuracy required for academic work.

(4) *Achilles Tatius*: I was glad at last to learn from Dr. Kroeger of the reference to the obscure Achilles Tatius, but to give a reference simply as "fr. 81.29," when the standard reference works (the preface to LSJ and the *Oxford Classical Dictionary*) do not list *any* work by *any* Achilles Tatius as "fr." is simply to consign all readers to the same kind of frus-

trating search of libraries that I experienced.[73] I was also surprised to find, when I finally did consult the work, that it did not contain the term κεφαλή at all but used ἀρχή though that fact had not been mentioned in Dr. Kroeger's 1998 response when she named the volume in which the text had been published.

(5) *The term* ἀρχή: I do not think it is correct that ἀρχή "almost never" denotes the person ruling. See the citations from Chrysostom (above) where the wife is a "second authority,"[74] or from Basil and Eusebius, where the Father is the "ruler" of the Son;[75] see also BAGD, meaning 3, "ruler, authority" (p. 112).

(6) *Chrysostom on the function of the head in the body*: I agree that Chrysostom thought that the senses had their origin in the head. But that is not the issue. He also thought that the head ruled the body.[76] The question is not what meaning he *could have* given to "head" when used in a metaphorical sense, but what meaning he *actually did* give. The nine citations given earlier where the "head" is specified as the ruling part or the person in authority make clear that Chrysostom used κεφαλή with the sense "authority over" (which Kroeger still did not acknowledge).

Her citation from Chrysostom is interesting, however, in what it omits. Here is her exact statement and the quotation that she gave from Chrystosom in her response (p. 3):

> One of the points of disagreement between my colleague and my own work was over the treatment of the term by John Chrysostom, one of the earliest exegetes, a fourth century scholar whose first language was Greek. The commonly held anatomical views of antiquity, that the head was the source of the body's exis-

---

[73]In this case I had also received help from David Chapman, a former student who was in Ph.D. studies at the University of Cambridge. He spent most of a day checking all the critical editions of Achilles Tatius, as well as papyrus fragments, but still found no work that could be identified as "fr. 81.29." We did not check the lesser-known Achilles Tatius because no reference work identified any work of his as "fr." I mention this only because the issue here is whether evangelical academic works should make it easy or hard for readers to check for themselves the sources quoted in an article.

[74]Citation (6) from Chrysostom, above.

[75]Patristic citations (5) and (8) above.

[76]Clinton E. Arnold, "Jesus Christ: 'Head' of the Church (Colossians and Ephesians)," *In Jesus of Nazareth: Lord and Christ*, eds. Joel B. Green and Max Turner (Grand Rapids, MI: Eerdmans and Carlisle, England: Paternoster, 1994), 346-366 shows that in the ancient world the head was commonly understood to be both the ruling part and the source of nourishment for the body. Similar conclusions are reached in an extensive study by Gregory W. Dawes, *The Body in Question: Meaning and Metaphor in the Interpretation of Ephesians 5:21-33* (Leiden: Brill, 1998), 122-149.

tence, led him to conventional metaphorical uses. From the head, he said, the senses "have their source and fount."

In the head are the eyes both of the body, and of the soul. . . . All the senses have thence their origin and their source. Thence are sent forth the organs of speech, the power of seeing, and of smelling, and all touch. For thence is derived the root of the nerves and of the bones. [*Commentary on I Thessalonians V:5*, p. 513]

This is one of the sections from Chrysostom that I quoted in the beginning of this paper—section B, citation (2) above. What is most interesting here is the material represented by the ellipsis in Dr. Kroeger's quotation of Chrysostom, as well as the two sentences immediately preceding this quotation and the two sentences immediately following it. This is highly relevant material that Dr. Kroeger omitted from this quotation in her attempt to argue that κεφαλή meant "source" and not "authority over." Here is the whole quotation, cited from the NPNF translation, with the words that Dr. Kroeger omitted underlined:

Thou art the head of the woman, let then the head regulate the rest of the body. Dost thou not see that it is not so much above the rest of the body in situation, as in forethought, directing like a steersman the whole of it? For in the head are the eyes both of the body, and of the soul. *Hence flows to them both the faculty of seeing, and the power of directing. And the rest of the body is appointed for service, but this is set to command.* All the senses have thence their origin and their source. Thence are sent forth the organs of speech, the power of seeing, and of smelling, and all touch. For thence is derived the root of the nerves and of the bones. *Seest thou not that it is superior in forethought more than in honor? So let us rule the women; let us surpass them, not by seeking greater honor from them, but by their being more benefited by us.*[77]

The words missing from her quotation disprove the point she is trying to make, for they show the head regulating the body, directing it, and commanding it. Both at the beginning and the end of this quotation Chrysostom makes explicit the parallel with the husband's governing role as "head" meaning "one in authority." When the words that one leaves out of a quotation do not change the sense, no reader will

---

[77]Chrysostom, *Homily 5 on 1-2 Thessalonians* (NPNF series 1, Vol. 13, 397). The relevant Greek portions are quoted at the beginning of this article in section II, citation (2).

object. But when the words that one leaves out are found to disprove the very point one is trying to make, readers will rightly conclude that one has not been truthful in handling the evidence.

(7) *Did Chrysostom understand* κεφαλή *as "source"?* Kroeger gives no further analysis of the quotation I listed above as Chrysostom (10), from Homily 26 on 1 Corinthians (TLG Work 156, 61.216.1-10). She simply repeats her translation of this section, except she changes "cause and primal source" to "primal cause and source." To put the matter plainly, this is assertion without argument, pure and simple. To reassert one's own idiosyncratic translation of a passage without further argument, and without giving reasons why it should be preferred to the commonly used NPNF translation of ἀρχή as "first principle" and also as "beginning" in this very passage, and without acknowledging that one's personal translation is a speculative one, hardly provides a reason for readers to be persuaded that she is correct.

(8) *What was not said:* What is interesting about this response is what was not said. No new evidence for κεφαλή as "source" was introduced. No objections were raised to my nine new citations of passages from Chrysostom where the meaning "authority over" was clear for κεφαλή. No answer was given for why she claimed a nonexistent quotation from Chrysostom to say that "only a heretic" would understand κεφαλή to mean "authority over." No explanation was given for why she said that the fathers vehemently argued for the meaning "source" when no reference she gave yielded any such vehement argument. No explanation was given for why she said the church fathers denied that Christ could be in a subordinate position relative to the Father when that very idea was seen several times in the actual references that she mentioned. No explanation was given for why she implied that the meaning "ruler, authority over" did not exist in the church fathers but failed to mention that Lampe's *Patristic Greek Lexicon* gave just this sense in its first five definitions of the metaphor as applied to persons. And no response was given to the important new letter from the editor of the Liddell-Scott *Lexicon: Supplement*, to which we now turn.

VII. RECENT LEXICOGRAPHICAL DEVELOPMENTS CONCERNING κεφαλή

1. *The letter from the editor of the Liddell-Scott Lexicon.* There have been some other recent developments regarding the meaning of κεφαλή. Of

considerable interest is a letter from the current editor of the *Supplement* to the Liddell-Scott *Lexicon*.

Most readers of this article will know that for several years a number of egalitarians have reinterpreted the verse, "for the husband is the *head* (κεφαλή) of the wife even as Christ is the head of the church" (Eph. 5:23). They were not inclined to agree that the husband's role as "head" meant he had authority to lead in the marriage. As an alternative interpretation that removed the idea of authority, they have said that "head" really means "source," because (they claimed) that is what the Greek word κεφαλή ("head") meant in ancient Greek literature. They went on to say that if the word "head" means "source," then there is no unique male authority in marriage and no male headship (in the commonly understood sense) taught in this verse or in the similar expression in 1 Corinthians 11:3.

A number of people did not find this explanation of "head" to be persuasive for Ephesians 5:23, because husbands are not the "source" of their wives in any ordinary sense of "source." But egalitarians continued to make this claim nonetheless and have said "source" was a common sense for κεφαλή in Greek.

The one piece of supporting evidence in Greek-English lexicons was claimed from the *Greek-English Lexicon* edited by H. G. Liddell and Robert Scott and revised by Henry Stuart Jones (ninth edition; Oxford: Clarendon, 1968, 945). This was important because this lexicon has been the standard lexicon for all of ancient Greek for over 150 years. Part of the entry for κεφαλή in the Liddell-Scott-Jones *Lexicon* (LSJ or simply Liddell-Scott) has the following headings:

II. 1. Of things, extremity

    a. In Botany

    b. In Anatomy

    c. Generally, *top, brim* of a vessel . . . *capital* of a column

    d. In plural, *source* of a river, Herodotus 4.91 (but singular, *mouth*); generally, *source, origin*, Orphic Fragments 21a; *starting point* [examples: the head of time; the head of a month].

Even this entry did not prove the egalitarian claim that a *person* could be called the "source" of someone else by using κεφαλή, because the major category for this lexicon entry had to do with the end-point of "things," not with persons (but persons are in view in Ephesians 5:23, with Christ and a husband being called "head").

In an article written in 1985, I argued that the reason κεφαλή could be applied to either the *source* or the *mouth* of a river was that in these cases κεφαλη was used in a fairly common sense to mean the end-point of something. In this way, the top of a column in a building was called the "head," and the ends of the poles used to carry the Ark of the Covenant are called the "heads" of the poles in the Septuagint translation of 1 Kings 8:8. This is a natural and understandable extension of the word *head* since our heads are at the top or end of our bodies. In fact, this is what the editors of Liddell-Scott-Jones intended, for they placed the river examples as a subcategory under the general category, "of things, extremity." In 1990 I wrote on this again and attempted to answer objections that had been brought against my 1985 article by several authors.[78]

In early 1997 I sent a copy of my 1990 article on κεφαλή to the editor of the Liddell-Scott lexicon in Oxford, England, so that their editorial team might at least consider the evidence and arguments in it. The *Lexicon* itself is not undergoing revision, but a Supplement is published from time to time. The current editor of the Liddell-Scott *Lexicon: Supplement*, P. G. W. Glare, responded in a personal letter dated April 14, 1997, which I quote here with his permission (italics used for emphasis have been added):

> Dear Professor Grudem,
> Thank you for sending me the copy of your article on κεφαλή. The entry under this word in LSJ is not very satisfactory. Perhaps I could draw your attention to a section of *Lexicographica Graeca* by Dr John Chadwick (OUP 1996), though he does not deal in detail with the Septuagint and NT material. I was unable to revise the longer articles in LSJ when I was preparing the latest Supplement, since I did not have the financial resources to carry out a full-scale revision.
> I have no time at the moment to discuss all your examples individually and in any case *I am in broad agreement with your conclusions*. I might just make one or two generalizations. κεφαλή is the word normally used to translate the Hebrew ראש, and this *does seem frequently to denote leader or chief* without much reference to its original anatomical sense, and here it *seems perverse to deny authority*. *The supposed sense 'source' of course does not exist* and it was at least unwise of

---

[78] Grudem, "Does *kephalē* ('Head') Mean 'Source' or "Authority Over' in Greek Literature?" 43-44; and Grudem, "Meaning of *kephalē*," 425-426, 432-433.

Liddell and Scott to mention the word. At the most they should have said 'applied to the source of a river in respect of its position in its (the river's) course'.

By NT times the Septuagint had been well established and one would only expect that a usage found frequently in it would come easily to such a writer as St. Paul. Where I would agree with Cervin is that in many of the examples, and I think all the Plutarch ones, we are dealing with similes or comparisons and the word itself is used in a literal sense. Here we are faced with the inadequacies of LSJ. If they had clearly distinguished between, for example, 'the head as the seat of the intellect and emotions' (and therefore the director of the body's actions) and 'the head as the extremity of the human or animal body' and so on, these figurative examples would naturally be attached to the end of the section they belong to and the author's intention would be clear. I hasten to add that in most cases the sense of the head as being the controlling agent is the one required and that *the idea of preeminence seems to me to be quite unsuitable*, and that there are still cases where κεφαλή can be understood, as in the Septuagint, in its transferred sense of head or leader.

Once again, thank you for sending me the article. I shall file it in the hope that one day we will be able to embark on a more thorough revision of the lexicon.

Yours sincerely,
Peter Glare[79]

This must be counted a significant statement because it comes from someone who, because of his position and scholarly reputation, could rightly be called the preeminent Greek lexicographer in the world.

2. *Other recent evidence.* The book to which Glare refers also provides evidence for the meaning "end point" and not "source" for κεφαλή— namely, John Chadwick's *Lexicographica Graeca: Contributions to the Lexicography of Ancient Greek.*[80] Chadwick, who before his recent death was a member of the Faculty of Classics at the University of Cambridge, says that his book "arose from working on the new supplement to Liddell and Scott as a member of the British Academy's Committee appointed to supervise the project" (p. v). He says, "*kephalē* can mean simply *either extremity of a linear object*" (p. 181) and then quotes the two examples where it can refer to either end of a river (what we

---

[79]Personal letter from P. G. W. Glare to Wayne Grudem, April 14, 1997. Quoted by permission.
[80]Oxford: Clarendon Press, 1996.

would call its "source" or its "mouth"). He then says the same variety
of usage is found with Greek *archē,* which can mean either "beginning"
or "end." He explains, "in English a rope has two ends, in Greek two
archai" (p. 181). Returning to *kephalē,* he mentions the quotation about
Zeus from the *Orphic Fragments* 21a and says, "On the same principle
as the rivers, it may also mean the *starting point.*"[81]

This analysis from Chadwick is consistent with the methodological warning that I cited from him early in this article, a warning that is
relevant for the few examples where the sense of κεφαλή is unclear
from the immediate context. It may be tempting to allow the meaning
"source" in such examples, even though the context does not require
it, but Chadwick says:

> A constant problem to guard against is the proliferation of mean-
> ings. . . . It is often tempting to create a new sense to accommo-
> date a difficult example, but we must always ask first, if there is any
> other way of taking the word which would allow us to assign the
> example to an already established sense. . . . As I have remarked in
> several of my notes, there may be no reason why a proposed sense
> should not exist, but is there any reason why it must exist?[82]

This does not mean that it is impossible that some persuasive
examples of κεφαλή meaning "source" when used metaphorically of a
person could turn up sometime in the future. If someone turns up new
examples in the future, we will have to examine them at that point, to
ask first whether they really mean "source," and second, whether they
mean "source" with no sense of authority (which would be necessary
for the egalitarian understanding of Ephesians 5:23). But Chadwick's
warning does mean that our wisest course with a few ambiguous
examples at the present time is to assign to them already established
meanings if it is possible to do so without doing violence to the text in
question. In the case of κεφαλή, the meanings "authority over" and
"beginning" will fit *all* the ambiguous texts where "source" has been
claimed as a meaning, and therefore (according to Chadwick's principle) we should not claim the meaning "source" when it is not necessary in any text and not an "already established sense."

---

[81]Chadwick, *Lexicographica Graeca,* 183, with reference to *Orphic Fragments* 21a; he also quotes
in this regard *Placita,* 2.32.2.
[82]Ibid., 23-24.

Another analysis of κεφαλή from the perspective of modern linguistic principles is found in Max Turner, "Modern Linguistics and the New Testament," in *Hearing the New Testament*.[83] Turner, who is Director of Research and Senior Lecturer in New Testament at London Bible College, analyzes the texts where the meaning "source" has been claimed and shows that other, established senses are preferable in each case. He says that the meaning "source," as claimed by some, "is not recognized by the lexicons, and *we should consider it linguistically unsound*" (p. 167, italics added).

Finally, the primary lexicon for New Testament Greek, the Bauer-Arndt-Gingrich-Danker *Greek-English Lexicon of the New Testament and Other Early Christian Literature*,[84] has now been replaced by a new, completely revised third edition, based on the sixth German edition. Due to the extensive work of Frederick W. Danker, this third edition is known as the Bauer-Danker-Arndt-Gingrich *Lexicon*, as announced at the 1999 Society of Biblical Literature meeting in Boston. In that new lexicon the entry for κεφαλή includes these meanings: "a being of high status, *head*, fig. 2a. In the case of living beings, to denote superior rank. . . . 2b. Of things, *the uppermost part, extremity, end point*."(p. 542). No mention is made of the meaning "source."

3. *Is there any dispute in the lexicons about the meaning of* κεφαλή? Where does this leave us with regard to the dispute over κεφαλη in the ancient world? Up to this time, Liddell-Scott was the only Greek-English lexicon that even mentioned the possibility of the meaning "source" for κεφαλή.[85] All the other standard Greek-English lexicons for the New Testament gave meanings such as "leader, ruler, person in authority" and made no mention of the meaning "source" (see BAGD,

---

[83]Joel Green, ed. (Grand Rapids, MI: Eerdmans, and Carlisle, England: Paternoster, 1995), 165-172.

[84]2nd edition; Chicago and London: University of Chicago Press, 1979. This is a translation based on the fifth German edition of Bauer's *Griechisch-Deutsches Wörterbuch* (1958).

[85]Professor Al Wolters has pointed out to me in private correspondence (December 7, 1997), however, that the recognition that Herodotus 4:91 gives to the "sources" of the Tearus River with the plural of κεφαλή is rather standard in Greek lexicons in other languages than English. I agree that κεφαλή is applied to the sources of the river in the Herodotus passage, but I would also agree with the analyses of Glare and Chadwick that this is simply an *application* of the word to the geographical end-points of a river and fits the common sense "extremity, end-point" for κεφαλή and should not be counted as an example of a new meaning, "source." (Wolters himself thinks the Herodotus reference is a result of semantic borrowing from Persian and so has a rather un-Greek character. This is certainly possible and would not be inconsistent with my understanding of κεφαλή.)

430; Louw-Nida, 1:739; also the older lexicons by Thayer, 345, and Craemer, 354; also TDNT, 3:363-372; as well as the sixth German edition of Walter Bauer, *Griechisch-deutsches Wörterbuch*,[86] 874-875; and most recently *A Greek-English Lexicon of the Septuagint*, edited by J. Lust, E. Eynikel, and K. Hauspie,[87] 254; similarly, for the patristic period see Lampe, *Patristic Greek Lexicon*, 749, as cited above).

But now the editor of the only lexicon that mentioned the meaning "source" in any connection says that κεφαλή "does seem frequently to denote leader or chief . . . and here it seems perverse to deny authority" and that "The supposed sense 'source' of course does not exist."

These recent developments therefore seem to indicate that there is no "battle of the lexicons" over the meaning of κεφαλή, but that the authors and editors of all the English lexicons for ancient Greek now agree (1) that the meaning "leader, chief, person in authority" clearly exists for κεφαλή, and (2) that the meaning "source" simply does not exist.

VIII. OTHER RECENT AUTHORS ON κεφαλή

At the end of this treatment of κεφαλή, it is appropriate to mention some recent discussions in commentaries and articles. Among the commentaries, most recent writers have agreed that the meaning "authority over" is the correct sense of κεφαλή when used in a metaphorical way to refer to one person as the "head" of another or of others.[88]

Among articles published since my 1990 analysis of κεφαλή, four in particular deserve mention. Joseph A. Fitzmyer, "*kephalē* in I Corinthians 11:3,"[89] thinks that the meaning "source" is appropriate in some extra-biblical passages, but he sees the meaning "leader, ruler,

---

[86]Berlin and New York: de Gruyter, 1988.

[87]Stuttgart: Deutsche Bibelgesellschaft, 1996.

[88]Since I completed my 1990 article, the following commentaries have advocated the meaning "authority over" (or its equivalent) for κεφαλή in 1 Corinthians 11:3 or Ephesians 5:23: Andrew T. Lincoln, *Ephesians* (Word Biblical Commentary; Dallas: Word, 1990), 368-369 ("leader or ruler" in Eph. 1:22 and 5:23); Simon Kistemaker, *Exposition of the First Epistle to the Corinthians* (New Testament Commentary; Grand Rapids, MI: Baker, 1993), 365-367; Craig Blomberg, *1 Corinthians* (NIV Application Commentary; Grand Rapids, MI: Zondervan, 1994), 208-209; and Peter T. O'Brien, *The Letter to the Ephesians* (Pillar New Testament Commentary; Cambridge: Apollos, and Grand Rapids, MI: Eerdmans, 1999), 413-415. All of these commentators except O'Brien also say that the meaning "source" is a possible sense for κεφαλή but choose "leader, authority over" mainly from the force of the context in these passages. (Blomberg also notes that "authority" was the understanding of the vast majority of the church throughout history.) On the other hand, Walt Liefeld, *Ephesians* (IVP New Testament Commentary; Downers Grove, IL and Leicester, England: InterVarsity Press, 1997), 110, 144-145 is undecided among meanings "source," "ruler," and "prominent one," all of which he sees as possible.

[89]"*kephalē* in I Corinthians 11:3," 52-59.

person in authority" as more frequent and thinks this is clearly the sense in 1 Corinthians 11:3. After citing significant patristic testimony to the meaning "leader, ruler" in this verse, Fitzmyer says,

> Given such a traditional interpretation of 1 Corinthians 11:3, one will have to marshall cogent and convincing arguments to say that Paul intended *kephalē* in that verse to mean "source" and not "one having authority over." Those who have claimed that "source" is the meaning intended by Paul have offered no other argument than their claim that *kephalē* would not have meant "ruler, leader, one having authority over" in Paul's day. The evidence brought forth above shows that it was certainly possible for a Hellenistic Jewish writer such as Paul to use the word in that sense. Hence, their argument has collapsed, and the traditional understanding has to be retained.[90]

Clinton E. Arnold, "Jesus Christ: 'Head' of the Church (Colossians and Ephesians),"[91] argues from first-century medical understanding that "the medical writers describe the head not only as the ruling part of the body, but also as the supply center of the body,"[92] which makes sense of the idea of the body being nourished through the head (as in Eph. 4:16) but in general supports the idea of "head" as "authority."

Gregory W. Dawes, *The Body in Question: Meaning and Metaphor in the Interpretation of Ephesians 5:21-33*,[93] has an entire chapter on "The 'Head' (κεφαλή) Metaphor" (122-149), in which he concludes that in Ephesians 1:22 and 5:22-24, the metaphor has the sense of "authority over." But in Ephesians 4:15 he thinks it conveys the sense of "source of the body's life and growth."[94] (He does not think the idea of authority is absent from that usage either.) He thinks the metaphor in which a person is spoken of as "head" is a live metaphor, and the sense has to be determined from what first-century readers would normally have

---

[90]Ibid., p. 57.

[91]*In Jesus of Nazareth: Lord and Christ*, eds. Joel B. Green and Max Turner (Grand Rapids, MI: Eerdmans and Carlisle, England: Paternoster, 1994), 346-366.

[92]Arnold, ibid., 366.

[93]Leiden: Brill, 1998.

[94]He says that a live metaphor can take such a meaning in this context, "even if this sense is unusual" (147). Dawes says several times that one of the characteristics of a live metaphor is that it can take senses other than known, established senses, and in that way authors create new meaning.

understood as the function of a literal head in relation to the body. He thinks the idea of leadership and control was clearly understood, and the idea of nourishment and provision was also understood.

Andrew Perriman, "The Head of a Woman: The Meaning of κεφαλή in 1 Cor. 11:3,"[95] argues that the meaning is "that which is most prominent, foremost, uppermost, preeminent." He raises several helpful objections against the meaning "source," but is less successful in removing the sense of authority from several passages in which he wants to see only "prominence," a sense that is not attested in the lexicons and not really required in any of the cases we have examined.

Anthony Thiselton,[96] in his massive and erudite recent commentary, *The First Epistle to the Corinthians*,[97] deals with κεφαλή in his treatment of 1 Corinthians 11:3. After an extensive review of the literature and the comment that "The translation of this verse has caused more personal agony and difficulty than any other in the epistle" (p. 811), he rejects both the translation "source" and the translation "head" (which, he says, has inevitable connotations of authority in current English). He says, "In the end we are convinced by advocates of a third view, even if barely" (p. 811)—namely, the idea of Perriman and Cervin that the main idea is that of "synecdoche and preeminence, foremost, topmost serving interactively as a metaphor drawn from the physiological head" (p. 816).[98] So Thiselton translates 1 Corinthians 11:3:

> *However, I want you to understand that while Christ is preeminent (or* head? source?*) in relation to man, man is foremost (or* head? source*) [sic] in relation to woman, and God is preeminent (or* head? source?*) in relation to Christ. (p. 800).*

His argument is that "head" (κεφαλή) is a "live metaphor" for Paul's readers, and therefore it refers to a "polymorphous concept," and that the word here has "multiple meanings" (p. 811). Since the actual

---

[95]*JETS* 45:2 (1994), 602-622.

[96]The following material interacting with Thiselton's view has been added to this article since I first published it in *JETS* 44/1 (March 2001), 25-65.

[97]Anthony Thiselton, *The First Epistle to the Corinthians*, NIGTC (Grand Rapids, MI: Eerdmans, and Carlisle, England: Paternoster, 2000), 800-822.

[98]He also claims Dawes, *The Body in Question: Meaning and Metaphor in the Interpretation of Ephesians 5:21-33* in support of this view, but he minimizes the conclusion of Dawes (cited above) that the idea of rule or authority is present in all the relevant metaphorical uses that Dawes examines in Ephesians, which is the focus of his study. Thiselton, in contrast to Dawes, is seeking for a translation that does not include the idea of rule or authority.

physical head of a person is what is most prominent or recognizable about a person, the metaphor of "head," Thiselton thinks, would convey "the notion of *prominence*; i.e., the most conspicuous or *topmost* manifestation of that for which the term also functions as *synecdoche for the whole*" (p. 821).

What is surprising, even remarkable, about Thiselton's treatment is that after his extensive reporting of material on κεφαλή in articles and lexicons, in the end he (like Cervin and Perriman before him) advocates a meaning for κεφαλή that is found in no Greek lexicon at all. Surely everyone would agree that in ordinary human experience a person's head is one prominent and visible part of the person (though one might argue that one's "face" is more prominent than the head generally); but in any case that does not prove that the word κεφαλή would have been used as a metaphor for "prominent part" in ancient Greek. Surely if such a meaning were evident in any ancient texts, we could expect some major lexicons to list it as a recognized meaning. Or else we should expect Thiselton to produce some ancient texts where the sense of "prominence" *absent any idea of authority* is clearly demonstrated. But we find neither.

And we suspect that there is something strange about a translation that cannot translate a simple noun meaning "head" with another noun (like "authority over" or even "source") but must resort to the convoluted and rather vague adjectival phrases, "prominent in relation to" and then "foremost in relation to."[99] Such phrases do not allow readers to notice the fact that even if Thiselton tried to translate the noun κεφαλή with a noun phrase representing his idea (for example, an expression like "prominent part"), it would produce the nonsensical statements, "Christ is the prominent part of man," "the man is the prominent part of the woman," and "God is the prominent part of Christ." Once we render Thiselton's idea in this bare-faced way, parallel to the way we would say that "the head is the prominent part of the body," the supposed connection with our physical heads and bodies falls apart, for while the head is a part of our physical body, a man is surely not a "part of a woman," nor is God a "part of Christ."

---

[99]I realize there are times when a word used as a metaphor in another language simply cannot be translated directly into English without significant loss of meaning and significant addition of incorrect meaning, such as Philippians 1:8, where the RSV's "I yearn for you all with the *affection* of Christ Jesus" is necessary instead of the KJV's literal "I long after you all in the *bowels* of Jesus Christ." But even here, some roughly equivalent noun ("affection," or in Philemon 7, "hearts") is able to provide the necessary substitute.

Moreover, while Thiselton rightly notes that metaphors usually carry multiple layers of meaning in any language, that is not true of his translation. The Greek text contains a metaphor of the head in relation to the body. But Thiselton "translates" not the mere word but the metaphor itself in a way that renders only one component of meaning (or what he claims is one component of meaning), yet he himself had said that the metaphor has "multiple meanings." In his rendering, there is no metaphor left for English readers, and no opportunity even to consider multiple meanings. But he says he cannot translate it simply as "head" because "in English-speaking contexts 'the head' almost always implies leadership and authority" (p. 817).

In fact, Thiselton's translation "preeminent" creates more problems than it solves, because it imports a wrongful kind of male superiority into the text. To be "preeminent" means to be "superior to or notable above all others; outstanding" (*American Heritage Dictionary*, 1997 edition, 1427). Does the Bible really teach that the man is "superior to" the woman? Or "notable above the woman"? Or "outstanding in comparison to the woman"? All of these senses carry objectionable connotations of male superiority, connotations that deny our equality in the image of God. And, when applied to the Father and the Son in the Trinity, they carry wrongful implications of the inferiority of the Son to the Father.

Perhaps a realization of the objectionable connotations of male superiority in the word "preeminent" made Thiselton unable even to use it consistently in translating κεφαλή in his rendering of 1 Corinthians 11:3:

> However, I want you to understand that while Christ is preeminent (or *head? source?*) in relation to man, man is foremost (or *head? source*) [sic] in relation to woman, and God is preeminent (or *head? source?*) in relation to Christ. (800)

But now what is gained by substituting the word "foremost"? Paul certainly cannot be speaking of location (as if a man always stands in front of a woman), for that would make no sense in this context. That leaves the sense "ahead of all others, especially in position or rank" (*American Heritage Dictionary*, 711). But if it means "the man is ahead of the woman in position or rank," then how has Thiselton avoided the sense of authority, except by cautious circumlocution that confuses more than clarifies?

Perhaps most telling of all is the fact that the one idea that Thiselton labors so long to avoid, the idea of one person having authority over another, is the one idea that is present in *every* ancient example of the construction that takes the form "Person A is the head of person or persons B." No counterexamples have ever been produced, so far as I am aware. It may be useful at this point to remind ourselves of what the ancient evidence actually says. Here are several examples:

1. David as King of Israel is called the "head" of the people he conquered (2 Sam. 22:44 [LXX 2 Kings 22:44]: "You shall keep me as the *head* of the Gentiles; a people which I knew not served me"; similarly, Psalm 18:43 (LXX 17:43).

2. The leaders of the tribes of Israel are called "heads" of the tribes (1 Kings [LXX 3 Kings] 8:1 (Alexandrinus text): "Then Solomon assembled the elders of Israel and all the *heads* of the tribes" (similar statements in Aquila, Deut. 5:23; 29:9(10); 1 Kings [LXX 3 Kings] 8:1).

3. Jephthah becomes the "head" of the people of Gilead (Judg. 11:11, "the people made him *head* and leader over them"; also stated in 10:18; 11:8-9).

4. Pekah the son of Remaliah is the head of Samaria (Isa. 7:9, "the *head* of Samaria is the son of Remaliah").

5. The father is the head of the family (Hermas, *Similitudes* 7.3; the man is called "the *head* of the house").

6. The husband is the "head" of the wife (Eph. 5:23, "the husband is *head* of the wife even as Christ is *head* of the church"; compare similar statements found several times in Chrysostom as quoted above).

7. Christ is the "head" of the church (Col. 1:18, "He is the *head* of the body, the church"; also in Eph. 5:23).

8. Christ is the "head" of all things (Eph. 1:22, "He put all things under his feet and gave him as *head* over all things to the church").

9. God the Father is the "head" of Christ (1 Cor. 11:3, "the *head* of Christ is God").

In related statements using not metaphors but closely related similes, (1) the general of an army is said to be "like the head": Plutarch, *Pelopidas* 2.1.3: In an army, "the light-armed troops are like the hands, the cavalry like the feet, the line of men-at-arms itself like chest and breastplate, and the general is like the *head*." Similarly, (2) the Roman Emperor is called the "head" of the people in Plutarch, *Galba* 4.3: "Vindix . . . wrote to Galba inviting him to assume the imperial power, and thus to serve what was a vigorous body in need of a *head*" (compare a related statement in Plutarch, *Cicero* 14.4). And (3) the King of Egypt is called "head" of the nation in Philo, *Moses* 2.30: "As the *head* is the ruling place in the living body, so Ptolemy became among kings."

Then there are the additional citations from Chrysostom quoted earlier in this article, where (1) God is the "head" of Christ; (2) Christ is the "head" of the church; (3) the husband is the "head" of the wife; (4) Christ is the "head" of all things; (5) church leaders are the "head" of the church; and (6) a woman is the "head" of her maidservant. In all six of these cases, as we noted, he uses language of rulership and authority to explain the role of the "head" and uses language of submission and obedience to describe the role of the "body."[100]

In addition, there are several statements from various authors indicating a common understanding that the physical head functioned as the "ruling" part of the body: (1) Plato says that the head "reigns over all the parts within us" (*Timaeus* 44.D). (2) Philo says, "the *head* is the ruling place in the living body" (*Moses* 2:30), and "the mind is *head* and ruler of the sense-faculty in us" (*Moses* 2.82), and "'*Head*' we interpret allegorically to mean the ruling part of the soul" (*On Dreams* 2.207), and "Nature conferred the sovereignty of the body on the *head*" (*The Special Laws* 184). (3) Plutarch says, "We affectionately call a person 'soul' or '*head*' from his ruling parts" (*Table Talk* 7.7 [692.e.1]). Clint Arnold and Gregory Dawes, in the studies mentioned above, adduce other examples of the physical head seen as ruling or controlling the body in ancient literature. Though they find examples where the head or the brain are seen as the source of something as well, they do not claim that these examples can be understood to deny a simultaneous ruling or governing function to the physical head. If the physical head was seen as a source of something like nourishment, it also surely was seen to have control and governance over the physical body.

Regarding "head" as applied metaphorically to persons, to my knowledge no one has yet produced one text in ancient Greek litera-

---

[100]See my two previous articles on κεφαλή, mentioned at the beginning of this article, for additional references like the ones cited here.

ture (from the eighth century B.C. to the fourth century A.D.) where a
person is called the κεφαλή ("head") of another person or group *and
that person is not the one in authority over that other person or group*. The
alleged meaning "prominent without authority," like the meaning
"source without authority," now sixteen years after the publication of
my 1985 study of 2,336 examples of κεφαλή, has still not been supported with *any* citation of *any* text in ancient Greek literature. Over
fifty examples of κεφαλή meaning "ruler, authority over" have been
found, but no examples of the meaning of "source without authority."

Of course, I would agree with Thiselton that in all of these cases
the person who is "head" is also "prominent" in some sense. That is
because some sense of prominence accompanies the existence of leadership or authority. And that overtone or connotation is not lost in
English if we translate κεφαλή as "head," for in English the "head
coach" or the "head of the company" or the "head of the household"
has some prominence as well. But why must we try to *avoid* the one
meaning that is represented in all the lexicons and is unmistakably
present in every instance of this kind of construction, the idea of
authority? One cannot *prove* that this great effort to avoid the idea of
authority is due to the fact that male authority in marriage is
immensely unpopular in much of modern culture, but we cannot help
but note that it is in this current historical context that such efforts
repeatedly occur.

In short, Thiselton has advocated a meaning that is unattested in
any lexicon and unproven by any new evidence. It fails fundamentally
in explaining the metaphor because it avoids the idea of authority, the
one component of meaning that is present in every ancient example of
κεφαλή that takes the form, "person A is the head of person(s) B."

Finally, some treatments of κεφαλή in egalitarian literature deserve
mention. Several treatments have been remarkably one-sided, particularly in their habit of failing even to mention significant literature on
another side of this question.[101] Grace Ying May and Hyunhye
Pokrifka Joe in a 1997 article, "Setting the Record Straight," say, "the
word translated 'head' in Corinthians and Ephesians does not suggest
male authority over women. . . . Paul . . . defines 'head' (*kephalē* in

---

[101]Kroeger herself is one example of this. Though she does cite my 1985 article in her bibliog-
raphy, along with Richard Cervin's 1989 response to that study, she surprisingly does not mention my much longer 1990 study, which includes a lengthy response to Cervin, though the
Dictionary of Paul and His Letters was published in 1993.

Greek) as the 'origin' of beings."[102] More remarkable is an article by Judy Brown, professor of church ministries at Central Bible College, Springfield, Missouri. Writing in the fall of 1999, Brown says of Ephesians 5:23, "the only thing that matters is the meaning of 'head' in first-century Greek, the language of Paul's letter. The evidence is overwhelming that the word meant 'source, supply' as in the 'fountainhead or headwaters of a stream or river.'"[103] Rebecca Groothuis in *Good News for Women* ignores the most significant opposing literature in the same way.[104] However, not all egalitarian treatments have been one-sided in the literature they mention. For example, Craig Keener, *Paul, Women, Wives*,[105] quotes significant treatments from both sides and says that "authority" is a possible sense for κεφαλή and thinks that would have been the acceptable sense in the culture to which Paul wrote.[106]

We may hope that articles and commentaries written in the future will take into account an increasing consensus in the major lexicons that the meaning "authority over" is firmly established for κεφαλή, and that the meaning "source," as Peter Glare says, "does not exist."

IX. A NOTE ON ACCURACY IN ACADEMIC WORK

One final comment should be made about the widely influential article on "head" with which we began. This article by Catherine Kroeger in *Dictionary of Paul and His Letters*, a major reference work, should be troubling to those who care about accuracy in scholarly work. The article is peppered with references to extra-biblical literature and therefore gives the appearance of careful scholarship. But only someone with

---

[102]*Priscilla Papers* 11/1 (Winter 1997), 3. In their footnotes on p. 9, only articles on κεφαλή representing the "source" interpretation are even mentioned, in spite of the fact that this 1997 article was published long after my 1985 and 1990 articles, and after Fitzmyer's 1993 article. When a writer gives readers access to only one side of the argument, it does not suggest confidence that one's position would be more persuasive if readers knew about arguments on both sides.

[103]Judy Brown, "I Now Pronounce You Adam and Eve," *Priscilla Papers* 13/4 (Fall 1999), 2-3. In the next sentence she refers readers to the literature on this question, but mentions only writings by Berkeley and Alvera Mickelsen (1986), Gilbert Bilezikian (1985), Gordon Fee (1987), and herself (1996). It is difficult to explain how Brown, as a college professor, could either be unaware of major studies on the other side of this question or else be aware of them and intentionally fail to mention them at all, and yet say that the evidence is "overwhelming" in favor of the meaning "source."

[104]Rebecca Groothuis, *Good News for Women* (Grand Rapids, MI: Baker, 1997) favors the meaning "source" (151) but does not even mention my studies or those of Fitzmyer in her endnotes (252-254, n. 13). Such oversight, whether intentional or accidental, does not inspire confidence that Groothuis's consideration of the matter has been thorough or careful.

[105]Peabody, Mass.: Hendrickson, 1992.

[106]Ibid., 34.

access to a major research library, the ability to translate extensive passages from untranslated ancient Greek literature, and many days free for such research could ever have discovered that this is not careful scholarship. In fact, in several sections its disregard of facts is so egregious that it fails even to meet fundamental requirements of truthfulness.

With respect to patristic material, the striking new quotation that she said was from Chrysostom does not exist. Her claims for the meaning of κεφαλή in Chrysostom are proven false by numerous statements in Chrysostom's writings. The other patristic references that she cites either give clear support to the meaning "leader, authority over" or else are ambiguous. She fails to mention that Lampe's *Patristic Greek Lexicon*, on the page on which several of her references are found, does not give the meaning "source," which she claims for κεφαλή. She also fails to mention that the meaning "chief, superior" or its equivalent occurs five times on that same page as the primary metaphorical meaning that attaches to κεφαλή when it is used of persons.

With respect to classical Greek material, of the fourteen sources she cites to prove "the classical view of head as source," four do not even contain the term κεφαλή. Of the remaining ten, only three are from the pre-New Testament "classical" period in Greek. No dates were provided for any references, some of which came from the third, fifth, and even ninth century A.D. Several references were cited in such obscure ways that they took literally days to locate. Six of the references repeat the same sentence about Zeus, in which Zeus is seen as the "beginning" or "first in a series," but not as the "source." Two of the references actually speak of "head" as "leader, one in authority." Several of the sentences use κεφαλή with ἀρχή, but the ambiguity of ἀρχή makes them inconclusive as evidence, and the clear use of ἀρχή in Chrysostom and others to mean "ruler" suggests this as a possible meaning in the ambiguous texts as well. In sum, no evidence clearly demonstrated the meaning "source," and several pieces of evidence argued against it.

In terms of accuracy with sources, only fourteen of the twenty-four references cited were both accurate citations and contained the word κεφαλή, "head."

Then in her 1998 response to all of these concerns about accuracy, rather than correcting these errors, Dr. Kroeger gave yet another citation from Chrysostom that, when checked, showed that she had omitted contrary evidence that was at the beginning, middle, and end of the very passage she cited. Sadly, this is not the first time concerns have been raised about the trustworthiness of materials written by this author.[107]

People who read reference books have a right to expect that they will be basically trustworthy, and that where evidence is cited it will, if checked, provide clear support for the points being claimed. When one does check the evidence in an article and it turns out to be unreliable, that undermines confidence in the trustworthiness of the author, editors, and publisher who have produced the work. Because this topic has been so controversial, one would expect that those responsible for the volume would have taken particular care to ensure accuracy. But did anyone check any of this evidence? Did any editor at IVP?[108]

Yet the primary responsibility for this article rests with Dr. Kroeger, and the article is troubling at its core, not only for what it claims, but for the model of scholarly work that it puts forth. The scholarly task is an exciting one, especially in the area of biblical studies. But it is too large for any one person, and scholarship can be advanced in a helpful way when we are able to read and benefit from one another's work. Even when we disagree with the conclusions of an article, we should be able to expect that the citations of evidence are fundamentally reliable.

But the lack of care in the use of evidence as manifested in this article, if followed by others, would throw the scholarly process into decline. We would wonder if we could trust anything that was claimed by anyone else unless we checked the original data for ourselves. For most topics there would never be time to do this, and thus all the gains of scholarship in our major reference books would no longer be useful, for neither scholars nor laypersons would know if any reference works could be trusted.

Such a threat to the trustworthiness of facts cited in academic articles and reference books is a far more serious matter than the meaning of an individual Greek word, even a word as important as κεφαλή. We may differ for our whole lives on the *interpretation* of facts, for that is the nature of the scholarly task. But if our citations of the facts themselves cannot be trusted, then the foundations are destroyed.

---

[107]See Albert Wolters's review of Catherine and Richard Kroeger, *I Suffer Not a Woman* (Grand Rapids, MI: Baker, 1992) in *Calvin Theological Journal* 28 (1993): " . . . their book is precisely the sort of thing that has too often given evangelical scholarship a bad name . . . there is a host of subordinate detail that is misleading or downright false" (209-210). See also Stephen Baugh's review of the same book in WTJ 56 (1994), 153-171, in which he says that the book "wanders widely from the facts" (155), is "wildly anachronistic" (163), and "contains outright errors of fact" (165).

[108]The editorial work for this volume was done by InterVarsity Press in the United States. The volume was also published (but not edited) by Inter-Varsity Press in the United Kingdom (IVP-UK), a separate company.

6

The Historical Novelty of Egalitarian Interpretations of Ephesians 5:21-22

Daniel Doriani[1]

—⠿⠿—

Introduction

Submit to one another out of reverence for Christ. Wives, submit to your husbands as to the Lord.

—Eph. 5:21-22

For over eighteen centuries the church was confident that it understood this and other biblical texts central to the Christian concept of marriage and gender relations. The church's leading pastors, theologians, and exegetes held that Ephesians 5 taught mutuality and service within the structure given by the leadership of a husband and father. The church judged Ephesians 5 and other passages, such as Genesis 2 and 1 Timothy 2, difficult to perform perhaps, but not difficult to understand.

A handful of Christians began to question this consensus in the 1800s, but the onslaught began with the onset of feminism a few decades ago. As it often does, the church started to echo a new cultural movement by adopting the questions and sensibilities of feminism, about a decade after its arrival. Theologians then began to read teachings about submission and leadership in new ways. Not surprisingly,

---

[1] I received research assistance from Bryan Stewart, M.Div., Covenant Seminary, Ph.D. candidate, University of Virginia, and from David Speakman, a current M.Div. candidate at Covenant.

feminist interpretations of Ephesians 5 started to appear in commentaries around 1970.[2] This chapter presents the church's mainstream of interpretation of Ephesians 5, especially regarding the question of mutual submission, describes the novel interpretations that arose in recent years, and briefly responds to them.

THE INTERPRETIVE ISSUES REGARDING EPHESIANS 5

Ephesians 5 is foundational for understanding the quality and structure of marriage and for understanding male-female relations in the family and in society. It has long been a pillar for the traditional theological teaching about the roles of men and women. It says plainly that wives should submit to their husbands and that a husband is the head of his wife (5:22-23).

Because Ephesians 5 appears so obviously to contradict their views, feminist interpreters are obligated to attend to it. Unless they are willing to renounce their feminism, evangelical feminists must argue that despite its apparent clarity, Ephesians 5 fails to endorse male headship and perhaps even undermines it. As uncomplicated and sweeping as Ephesians 5 seems to be in its promotion of male leadership, it is neither, says the evangelical feminist, and so it cannot be taken at face value. It is noteworthy that critical scholars who feel no compunction to heed the text commonly interpret Ephesians 5 the traditional way. For example, Elizabeth Schussler Fiorenza says, "The general injunction for all members of the Christian community, 'Be subject to one another in the fear of Christ,' is clearly spelled out for the Christian wife as requiring submission and inequality."[3]

Evangelical feminist interpretations of Ephesians 5 may adopt four types of argumentation:

1. Ephesians 5 has exegetical mysteries that make its teaching unclear, and therefore unusable for either side of the gender debate. They assert that the command to submit in 5:22 is rendered unstable by the requirement of mutual submission in 5:21.

[2] A survey of nearly one hundred available commentaries shows that feminist interpretations began to appear with J. P. Sampley, *And the Two Shall Become One Flesh* (Cambridge: Cambridge University Press, 1971) and Markus Barth, *Ephesians 4-6* (Garden City, NJ: Doubleday, 1974), 609-611.

[3] Elizabeth Schussler Fiorenza, *Bread Not Stone: The Challenge of Biblical Feminist Interpretation* (Boston: Beacon, 1984), 269.

Christian egalitarians also argue that the term "head" (5:23) is unclear, since it may mean source or leader.[4]

2. Ephesians 5 presents a temporary injunction, adapted to local conditions that no longer obtain, so that the teaching no longer requires literal obedience.

3. The Bible does teach that women ought to be subordinate to men, but the subordination of women to men is a consequence of the curse. Since we should ever seek to reverse the effects of the curse, the church should steadily strive to eradicate female subordination.

4. Ephesians 5 does not support the traditional view at all. Rather, when Paul commands Christians to "submit to one another," he abolishes authority structures in the family, forbidding it even as a temporary measure. Ephesians 5:21 overrides or trumps 5:22.[5]

Gilbert Bilezikian illustrates all four approaches to some degree. In *Beyond Sex Roles*, Bilezikian declares, "Since mutual submission is the rule for all believers, it also applies to all husbands and to all wives who are believers."[6] As for Ephesians 5:21, the reciprocal pronoun "to one another" changes everything. "'Being subject to one another' is a very different relationship from 'being subject to the other.'"[7] Regarding headship, Bilezikian asserts that the headship of Christ means He is the "fountainhead of life and growth" and that He takes "the servant role of provider and reciprocity." There is no New Testament text where "Christ's headship . . . connotes a relationship of authority," nor is there one "where a husband's headship to his wife connotes a relationship of authority."[8] Further, "Wives are never commanded to obey their husbands or to submit to the authority of their husbands." Submission to authority is "so radical in its demands and so comprehensive in its scope that it

---

[4]In a singular case of pleading that uncertainty vitiates key texts, Sanford Hull lists every uncertainty regarding 1 Corinthians 11:2-16, 1 Corinthians 14:33-36, and 1 Timothy 2:8-15, then reasons that the uncertainties make it impossible to use the texts to construct a concept of women's roles. He fails to observe that the same gambit could be used with egalitarians' favored texts. Further, his approach unintentionally shares deconstruction's pessimism about the possibility of communication. See Sanford Hull's "Exegetical Difficulties in the 'Hard Passages,'" in Gretchen Hull, *Equal to Serve* (Tarrytown, NY: Revell, 1987), 251-266.

[5]Curiously, even among feminist commentaries in the survey (note 2 above), several imply but not one explicitly argues that mutual submission (5:21) nullifies a husband's authority (5:22). That is left to the monographs.

[6]Gilbert Bilezikian, *Beyond Sex Roles* (Grand Rapids, MI: Baker, 1985), 163.

[7]Ibid., 154.

[8]Ibid., 161

causes 'obedience to authority' to pale into insignificance." If husbands are supposed to follow Christ's example, it is not His power or authority they are to imitate but "his humility . . . abnegation and . . . servant behavior."[9]

Aida Spencer exemplifies argument 3, that woman's subordination is strictly a result of the Fall. In *Beyond the Curse*, Spencer said that for the woman:

> Her curse now was to be ruled, perversely to long for her husband and he to rule over her. She would want to be dominated by her husband and he would submit[!] to this desire. God does not command Adam to rule or govern his wife. Rather the curse is Eve's. The ruling is a consequence of Eve's longing and her fall.[10]

Originally, God intended Eve to be Adam's equal—if not his superior.[11] The ideal is mutual respect and partnership in marriage, parenting, and ministry.[12]

Similarly, Gilbert Bilezikian says, "Male rulership was precipitated by the fall as an element of the curse. . . . [It] is announced in the Bible as the result of Satan's work at the fall."[13] Further, "Where the curse had predicted, 'He shall rule over you' the gospel orders that 'husbands should love their wives as their own bodies.'"[14]

Egalitarians commonly assert that Paul may require wives to submit to their husbands, but in a manner not so very different from the mutual submission all Christians owe each other. That is, wives must submit to their husbands, but husbands must also submit to their wives, so that mutual submission, not authority, is the final word. This is often assumed rather than argued. Gretchen Hull says that "when both sexes are seen as equally human and equally redeemed . . . [they are] equally free to practice the mutual submission commanded for all believers by Ephesians 5:21. . . . The general admonition in verse 21 is that all believers be mutually submissive . . . with each other."[15] In informal settings, one can hear Christian feminists say, "I'll submit to my husband if he also submits to me."

---

[9]Ibid., 168-169.

[10]Aida Spencer, *Beyond the Curse* (Peabody, MA: Hendrickson, 1985), 36.

[11]Ibid., 25.

[12]David Spencer, in ibid., 138ff.

[13]Bilezikian, *Beyond Sex Roles*, 227, n. 12.

[14]Ibid., 80.

[15]Hull, *Equal to Serve*, 194-196.

Bilezikian, Spencer, and Hull are widely known, but pride of place among egalitarian interpreters of Scripture goes to Craig Keener, an erudite and gracious scholar. In *Paul, Women & Wives*, Keener has composed a thorough feminist interpretation of Ephesians 5.[16] Why, he asks, does Paul, "who calls for mutual submission, deal more explicitly with the submission of wives than with that of husbands?" Keener answers, "Because he was smart."[17]

Keener explains that the Roman aristocracy lived in fear of "the upward mobility of socially inferior elements, such as former slaves, foreigners, and women." Further, the aristocrats viewed foreign religions as agents in the "subversion of the appropriate moral order." Since they opposed foreign cults, including Judaism and Christianity, and since they feared the "increase of women's social power," it was essential that Christianity demonstrate its "lack of subversiveness" by avoiding radical challenges to "Roman social structures."[18] In other words, Paul's instructions are a temporary measure, designed to make Christianity inoffensive (argument #2).

Yet, Keener continues, Paul's ethics are "more revolutionary than they appear." It is noteworthy that Paul even addresses women.[19] Further, Paul does not command women to obey, nor does he order men to rule.[20] Rather, he requires husbands to love, which is nothing more than he requires of all Christians. When he calls wives to submit, this is no more than "a particular example of the submission of all believers to one another" from Ephesians 5:21, "the kind that Christian husbands . . . also need to render to their wives"[21] (argument #4). Further, unlike his Jewish and Greek contemporaries, Paul does not ascribe moral or spiritual inferiority to women.[22]

Though Keener cites Plutarch's gentle advice that husbands and wives should live in "harmonious consent," he claims Paul's exhortations are "quite weak by ancient standards."[23] Having discussed ameliorating cultural considerations, Keener is prepared to overturn the historic Christian interpretation of Ephesians 5.

---

[16]Craig Keener, *Paul, Women & Wives* (Peabody, MA: Hendrickson, 1990), 139-224.
[17]Ibid., 139.
[18]Ibid., 144-147.
[19]Ibid., 168.
[20]Ibid., 147, 157.
[21]Ibid., 157, 169.
[22]Ibid., 158-167.
[23]Ibid., 169.

Keener is well aware of the complementarian interpretation of Ephesians that would best incorporate his cultural insights. He knows that Paul might mean that "wives should always submit," whereas "husbands should submit only in the sense that they lovingly look out for their wives' interests." He knows the strongest complementarian interpretation of Ephesians 5:21-22. Paul's summons to mutual submission could mean that "all Christians should submit to one another, but they should submit in different ways, as detailed in his list of duties in 5:22—6:9." Indeed, most of the church has seen it just that way. But for Keener, Paul's summons to mutual submission rules that out. Paul "subordinates wives so weakly, and emphasizes mutuality so strongly, that it is difficult to believe that he is arguing for their transcultural subordination."[24]

Keener continues, "Paul is responding to a specific cultural issue for the sake of the gospel, and his words should not be taken at face value in all cultures." Paul only asked women "in his day" to conform "to the general social ideal without fighting it."[25] But the call to submission no longer obtains today. Keener asserts that the key, in moving from then to now, is to note that Paul also assumes slavery in Ephesians and commands slaves to submit to masters. If that command is passé, then so is the command to wives.[26]

To isolate the essential argument, Keener says the command, "Wives, submit to your husbands" cannot be taken at face value because it appears with similar instructions regarding slavery. If the instructions regarding slavery do not hold, then neither do those regarding marriage.[27] Keener's reliance on an analogy between marriage and slavery fails because God instituted marriage before the Fall, whereas mankind instituted slavery after it. Ever a tragic estate, Scripture acknowledges, then regulates and mitigates the evils of slavery. No wonder, then, that commands about slavery are temporary. But God instituted marriage. It is good in itself, and so we may not assume its regulations are temporary. Indeed, when Keener judges them temporary, he assumes what is to be proved, and so his argument is invalid. Worse, he ignores the teaching about parent-child relations, though the texts are closer to

---

[24]Ibid., 170.

[25]Ibid., 171.

[26]Ibid., 184-211, especially 207-211.

[27]The long, tragic continuance of slavery prevented the formation of his argument in prior centuries.

each other than those on marriage and slavery. No one argues that parental authority is passé, and the analogy between marriage and parenthood is closer than the analogy between marriage and slavery.

But my primary task is to show that the current feminist interpretation of mutual submission in Ephesians 5 is novel in church history, not that it is false. To the evidence we turn.

OVERVIEW OF THE TEXT AND ITS INTERPRETATION

Before we proceed, for the sake of accuracy, some grammatical features of Ephesians 5 should be explained. Though we will often speak of the imperatives or commands of Ephesians 5:21-22, the verbs in question are, technically speaking, imperatival participles. Grammatically, the phrase "submit to one another" is the last of five participles that depend on the imperative "be filled with the Spirit" in 5:18b. Literally Paul says, "Be filled with the Spirit, *speaking* to one another with psalms, hymns and spiritual songs, *singing* and *making music* in your heart to the Lord, always *giving thanks* to God the Father for everything . . . *submitting* to one another out of reverence for Christ . . . wives . . . to your husbands as to the Lord." (5:19-22). The phrase "submitting to one another" functions as an imperative in 5:21, and that functional imperative is borrowed by 5:22. The phrase "submitting to one another" therefore is both the last thought on the Spirit-filled life and the first thought on a spiritual household. There is no significant debate about these points.[28]

Instead, interpreters focus on the unusual object of the verb "submit"—"to one another."[29] It is unusual because the object of "submit" (Greek *hypotassō*) is ordinarily some authority, such as God, the Law, husbands, masters, or kings. Ordinarily it is clear that one person bows to the will or decree of someone in authority. In all uses other than the one being considered, "submit" is one-directional. A person who is lower in rank, age, position, or power yields to one with greater rank or power. What then does "submit to one another" mean? How can husband and wife both submit to the other? We seem to have an oxymoron.

This unusual object "one another" can be interpreted in three ways. Option #1: Believers should submit to whatever authority is over them. On this view, the command to submit to each other does not mean everyone submits to everyone, thereby annulling all author-

---

[28]All parties agree that the imperatival participles function as finite imperative verbs, and no one questions the functioning of the ellipsis in 5:22.

[29]The Greek is a single word, the dative plural of a reflexive pronoun, ἀλλήλοις.

ity relationships. Rather, the passage tells the congregation as a whole that each member should yield in all relationships where someone has some authority over him or her.

Option #2: The command to submit to one another spells the end of all divinely ordered authority relationships. One person or group may, by mutual agreement, cede authority to another for the sake of convenience, but no one has the right to exercise authority over anyone else.

Option #3: Paul is altering the meaning of submission. He means that the Ephesians should yield to the needs of others and serve them in self-sacrificial love, not that they literally submit to each other's orders.

Almost all parties agree that Ephesians 5 at least partially redefines the meaning of submission in marriage. But in recent years advocates of the traditional view of Ephesians 5 have also defended option #1. They point out that in all other New Testament uses, "submit" means to yield to authority. They show that the Greek term *allelois*, translated "to one another," may or may not indicate full reciprocity, depending on the context.[30] So, they say, Paul means that all Christians should submit to those who have authority over them, according to God-ordained role relationships. That is, they should submit whenever submission is relevant. This argument has much to commend it, and I adhere to it, but we must note that it does not have a centuries-old pedigree either.[31]

In the past, exegetes and theologians were content to make two statements and let them stand side by side without lengthy explanation. We may plausibly surmise that they had the liberty to do so because they hardly had to defend the notion that God created an ordered society where husbands had authority over their wives roughly as magistrates led the state, ministers of the Gospel led the church, and parents led their children. They took married couples to have something quite close to a relationship between equals, but they still believed godly husbands led.

---

[30]Full reciprocity is in view in Philippians 2:3, "Consider others [one another] better than yourselves," and in Mark 9:50, "be at peace with each other." But in Galatians 6:2, "Carry each other's burdens" does not mean "exchange burdens," but that *some* should help others. Again Revelation 6:4, "Men slay each other," does not mean all murders are fully reciprocal, ending in double death, but that some men kill others.

[31]See James Hurley, *Man and Woman in Biblical Perspective* (Grand Rapids, MI: Zondervan), 139ff. and Wayne Grudem, in note 6 for "Husbands and Wives as Analogues of Christ and the Church" by George Knight, in *Recovering Biblical Manhood and Womanhood*, eds. John Piper and Wayne Grudem (Wheaton, IL: Crossway Books, 1991), 493-494.

COMMENTARIES ON EPHESIANS 5

As we begin, let us remember our duty to let historical sources be what they are. We must realize that until the Reformation, there was very little exegesis as we understand it today. Further, this question was not controversial, and therefore sources are relatively slender.[32] To my knowledge, Augustine never comments on our question, and many commentators are quite terse. Still, there is ample record that older theologians adopted the traditional view.

Clement of Alexandria (c. 150-215)

In perhaps the earliest recorded Christian remarks on women's roles, Clement of Alexandria said, "There is sameness" concerning the souls of men and women, so that they can "attain to the same virtue." Yet women are "destined for child-bearing and housekeeping," but not for war or "manly work and toil." Clement verified his view that the souls of women are equal to men but that their roles are different from men by citing 1 Corinthians 11:3, 8, 11 and Ephesians 5:21-29, essentially without comment.[33]

John Chrysostom (345-407)

Chrysostom epitomizes the tendency of ancient, medieval, and Reformation theologians to let the two imperatives of Ephesians 5:21-22 stand side by side without resolution. Thus he declared there must be "an interchange of service and submission" between slave and freeman, between master and slave, between friend and friend. Christians should submit themselves to all, "as if all were their masters."[34] Yet in the next homily, Chrysostom said the husband is the head and has "authority and forethought," whereas the wife is the body, so that her place is submission. He counseled men to seek "a wife obedient unto thee" and to care for their wives as Christ does the church.[35]

---

[32]An indirect corroboration appears in the Ancient Christian Commentary on Scripture series, whose citations contain nothing that is amenable to the egalitarian perspective. See *Galatians, Ephesians, Philippians*, ed. Mark J. Edwards (Downers Grove, IL: InterVarsity Press, 1999), 194.

[33]Clement of Alexandria, "The Stromata or Miscellanies," in *Ante-Nicene Fathers*, eds. Alexander Robertson and James Donaldson (Grand Rapids, MI: Eerdmans, 1956), 2:419-420.

[34]Chrysostom, "Homily 19 on Ephesians," in *The Nicene and Post-Nicene Fathers*, ed. Philip Schaff (Grand Rapids, MI: Eerdmans, 1956), 13:142.

[35]Chrysostom, "Homily 20 on Ephesians," in ibid., 13:144.

Thomas Aquinas (1225-1274)

Much like Chrysostom, Aquinas said, "The relation of a husband to his wife is, in a certain way, like that of a master to his servant, insofar as the latter ought to be governed by the commands of his master."[36] Though husband and wife share a life, so that he is only *like* a lord, and not literally one, a wife is still subject to her husband. Indeed, she is "obedient to her husband as the church is subject to Christ," for he is her head. Beyond this, Aquinas essentially paraphrased Ephesians 5, with parallel passages adduced. He urged husbands to follow the example of Christ in loving their wives, sanctifying them and presenting them pure to God.[37] Few are more diligent than Aquinas at addressing objections to his views, but it did not even occur to Aquinas that someone might think Paul advocated reciprocal leadership or role reversals.

Henry Bullinger (1504-1575)

The earliest reformers, busy restoring the foundations of theology, left few remarks on Ephesians. But at last the Reformers brought us commentary on Ephesians 5 by *married* men. Bullinger, the near contemporary of Zwingli in the Swiss Reformation, was one of the first to write about Ephesians 5, in *The Christen State of Matrimonye*. Bullinger viewed women's subordination to men as a consequence of the Fall. Yet he did not call for the abolition of male leadership. The Lord commanded wives "to obey their husbands." He declared, "The husband . . . is the wife's head even as Christ is the head of the congregation."[38]

John Calvin (1509-1564)

Calvin is one of the first commentators to note the strangeness of the language of Ephesians. Calvin took the call to mutual submission to mean that God's children must "act for one another's good . . . to serve one another" and to remember that they "are joined together in one mutual bond of charity."[39] That, said Calvin, is the sense of Ephesians 5. He continued:

---

[36]Thomas Aquinas, *Commentary on Saint Paul's Epistle to the Ephesians*, trans. Matthew Lamb (Albany, NY: Magi Books, 1966), 217-218.

[37]Ibid., 218-220.

[38]Heinrich Bullinger, *The Christen State of Matrimonye*, trans. Miles Coverdale (1541), Dii (sic).

[39]John Calvin, *Sermons on the Epistles to the Ephesians* (Carlisle, PA: Banner of Truth, 1562, reprint 1973), 560.

> Now a man may think it strange . . . that he should say that we ought to be subject to one another. For it does not seem fitting that a father should be subject to his children, the husband to his wife, or the magistrate to the people whom he governs or even that . . . equal[s] . . . should be subject to one another.[40]

Calvin explained that Paul places all Christians under subjection. So those "who are exalted in authority and glory above other men" should see that they do not rule for their own sake, "but for the sake of the common well-being." For example, magistrates serve the state by putting wise laws over citizens. They "serve in ruling," as do fathers. He viewed a husband's subjection similarly:

> Similarly between the husband and the wife. For is it not a subjection that the husband supports the frailty of his wife, and is prudent enough not to use rigor towards her, holding her as his companion, and taking upon him a part of her burden both in sickness and in health? Is that not a subjection?[41]

So Calvin held that men of every condition and rank are subject to one another. Yet he did not think the idea of submission spells the end of authority structures. Rather, he believed Ephesians 5 "shows that there are certain orders among men." There is universal submission among all men; nonetheless, "there is also a greater subjection of the son to the father, of the wife to her husband and of underlings to their superior." Specifically, "although the husband may be superior in authority," yet he remains "under obligation to his wife" and is not free to lord it over her or act tyrannically.[42]

Our obligation, both to God's authority structure and to His commands for operating within them, is absolute. Husbands must still love "dreadful and stubborn" wives. And "the vices that are in a man must not hinder the subjection and obedience to him," for rejection of a husband's authority is rejection of God's authority.[43]

---

[40]Ibid.
[41]Ibid., 561.
[42]Ibid., 565.
[43]Ibid., 566, 569.

William Perkins (1558-1602)

The English Puritans commented far more extensively on marriage and its authority structure than any comparable group had done until their time, more than any group until the twentieth century. We will cite five representatives, from William Perkins to Richard Steele.

Perkins defined husbands in terms of their authority: "The husband is he which hath authority over the wife." He is "head over his wife." Perkins said husbands have three duties: to love their wives (citing Ephesians 5:25), to provide for them, and to honor them. Perkins's commentary can sound nearly contemporary. A husband renders honor to his wife, Perkins said, by treating her as his companion, by patiently bearing her infirmities, and "by suffering himself sometimes to be admonished or advised by her" and leaving some matters to her judgment. Wives have two duties. "The first is to submit herself to her husband and to . . . reverence him as her head in all things [citing Ephesians 5:22]. . . . The second duty is to be obedient to her husband in all things."[44]

Paul Bayne (?-1617)

Bayne said that Ephesians 5:21 did not teach "inferiors" their duty to "superiors." Rather, "it commandeth such a submission as all owe interchangeably one to another. . . . The thing here laid down is this, that the highest must shew submission toward the lowest." He added, "The superior must honor the inferior, as well as receive honor from him." Thus Bayne lamented the many superiors who hold their inferiors in contempt and refuse ever to alter their preferences to please their servants.[45] Still, Bayne took 5:22 at face value, requiring, in the home, that wives show subjection to their husbands, as to the Lord, for both "nature itself" and "God's ordinance" show that "man is the head." Bayne defined subjection as obedience to a husband's commands, receptiveness to his rebukes, and submission to his desires. He chided women who have "no awe of their husbands" and refuse to submit to them with constant obedience.[46]

---

[44]William Perkins, "Christian Oeconomy," in *The Workes of William Perkins* (Cambridge: Cantrell Legge, 1616-1618), 3:692.

[45]Paul Bayne, *Commentary on Ephesians* (London, 1618; reprint Edinburgh: James Nicholl, 1866), 335-336.

[46]Ibid., 337-339.

Henry Smith (1560-1591)

Smith urged husbands to love their wives with a holy, hearty, and constant love. Husbands and wives, he said, are partners "like two oars in a boat." But the wife is also "an under officer in his commonweal." Therefore she should be obedient and submit herself to her husband.[47]

William Gouge (1578-1653)

Gouge's 180-page exposition of Ephesians 5:21—6:9 often probed the proper structure and use of authority in marriage. First, he asserted, "It is a general mutual duty appertaining to all Christians, to submit themselves one to another." In explaining mutual submission, Gouge understood "without question" that "inferiors" owe submission to their "superiors" and that equals owe one another honor; but there is "just question" whether superiors must submit themselves to their inferiors.[48] Gouge answered by distinguishing. "Subjection of reverence" is the duty of inferiors, who must show respect to their leaders by their speech, their deportment, and their ready obedience. "Subjection of service" is the duty of every Christian "to do what good he can to another." By serving, magistrates submit to subjects, parents submit to children, and husbands submit to wives. Authorities submit when they see that God set them in their place "for the good of their subjects," not for their own honor.[49]

According to Gouge, all Christians must serve in their God-given place. "A wife must yield a chaste, faithful, matrimonial subjection to her husband." The husband is the head of the wife. As head, he is "more eminent and excellent," and as head he governs, protects, preserves, and provides for the body, his wife. A husband subjects himself to his wife by fulfilling his role of leading-serving in love.[50] This is a man's duty, and he must not abdicate it by yielding to a discontented wife, nor abuse it by the selfish use of force.[51] A wife must accept her husband's lead, even if she is sober and religious and he is a drunkard

---

[47]Henry Smith, "A Preparative to Marriage," in *The Works of Henry Smith* (London, 1592; reprint Edinburgh: James Nicholl, 1866), 1:24-25, 30-31.

[48]The terms *superior* and *inferior* were, in Gouge's day, the labels for those who held positions of authority and those who were under authority. Gouge makes it very clear that he does exalt the value of one person or diminish the other.

[49]William Gouge, *Of Domesticall Duties* (London, 1622), 4-7.

[50]Ibid., 16-17, 26-29.

[51]Ibid., 355, 377-379.

and a blasphemer.[52] But a husband must exercise authority with a Christlike love and sacrifice, so that he is easy to respect.[53]

Richard Steele (1629-1692)

Steele assumed that husbands are their wives' spiritual heads. Husbands, he said, should instruct their wives if ignorant, should reprove their errors, and should seek to be a good example to them. Yet husbands should yield to their wives' reasonable requests[54] and show love by their "mild use" of authority. A wise husband will remember "that though he be superior to his wife, yet . . . their souls are equal; that she is to be treated as his companion; that he is not to rule her as a king doth his subjects; that . . . she was not taken out of Adam's head, so neither out of his foot, but out of his side near his heart." Therefore he must be gentle, and neither abject nor magisterial.[55]

Jonathan Edwards (1703-1758)

Edwards faulted unkind, imperious husbands who treat their wives "as if they were servants" and lay unreasonable restraints on them. Yet he cited Ephesians 5:22 to show that wives should submit to their husbands. He added, "The person who lightly violates these obligations will doubtless be treated as one who slights the authority of God."[56]

John Wesley (1703-1791)

Like many before him, Wesley noted Paul's call to mutual submission in Ephesians 5:21 but could not see that it undercut the responsibility of wives, children, and slaves to submit to husbands, parents, and masters. The idea of Christians subjecting themselves to one another is comprehensive. Still, Paul's main message concerns sub-

---

[52]Ibid., 355, 272-277.

[53]Ibid., 43, 50, 75, 354. As Gouge's contemporary, William Whately (1583-1639), put it, "I am the chief, that all may fare the better for me, that by using more wisdom, and taking more pains, and showing more virtues . . . all of my family, and especially my wife, may live more . . . comfortably . . . and get more grace." See William Whately, *Directions for Married Persons* (London, 1623; reprinted in *A Christian Library*, ed. John Wesley (London, 1821), 12:304.

[54]Richard Steele, "What Are the Duties of Husbands and Wives to Each Other?" in *Puritan Sermons, 1659-1689* (Wheaton, IL: R. O. Roberts, 1981), 2:286-288.

[55]Ibid., 286-290.

[56]Jonathan Edwards, sermon on self-examination, in *The Works of President Edwards*, ed. C. C. Goen (New Haven, CT: Yale University Press, 1972), 4:524.

mission. Thus, "inferiors ought to do their duty, whatever their superiors do."[57]

Charles Hodge (1797-1878)

Hodge represents mainstream nineteenth-century American exegesis and agreed with his forebears. Hodge acknowledged "the mutual dependence of the sexes and their essential equality of nature." Further, a wife is "the companion and ministering angel to the husband." Yet, he said, a wife's "obedience to her husband is to be regarded as part of her obedience to the Lord." It is a service rendered to Christ, and therefore easy and light.[58] Like a few others, Hodge wondered if wives should permanently stand under their husbands' authority. Hodge answered that the command has "a foundation in nature." Specifically, a husband has a natural "eminency," a superiority that does "enable and entitle him to command. He is larger, stronger, bolder," and therefore he leads.[59]

CONCLUSIONS AND IMPLICATIONS

To summarize, traditional commentaries on Ephesians 5 typically proceed by reiterating the two main imperatives of Ephesians 5:21-22. They affirm that all Christians should submit to each other (5:21). Yet they take Ephesians 5:22-33 at face value, affirming that authority structures remain, so that wives must submit to husbands, children to parents, and slaves to masters. Commentators do not hold the phrase "Submit to one another" to require full mutuality. Traditional interpreters summon all Christians to a submissive spirit, so that each prefers the good of the other, but they never say that husbands should submit to their wives just as wives submit to their husbands. They let Ephesians 5:21 and 5:22 interpret each other. They say, "All Christians submit to one another" and explain that Christians practice mutual submission when wives submit to their husbands and husbands love their wives.

The history of the interpretation of Ephesians 5 shows that the concept of mutual submission is not entirely novel; that language has been used occasionally since the Reformation. But past theologians and

---

[57]John Wesley, *Explanatory Notes Upon the New Testament* (London: The Epworth Press, 1952), 718.

[58]Charles Hodge, *A Commentary on the Epistle to the Ephesians* (Grand Rapids, MI: Eerdmans, 1954), 312-313.

[59]Ibid. For others who believe male leadership can be traced to male characteristics, see Daniel Doriani, "History of the Interpretation of 1 Timothy 2," in *Women in Church: A Fresh Analysis of 1 Timothy 2:9-15*, eds. Andreas Kostenberger, Thomas Schreiner, and Scott Baldwin (Grand Rapids, MI: Baker, 1995), 230-232, 245-246.

exegetes defined mutual submission as a quality that modified relationships, not as a structure that defined relationships. "Submitting to one another" meant serving and caring for others; it did not mean handing authority to them. In prior centuries no one questioned that husbands, fathers, masters, and magistrates must exercise a loving but undeniable authority over their wives, children, servants, and subjects respectively. Again, they judged Ephesians 5:21 and 5:22 to be mutually interpretive. In their view, the phrase "submitting to one another" in 5:21 told leaders how to conduct themselves within the authority structure described in 5:22—6:9. It is a historical novelty to assert that mutual submission means husbands should submit to their wives just as wives submit to their husbands.

In recent times, however, biblical feminists have adopted several lines of argument in an attempt to show that the command "Wives, submit to your husbands" should not be taken at face value. Either 1) the command is judged unclear, or 2) it is viewed as a temporary injunction, or 3) it is viewed as a reversible element of the curse, or 4) the prior command, "Submit to one another," is held to annul authority structures.

The fourth approach is perhaps most common. It operates, in the final analysis, by pitting Ephesians 5:21 against 5:22. Mutual submission is judged the clear, general principle that becomes the ground for critique of following sentences. Egalitarians reason as follows: Given that "submit to one another" is the general principle standing over Paul's instruction for household relationships, no subsequent portion can be contrary to it. Therefore, feminists say, the command "wives submit" cannot be taken as a literal and permanent mandate since it contradicts the ideal of mutual submission.

This approach has several flaws. First, it rejects the age-old wisdom of the church. Second, it potentially undermines the orthodox view of Scripture, since it reads imperatives in consecutive verses as if they are irreconcilable. We do not charge our evangelical friends with denying Scripture's infallibility and authority, but playing text against text is dangerous, and it happens elsewhere too. For example, feminist interpretations of 1 Timothy 2:12 ("I do not permit a woman to teach or to have authority over a man") often dismantle the text by alleging 1) that it contradicts the examples of women who engage in blessed ministry (e.g., Deborah or Huldah) and 2) that it contradicts Paul's general principle that "There is neither . . . male nor female . . . in Christ Jesus"

(Gal. 3:28). By playing text against text, feminists deny the permanence of both Ephesians 5:22 and 1 Timothy 2:12.

Third, it uses erroneous patterns of interpretation. A leading principle of interpretation says that texts by the same author must be assumed to interpret, not contradict, each other. For example, the Old Testament case laws regarding property offenses clarify the meaning of the general principle, "You shall not steal" (Exod. 20:15). Some case laws develop the eighth commandment in unexpected ways, but we assume that they rightly develop the Law's intent. Similarly, it may be unexpected that Paul follows "submit to one another" with the command that wives submit to husbands, and yet we ought to assume that it truly develops the first command's original intent.[60]

Finally, the feminist interpretation proves too much. If the principle of mutual submission annuls the command that wives should submit to husbands, then logically it also nullifies the command that children should obey their parents. Indeed, the underlying principle potentially undermines authority structures at work, in the church, in schools, and in the state as well. With good biblical warrant, theologians of the past asserted that God ordained authorities in all these spheres for the good, especially the good order of society.[61] Of course, no one pushes the principle of mutual submission to its end. No one thinks parents should tell their young children, "It's time for you to go to bed" and expect rejoinders such as, "OK, but it's time for you to go to bed too." But if feminists do not follow the idea of mutual submission to its conclusion, they must explain why they follow it one time and not another.[62]

Readers surely recognize that I believe the traditional interpretation to be exegetically correct and theologically sound. The particular purpose of this chapter is to show that the church thought the same throughout the great bulk of its history. For over eighteen centuries the church's leaders believed that Ephesians 5 taught mutuality and service within the leadership of a husband and father.

---

[60]On the interpretation of biblical law, see Daniel Doriani, *Putting the Truth to Work: The Theory and Practice of Bible Application* (Phillipsburg, NJ: Presbyterian & Reformed, 2001), Chapters 10 and 11.

[61]Notice, for example, that Paul commands Christians to submit to government authorities, but he never commanded authorities to submit to the people (Rom. 13). Likewise, the book of Hebrews commands the church to submit to its elders but never tells elders to submit to the people (13).

[62]Of course, some do argue for the overthrow of *all* authorities. But they contradict the biblical plan for society that places kings, priests, judges, and prophets over Israel and apostles, pastors, teachers, and elders over the church.

7

THE MYTH OF MUTUAL SUBMISSION AS AN INTERPRETATION OF EPHESIANS 5:21

Wayne Grudem

BACKGROUND

For nineteen centuries Christians understood without confusion the plain words of Ephesians 5:22-24:

> *Wives, submit to your own husbands, as to the Lord. . . . Now as the church submits to Christ, so also wives should submit in everything to their husbands.*[1]

They also understood, for nineteen centuries, Colossians 3:18:

> *Wives, submit to your husbands, as is fitting in the Lord.*

And they had no problem understanding Titus 2:5, where Paul says that older women are to train young women to be "submissive to their own husbands, that the word of God may not be reviled."

---

[1]The word *hypotassō*, "be subject to" or "submit to," is missing from some significant early manuscripts of Ephesians 5:22, such as p[46] and B. This makes little difference to the sense, because if it is not there, it is the verb that Paul obviously intended readers to supply from verse 21 in any case, and the verb is found again in verse 24, "as the church submits to Christ, so also wives should submit in everything to their husbands."

Nor did they have trouble understanding 1 Peter 3:1:

Likewise, wives, be subject to your own husbands, so that even if some do not obey the word, they may be won without a word by the conduct of their wives.

But these verses became an embarrassment to many Christians as feminism began to gain influence in the mid-twentieth century. How could Paul dare to tell women to be submissive to their husbands? If these submission verses were allowed to have their plain force today, it would be impossible to support the egalitarian agenda of abolishing any unique male leadership in marriage.

Then suddenly, in the second half of the twentieth century, egalitarians "discovered" a wonderful solution to these troublesome verses.[2] Their solution was to claim "mutual submission": Not only did wives have to submit to their husbands, but husbands also had to submit to their wives! The proof for this was seen one verse earlier, in Ephesians 5:21, "submitting *to one another* out of reverence for Christ."

And so egalitarians began to claim that Ephesians 5:22 did not really teach any unique authority for the husband in a marriage, because Ephesians 5:21 nullified that idea. Any submission in marriage has to be mutual, and thus male headship in marriage evaporates.

For example, Gilbert Bilezikian says that Ephesians 5:21 teaches "mutual submission." He says that "'Being subject to one another' is a very different relationship from 'being subject to the other' . . . by definition, mutual submission rules out higher hierarchical differences. Being subject to one another is only possible among equals. It is a mutual (two-way) process that excludes the unilateral (one-way) subordination implicit in the concept of subjection without the reciprocal pronoun. Mutual subjection suggests horizontal lines of interaction among equals."[3]

Rebecca Merrill Groothuis, to take another example, says, "The call to mutual reciprocal submission in Eph. 5:21 establishes the framework for the instructions to wives and husbands that follow."[4] She goes on to say that wives "are to submit to their husbands in the same way that all

---

[2]The history of interpretation of Ephesians 5:21 is traced by Daniel Doriani, "The Historical Novelty of Egalitarian Interpretations of Ephesians 5:21-22," in Chapter 6 in this volume.

[3]*Beyond Sex Roles*, 2nd edition (Grand Rapids, MI: Baker, 1990), 154.

[4]*Good News for Women: A Biblical Picture of Gender Equality* (Grand Rapids, MI: Baker, 1997), 164.

believers are to submit to one another. This text is not advocating a uni-lateral female submission to male authority. Rather, it is presenting the submission of wives as one application of the basic principle of basic sub-mission that is to be applied by all believers within the Body of Christ."[5]

Sometimes egalitarians will say something like this: "Of course I believe a wife should be subject to her husband. And a husband should also be subject to his wife." Or an egalitarian might say, "I will be sub-ject to my husband as soon as he is subject to me." And so, as egalitar-ians understand Ephesians 5:21, it tells us that there is no difference in roles between men and women. There is no unique leadership role for the husband. There is simply "mutual submission."[6]

But is this the correct understanding of Ephesians 5:21? Does it really nullify all unique male leadership and male authority in marriage? In the material that follows, I will attempt to show that the egalitarian interpretation cannot be a correct understanding of Ephesians 5:21.

AN ACCEPTABLE SENSE OF MUTUAL SUBMISSION

I have to affirm at the outset that people can mean different things by *mutual submission*. There is a sense of the phrase *mutual submission* that is different from an egalitarian view and that does not nullify the hus-band's authority within marriage. If mutual submission means being considerate of one another, and caring for one another's needs, and being thoughtful of one another, and sacrificing for one another, then of course I would agree that mutual submission is a good thing.

However, egalitarians mean something so different by this phrase, and they have used this phrase so often to nullify male authority within marriage, that I think the expression "mutual submission" only leads to confusion if we go on using it.[7]

---

[5]Ibid., 164-165.

[6]In fact, our egalitarian friends have a journal called *Mutuality,* published by the organization Christians for Biblical Equality.

[7]When the Southern Baptist Convention was debating its statement on marriage and the fam-ily, I am told that there was a motion from the floor to add "mutual submission" to the state-ment. Dorothy Patterson, a member of the drafting committee for the statement and one of the original members of the Council on Biblical Manhood and Womanhood, spoke against the motion and explained how egalitarians have used it to deny any sense of male authority within marriage. The motion was defeated, and appropriately so. If "mutual submission" had been added to the Southern Baptist statement, in effect it would have torpedoed the whole statement, because it would have watered it down so much that people from almost any position could sign it, and it would have affirmed no unique male authority within marriage. (These events were reported to me by friends who were present when the statement was being debated on the floor of the Southern Baptist Convention in the summer of 1998.)

In previous generations some people did speak about "mutual submission," but never in the sense in which egalitarians today understand it. In his study of the history of the interpretation of Ephesians 5:21, Daniel Doriani has demonstrated that a number of earlier writers thought there was a kind of "mutual submission" taught in the verse, but that such "submission" took very different forms for those *in authority* and for those *under authority*. They took it to mean that those in authority should govern wisely and with sacrificial concern for those under their authority. But Doriani found no author in the history of the church prior to the advent of feminism in the last half of the twentieth century who thought that "submitting to one another" in Ephesians 5:21 nullified the authority of the husband within marriage.[8]

OBJECTIONS TO THE EGALITARIAN SENSE OF MUTUAL SUBMISSION IN EPHESIANS 5:21

What exactly is wrong with understanding Ephesians 5:21 to teach mutual submission? There are at least four reasons why I think this understanding is incorrect:

(1) *The following context specifies the kind of submission Paul has in mind*: Paul explains in the following context that wives are to be subject to their husbands (Eph. 5:22-23), children are to be subject to their parents (Eph. 6:1-3), and slaves (or bondservants) are to be subject to their masters (Eph. 6:5-8). These relationships are never reversed. He does not tell husbands to be subject to wives, or parents to be subject to their children (thus nullifying all parental authority!), or masters to be subject to their servants.

In fact, Paul does not tell husbands and wives generally to be subject to each other, nor does he tell wives to be subject to other people's husbands! He says, "Wives, submit to *your own husbands*, as to the Lord" (Eph. 5:22).[9]

Therefore, what Paul has in mind is not a vague kind of mutual submission where everybody is considerate and thoughtful to everybody else, but a specific kind of submission to an authority: the wife is subject to the authority of her own husband. Similarly, parents and children aren't told to practice mutual submission, but children are to be subject to (to "obey") their parents (Eph. 6:1-3), and servants are

---

[8]See Doriani, "Historical Novelty," as mentioned in footnote 2, above.
[9]The Greek text has the adjective *idios*, meaning "your own."

told to be subject to (to "obey") their masters (Eph. 6:5-8). In each case, the person in authority is not told to be subject to the one under authority, but Paul wisely gives guidelines to regulate the use of authority by husbands (who are to love their wives, Eph. 5:25-33), by parents (who are not to provoke their children to anger, Eph. 6:4), and by masters (who are to give up threatening their servants and to remember that they too serve Christ, Eph. 6:9). In no case is there mutual submission; in each case there is submission to authority and regulated use of that authority.

And then Paul says that the kind of submission wives are to exercise is like the submission of the church to Christ: "Now as the church submits to Christ, so also wives should submit in everything to their husbands" (Eph. 5:24). This is surely not a mutual submission, for the church is subject to Christ's authority in a way that Christ is not, and never will be, subject to us.

This clear evidence in the context is why people didn't see mutual submission in Ephesians 5:21 until feminist pressures in our culture led people to look for a way to avoid the force of Ephesians 5:22, "Wives, submit to your own husbands, as to the Lord." For centuries no one thought mutual submission was there in Ephesians 5:21, for they recognized that the verse teaches that we should all be subject to those whom God has put in authority over us—such as husbands, parents, or employers. In this way, Ephesians 5:21 was rightly understood to mean, "being subject to one another (that is, *some to others*), in the fear of Christ."

(2) *The absence of any command for husbands to submit to wives*: There is one more fact that egalitarians cannot explain well when they propose mutual submission as an understanding of this verse. They fail to account for the fact that while wives are several times in the New Testament told to be subject to their husbands (Eph. 5:22-24; Col. 3:18; Titus 2:5; 1 Pet. 3:1-6), the situation is never reversed: *Husbands are never told to be subject to their wives*. Why is this, if Paul wanted to teach mutual submission?

The command that a *husband should be subject to his wife* would have been startling in an ancient male-dominated culture. Therefore, if the New Testament writers thought that Christian marriage required husbands to submit to their wives, they would have had to say that very clearly in their writings—otherwise, no early Christians would have ever known that was what they should do! But nowhere do we find such a command. It is surprising that evangelical feminists can claim that the New Testament teaches this when it is nowhere explicitly stated.

(3) *The meaning of "be subject to" (hypotassō).*

When we look at the word that Paul used when he said "submitting to one another" in Ephesians 5:21, we find that this word (Greek *hypotassō*) in the New Testament is always used for *submission to an authority.* Here are some examples:

• Jesus was subject to the authority of His parents (Luke 2:51).

• Demons were "subject to" the disciples (Luke 10:17; it is clear that the meaning "be considerate of, be thoughtful toward" cannot fit here, for the demons were certainly not considerate of or thoughtful toward the disciples!).

• Citizens are to be "subject to" the governing authorities (Rom. 13:1, 5; see also Titus 3:1; 1 Pet. 2:13).

• The universe is "in subjection" to Christ (1 Cor. 15:27; see also Eph. 1:22).

• Angels and other spiritual beings have been "subjected to" Christ (1 Pet. 3:22).

• Christ is "subjected to" God the Father (1 Cor. 15:28).

• Church members are to be "subject to" the elders in the church (1 Pet. 5:5[10]).

• Wives are told to "submit to" their husbands (Eph. 5:22, 24; Col. 3:18; Titus 2:5; 1 Pet. 3:5).

• The church "submits to" Christ (Eph. 5:24).

• Servants are to be "submissive to" their masters (Titus 2:9; 1 Pet. 2:18).

• Christians are to be "subject to" God (Heb. 12:9; Jas. 4:7).

What this list should demonstrate clearly is that to be "subject to" or "submissive to" someone in the sense that is signified by the word *hypotassō* always means to be subject *to the authority* of that other person. In all of these examples, there is no exception. The subjection is one-directional, and the person who is under authority is subject to the person who has authority over him or her. The relationships indicated by the word *hypotassō* simply do not envision relationships where the

---

[10]First Corinthians 16:15-16 should also be placed in this category, because it seems from 1 Clement 42:4, a letter written from Clement of Rome to the church of Corinth in A.D. 95, that the elders in the church at Corinth came from the household of Stephanas (note the allusion to 1 Cor. 16:15 with the expression "first converts" (Greek *aparchē*). Therefore, when Paul tells the Corinthians to be "subject to" the household of Stephanas, he is telling them to be subject to those who were elders in Corinth.

authority is mutual, or where it is reciprocal, or where it is reversed. It is only one-directional.

Egalitarians have to introduce some new sense for the word *hypotassō*, a sense like "be thoughtful of, be considerate of (someone)." These are good Christian virtues, and we surely should be considerate of one another, but these are simply not what *hypotassō* means.[11]

(4) *The lack of evidence for the egalitarian meaning of hypotassō*: In all of this controversy over roles for men and women, no one has yet produced any examples in ancient Greek literature (either inside or outside the New Testament) where *hypotassō* is applied to a relationship between persons and where it does not carry the sense of being *subject to an authority*.

I have been asking a particular question in one form or another for more than fifteen years now (since I first asked it in the plenary sessions of the 1986 meetings of the Evangelical Theological Society in Atlanta, Georgia), and I have not received an answer yet.[12] The question is

---

[11]With respect to persons, the BDAG lexicon gives the meanings: [active] "to cause to be in a submissive relationship, to subject, to subordinate"; [passive] "become subject . . . subject oneself, be subjected or subordinated, obey" (1042).

Some, such as Gilbert Bilezikian, claim that the meaning of *hypotassō* is changed when the pronoun "to one another" (Greek *allēlous*) is added to it. So Bilezikian says, "The addition . . . of the reciprocal pronoun 'to each other' changes its meaning entirely," 154.

How can he claim that the meaning is changed? He says, "There are several words in the New Testament whose meaning is changed by the addition of the reciprocal pronoun *allēlōn*. Thus, the verb for 'steal' becomes 'deprive' with the addition of the reciprocal pronoun, without any idea of fraud (1 Cor. 7:5). Likewise, the verb for 'worry' becomes 'care for each other' with the reciprocal pronoun (12:25)" (288, n. 30).

However, his argument is incorrect for two reasons. First, the other examples he cites are recognized, established meanings supported in the standard Greek lexicons. But his "change of meaning" for *hypotassō* has no support in the lexicons. Second, his other examples are not parallel to the case of *allēlous*. He fails to realize that what he calls a "change" of sense in 1 Corinthians 7:5 is not due to the presence of the phrase "to one another" but rather to the fact that it is a figurative usage of the word rather than a literal usage. It is the sense we would expect to attach to a figurative usage of the word applied to marital rights rather than to literal stealing of goods (see BDAG, 121). With regard to 1 Corinthians 12:25, Bilezikian's statement is simply incorrect: The meaning is not "changed" by the presence of a reciprocal pronoun, but 1 Corinthians 12:25 is just one of several examples in the New Testament where the sense of *merimnaō* is "to attend to, care for, be concerned about" (see BDAG, 632), and the other verses where it has this sense do not have the reciprocal pronoun.

[12]Some people have sent me e-mails saying that the example I am asking for is found in Ephesians 5:21, where *hypotassō* "obviously" means mutual submission and therefore it can't mean to be subject to an authority. Their claim simply shows that they have not understood the question.

We are not free, in interpreting the Bible, to give a word any meaning we might think "fits." Words have established ranges of meanings that were familiar to native speakers of Greek in the ancient world and that allowed them to understand one another (that is how all language functions—speakers and hearers have in their minds shared meanings of thousands of words). Those established meanings are what are listed in dictionaries (or "lexicons") of ancient Greek. I am simply asking for some evidence showing that "be considerate of" with no idea of submission to an authority was an established, shared meaning of *hypotassō* in the ancient world. No one has produced any evidence.

addressed to our egalitarian friends, and the question is this: Why should we assign to *hypotassō* in the New Testament a meaning ("defer to" or "be considerate of, be thoughtful of") that it is nowhere attested to have, and that no Greek lexicon has ever assigned to it, and that empties it of a meaning (one-directional submission to an authority) that it always has when speaking of relationships between persons?

The question remains to be answered.

The Meaning of "One Another"

The Greek term translated "one another" (the word *allēlous*) can have two different meanings. Sometimes in the New Testament it means something like "everyone to everyone," as we see in verses such as John 13:34, "a new commandment I give to you, that you *love one another.*" Everyone would agree that this means that all Christians are to love all other Christians. It has the sense "everyone to everyone."

But here is the crucial mistake made by egalitarians: They assume that because *allēlous* means "everyone to everyone" in some verses, it must mean that in all verses. When they assume that, they simply have not done their homework—they have not checked out the way the word is used in many other contexts, where it doesn't mean "everyone to everyone," but "some to others."

For example, in Revelation 6:4 the rider on the red horse "was permitted to take peace from the earth, so that men should *slay one another.*" This does not mean that every person first got killed and then got back up and killed the one who had murdered him! It simply means that *some* killed *others.* Here the word *allēlous* does not mean "everyone to everyone" but "some to others."

We see a similar example in Galatians 6:2, "bear *one another's* burdens, and so fulfill the law of Christ." Here Paul does not mean that

---

To claim (as these e-mail writers have claimed to me) that *hypotassō* means something in Ephesians 5:21 that it nowhere meant at any other time or place in history would require (1) that Paul wrote a word with a new, secret meaning that Greek-speaking people had never known before, and (2) that Paul expected that all the Christians in all the churches to which the epistle to the Ephesians went would know this new, secret meaning and understand what he meant, and (3) that they would know that he did not mean by *hypotassō* what all Greek speakers everywhere had previously meant when they used it in conversation and even what Paul himself meant by it in all his other writings, and (4) that all subsequent writers in over 1,900 years of church history have failed to discern this non-authoritative meaning for *hypotassō*, and (5) that the meaning is now suddenly so "obvious" from the context that everyone should see it.

People may believe such a position if they wish, but it will be for reasons other than evidence or facts.

everybody should switch burdens with everybody else, but only that some who are more able should bear the burdens of others who are less able to bear their burdens. And in 1 Corinthians 11:33 Paul says, "When you come together to eat, wait for *one another*." This does not mean that those who come early should wait for those who are late and those who are late should wait for those who are there early! It only means that those who are early should wait for the others who are late. Here again *allēlous* means "some to others"—"some" are to wait for "others." The New Testament has many other examples of this type (see Matt. 24:10; Luke 2:15; 12:1; 24:32; and so forth). In these verses *allēlous* means "some to others."

Therefore, "submitting to one another" in Ephesians 5:21 *can* take the sense "some be subject to others" if the context fits or requires this meaning. And as we have seen above, the word translated "submitting to" (Greek *hypotassō*) requires this sense, because it is never used to speak of a reciprocal relationship between persons but always signifies one-directional submission to an authority.

Therefore we can paraphrase Ephesians 5:21 as follows: "Be subject to others in the church who are in positions of authority over you."[13]

No idea of mutual submission is taught, then, in Ephesians 5:21. The idea itself is self-contradictory if *hypotassō* means here (as it does everywhere else) "be subject to an authority."

The Meaning of Colossians 3:18, Titus 2:5, and 1 Peter 3:1

One other fact warns us that the egalitarian claim of mutual submission should not be used as a magic wand to wave away any claims of male leadership in marriage: There is no statement about "submitting to one another" in the context of Colossians 3:18, Titus 2:5, or 1 Peter 3:1. Yet, as we saw at the outset of this chapter, those verses also explicitly teach wives to be submissive to their husbands. And they say nothing about husbands being submissive to their wives.

This leaves egalitarians in a dilemma. Nothing in these letters would have even hinted to Paul's original readers in Colosse or to Titus and the church in Crete or to Peter's readers in hundreds of churches

---

[13]It is interesting that the King James Version showed an understanding of the sense of *allēlous* in this passage. It translated the verse, "submitting yourselves one to another in the fear of God." In fact, when *allēlous* takes the sense "some to others," the King James Version often signaled that by phrases such as "one to another."

in Asia Minor anything like the mutual submission that egalitarians advocate. But that means (from an egalitarian standpoint) that these three letters would have taught a wrong idea—the idea that wives should submit to the authority of their husbands in marriage. Did the letters of the apostles Paul and Peter then lead the church astray? Would it have been sin for the original readers to obey the letters of Paul and Peter and teach that wives should be subject to their husbands? This would contradict our doctrine of Scripture as the inerrant, absolutely authoritative Word of God.[14]

For all of these reasons, the egalitarian idea of mutual submission in Ephesians 5:21 should be seen as merely a myth. It has no sound basis in the text of Scripture.

PRACTICAL APPLICATION

With respect to your own churches, if you want to add a statement on men and women in marriage to your governing document or publish it as a policy statement (as did the Southern Baptist Convention and Campus Crusade for Christ), and if in the process someone proposes to add the phrase "mutual submission" to the document, I urge you strongly not to agree to it. In the sense that egalitarians understand the phrase "mutual submission," the idea is found nowhere in Scripture, and it actually nullifies the teaching of significant passages of Scripture.

How then should we respond when people say they believe in "mutual submission"? We need to find out what they mean by the phrase, and if they do not wish to advocate an egalitarian view, we need to see if we can suggest alternative wording that would speak to their concerns more precisely. Some people who hold a fully complementarian view of marriage do use the phrase "mutual submission" and intend it in a way that does not nullify male leadership in marriage. I have found that some people who want to use this lan-

---

[14] I agree, of course, that teachings in one part of the Bible can modify or refine our understanding of teachings in another part of the Bible. In this way the teachings of the different sections are complementary. But in the egalitarian claim that mutual submission nullifies a husband's authority and gives an entirely different sense to submission, we are talking not just about a complementary teaching in another part of the Bible but about something that fundamentally denies and even contradicts the meaning of these verses in Colossians, Titus, and 1 Peter. Even if we were to grant Bilezikian's claim that the addition of "to one another" to *hypotassō* "changes its meaning entirely," that would not help him in Colossians, Titus, and 1 Peter, where there is no statement about "one another," but just "wives, be subject to your own husbands."

guage may simply have genuine concerns that men not act like dictators or tyrants in their marriages. If this is what they are seeking to guard against by the phrase "mutual submission," then I suggest trying this alternative wording, which is found in the Campus Crusade for Christ statement:

> In a marriage lived according to these truths, the love between husband and wife will show itself in listening to each other's viewpoints, valuing each other's gifts, wisdom, and desires, honoring one another in public and in private, and always seeking to bring benefit, not harm, to one another.[15]

---

[15]Policy statement announced and distributed to Campus Crusade staff members at a biannual staff conference, July 28, 1999, at Moby Arena, Colorado State University, Fort Collins, Colorado. The statement was reported in a Religion News Service dispatch July 30, 1999, a Baptist Press story by Art Toalston on July 29, 1999 (www.baptistpress.com), and an article in *World* magazine September 11, 1999 (32), and it was also quoted in full in James Dobson's monthly newsletter *Family News from Dr. James Dobson* (Sept. 1999, 1-2). The statement is also reproduced and discussed in Dennis Rainey, *Ministering to Twenty-First Century Families* (Nashville: Word, 2001), 39-56.

Tampering with the Trinity: Does the Son Submit to His Father?[1]

Bruce A. Ware

⸺❦⸺

Introduction

To someone not conversant with contemporary theological writings, it may come as something of a surprise to learn that the historic doctrine of the Trinity is undergoing considerable scrutiny, reassessment, reformulation, and/or defense.[2] To many this doctrine, perhaps as much or more than any other, seems so abstract and unrelated to life that they might wonder just why the interest. What is *here* that would warrant and elicit such concentrated attention? What is at stake in *this doctrine* that would provoke such interest and concern?

To many, what is at stake is simply this: the integrity and reality of the Christian faith itself. Donald Bloesch surprised many in the theological world with the publication in 1985 of his book entitled *The Battle*

---

[1] An expanded and edited version of this chapter will appear as part of a forthcoming chapter, "The Doctrine of the Trinity," in *God Under Fire: Modern Scholarship Reinvents God*, eds. Douglas S. Huffman and Eric L. Johnson (Grand Rapids, MI: Zondervan, upcoming).

[2] Consider a sampling of recently published works, and notice the variety of theological perspectives and interests represented among their authors: Colin E. Gunton, *The Promise of Trinitarian Theology* (Edinburgh: T. & T. Clark, 1991, 2nd ed. 1997); Ted Peters, *God as Trinity: Relationality and Temporality in Divine Life* (Louisville: Westminster/John Knox, 1993); Thomas F. Torrance, *Trinitarian Perspectives: Toward Doctrinal Agreement* (Edinburgh: T. & T. Clark, 1994); Duncan Reid, *Energies of the Spirit: Trinitarian Models in Eastern Orthodox and Western Theology* (Atlanta: Scholars Press, 1997); Kevin Vanhoozer, ed., *The Trinity in a Pluralistic Age: Theological Essays on Culture and Religion* (Grand Rapids, MI: Eerdmans, 1997).

for the Trinity.[3] He charged the feminist rejection of the Bible's and traditional theology's predominantly masculine language for God as a rejection of the Trinity itself and as such the imposition of a different faith (i.e., not the *Christian* faith) onto those quarters of the church inclined to accept the feminist critique. And such charges and concerns have continued unabated. Consider, for example, the sobering words of Duke University Professor of Systematic Theology Geoffrey Wainwright:

> The signs of our times are that, as in the fourth century, the doctrine of the Trinity occupies a pivotal position. While usually still considering themselves within the church, and in any case wanting to be loyal to their perception of truth, various thinkers and activists are seeking such revisions of the inherited doctrine of the Trinity that their success might in fact mean its abandonment, or at least such an alteration of its content, status, and function that the whole face of Christianity would be drastically changed. Once more the understanding, and perhaps the attainment, of salvation is at stake, or certainly the message of the church and the church's visible composition.[4]

What are some of these contemporary proposed revisions of the doctrine of the Trinity that would provoke such strong reaction? This paper proposes to focus on two dimensions of trinitarian reconstruction, both of which are the result of feminist revisionism. First, mainline church rejection of masculine trinitarian language (or any masculine God-language, more generally) has been occurring for nearly three decades. Whether emasculating God's name leaves us with the God named in the Bible will be explored here, with argumentation offered to support traditional and biblical masculine language for the triune God. Second, many contemporary evangelical egalitarians are urging the church to retain masculine language for God while denying that this masculine language indicates any kind of inner-trinitarian distinction of authority. These arguments will be weighed, and support will be offered for the church's long-standing commitment to the trinitarian persons' full equality of essence and differentiation of persons, the lat-

---

[3]Donald Bloesch, *The Battle for the Trinity: The Debate over Inclusive God Language* (Ann Arbor, MI: Servant, 1985).

[4]Geoffrey Wainwright, "The Doctrine of the Trinity: Where the Church Stands or Falls," *Interpretation* 45 (1991), 117.

ter of which includes and entails the eternal functional subordination of the Son to the Father, and of the Spirit to both Father and Son.

MAINLINE FEMINIST REJECTION OF MASCULINE LANGUAGE FOR THE TRIUNE GOD

Central Feminist Arguments for Rejecting Masculine Trinitarian Language

Admittedly a radical representative of the feminist movement, Mary Daly has nonetheless captured the heart of the feminist criticism of the church's biblical and historic adherence to masculine God-language in her claim, "If God is male, the male is god."[5] While *no* respected theologian of the church has claimed that God is *male*, the force of Daly's objection is simply that to refer to God with masculine language gives the impression that masculinity is more Godlike. By this impression, then, women are held in subservient positions and are granted less than their rightful dignity, so it is asserted. The only corrective can be to remove the predominance of masculine God-language from our Scripture, liturgy, and preaching. While some (like Daly herself) have moved to an exclusive use of feminine, earthly, even neo-pagan language for deity, most in the mainline churches who share this fundamental concern call for a balance of masculine and feminine references (e.g., God as Father and Mother) or for a fully gender-neutral language altogether in reference to God (e.g., Creator, Redeemer, Sustainer to replace Father, Son, Holy Spirit).[6]

Only brief attention can be given here to the several lines of argument put forth for inclusive God-language,[7] and our focus will be particularly on the concern over the traditional masculine trinitarian formulation. First, appeal is made to the metaphorical nature of the Bible's own masculine language for God. All agree that when Scripture

---

[5]Mary Daly, *Beyond God the Father: Toward a Philosophy of Women's Liberation* (Boston: Beacon, 1973), 19.

[6]See, e.g., Carol Christ and Judith Plaskow, eds., *Womanspirit Rising: A Feminist Reader in Religion* (San Francisco: Harper & Row, 1979); Virginia Mollenkott, *The Divine Feminine: The Biblical Imagery of God as Female* (New York: Crossroad, 1983); Rosemary Radford Ruether, *Sexism and God-Talk: Toward a Feminist Theology* (Boston: Beacon, 1983); Ruth Duck, *Gender and the Name of God: The Trinitarian Baptismal Formula* (New York: Pilgrim, 1991); Elizabeth Johnson, *She Who Is: The Mystery of God in Feminist Theological Discourse* (New York: Crossroad, 1992); Gail Ramshaw, *God Beyond Gender: Feminist Christian God-Language* (Minneapolis: Fortress, 1995); Aida Besançon Spencer, et. al., *The Goddess Revival* (Grand Rapids, MI: Baker, 1995).

[7]For very careful and thorough study and critique of this argumentation, see Alvin F. Kimel, Jr., ed., *Speaking the Christian God: The Holy Trinity and the Challenge of Feminism* (Grand Rapids, MI: Eerdmans, 1992); and John W. Cooper, *Our Father in Heaven: Christian Faith and Inclusive Language for God* (Grand Rapids, MI: Baker, 1998).

calls God "Father" or "King," we are not to understand by these that God is literally male. These terms function metaphorically to speak of fatherly and kingly functions such as provision, protection, and rulership. So, while God literally is provider, protector, and ruler, He is metaphorically father and king. This being so, feminists argue that we ought, then, to describe God with feminine metaphors that express some other functions of God more characteristically feminine, such as God as comforter, healer, and sympathizer. So while God is (literally) neither father or mother, the metaphors *father* and *mother* are equally appropriate in describing qualities and functions literally true of Him. We ought, then, it is said, to balance feminine names of God with traditional masculine names to give a more complete view of God, or else we ought to avoid such gender-specific terms altogether if the risk is just too great that people might take these to think God *is* a sexual being. As applied to language for the Trinity, feminist advocates have suggested revised language in both directions. Either we should speak of the first person of the Trinity as Father/Mother and the second as the Child of God,[8] or we should move to a strictly gender-neutral trinitarian language, such as Creator, Redeemer and Sustainer. Both approaches are advocated within mainline feminism, and what both have in common is the avoidance of the dominant masculine language for the triune God due to its being both false and misleading.

Second, another important feminist argument claims that when one inquires why both biblical and traditional ecclesial language for God have been predominantly masculine, one immediately realizes the intrinsically culturally conditioned nature of the Bible's and the church's God-talk. Patriarchal culture in biblical days and throughout the history of the church has given rise to this predominantly masculine language for God. For feminism, upon realizing this reality, it seems both obvious and necessary that we work to revamp our God-talk. We can maintain this predominantly masculine language for God only at the expense of perpetuating the illicit patriarchy that gave rise to it. While most mainline feminists would not agree wholly with Mary Daly, they would adjust her claim to say that if God is seen and spoken of as masculine, what is masculine will be viewed, naturally and

---

[8]Note that the early creeds speak of the second person as "begotten, not made," which, as such, contains no gender connotation. So, to speak of the Child begotten of the Father/Mother is consistent with the language of the early church and preserves continuity while making a needed correction.

unavoidably, as of higher value and authority. Again, then, the claim is made that one of two lines of response is needed: Either we must balance traditional masculine usage with appropriate and meaningful feminine language of God, or we should leave behind all gender-specific God referencing altogether.

Third, following from the above two items, feminist political and ideological advancement requires that we reject the biblical and traditional dominance of the masculine in regard to God. The true liberation of women generally, and the cause of women's rights to serve in all levels of church and denominational leadership in particular, can never happen when God, our highest authority and only rightful object of worship, is spoken of in masculine terms. Perpetuating the masculinity of God perpetuates the servile nature of the feminine. Since God is above gender, and since He created both genders in His image, then we dare not continue to focus our discussion of God on one gender, thus subordinating the other as inferior and subservient.

Responding to the Feminist Case Against Masculine Trinitarian Language

Interestingly, many from within mainline churches as well as the majority of evangelical feminists (i.e., egalitarians) from within and without mainline denominations are opposed to this revisionist feminist agenda. While claiming fully to identify with the values and aspirations of Christian feminism, these opponents claim boldly that to change the language of the Bible and church tradition in which God is revealed as Father, Son, and Holy Spirit is to jeopardize the integrity of Christianity itself and to promote what is truly, in fact, another deity and another faith.[9] Their argumentation is complex and involved, but we will sketch some of their main concerns.

First, while it is true that the Bible uses masculine metaphorical language for naming God (though God is never literally male), it is also true that the Bible never employs feminine metaphorical language to *name* God. True, God is sometimes said to be or act in ways *like* a mother (or some other feminine image),[10] but never is God called

---

[9]Note the telling title of an article opposed to feminist God-language revisionism, viz., Elizabeth Achtemeier, "Exchanging God for 'No Gods': A Discussion of Female Language for God," in Kimel, ed., *Speaking the Christian God*, 1-16.

[10]For an exhaustive discussion of biblical references to God employing feminine imagery, see Cooper, *Our Father in Heaven*, chapter 3, "The Bible's Feminine and Maternal References to God," 65-90.

"Mother" as He is often called "Father." Respect for God's self-portrayal in Scripture requires that we respect this distinction. While we have every right (and responsibility) to employ feminine images as analogies to some aspects of God's nature and ways, as is done often in Scripture itself, we are not permitted, by biblical precedence, to go further and to name God in ways He has not named Himself. He has named Himself "Father" but not "Mother." This stubborn fact of scriptural revelation must itself restrain our talk of God.

Second, one might be tempted to dismiss the above "factual" point by appeal to the inherently patriarchal culture in which our biblical language of God was framed. But appeal to culture shows just how odd and even unique it is that Israel chose to use only masculine (and *not* feminine) language when naming God. The fact is that the most natural route Israel might have taken is to follow the lead of the nations surrounding her, which spoke with regularity and frequency of their deities as feminine.[11] That Israel chose not to do this shows her resistance to follow natural and strong cultural pressures, and it indicates that she conceived of the true God, the God of Israel, as distinct from these false deities.

In defending her assertion that "the Bible's language for God is masculine, a unique revelation of God in the world," Elizabeth Achtemeier continues:

> The basic reason for that designation of God is that the God of the Bible will not let himself be identified with his creation, and therefore human beings are to worship not the creation but the Creator. . . . It is precisely the introduction of female language for God that opens the door to such identification of God with the world, however.[12]

Whether one follows Achtemeier here fully or not,[13] what is clear is that Scripture never names God as "Mother" or with any other fem-

---

[11]Elaine Pagels, "What Became of God the Mother? Conflicting Images of God in Early Christianity," in Christ and Plaskow, eds., *Womanspirit Rising*, 107 comments that "the absence of feminine symbolism of God marks Judaism, Christianity, and Islam in striking contrast to the world's other religious traditions, whether in Egypt, Babylonia, Greece and Rome, or Africa, Polynesia, India, and North America."

[12]Achtemeier, "Exchanging God for 'No Gods,'" 8-9.

[13]See, ibid., 12, where Achtemeier acknowledges that many feminists deny that naming God as feminine links God with creation but asserts and then supports with numerous citations her claim, "But feminist writings themselves demonstrate that it does."

inine ascription, and this stands clearly against the prevailing practice of the cultures surrounding Israel and the early church.

Third, while Scripture surely does reflect the various cultural and historical settings in which it was written, the God of the Bible is presented, ultimately, by self-revelation or self-disclosure. The Bible's language of God, then, must be received with respect and gratitude as the divinely ordained conveyer of the truth God Himself intended His people to know about Him. To alter biblical language for God is to deny and reject God's self-disclosure in the terms that He chose and that He used in making Himself known to us. Clearly, at the pinnacle of this self-disclosure of God stands the revelation of Jesus the Christ who became flesh that we might know in visible, physical form what God is like (John 1:14-18). And throughout His ministry, with shocking regularity, Jesus refers to God, in a manner scandalous to His Jewish listeners, as none other than "Father." That Jesus is the *Son* sent by the *Father* is so deeply and widely reflective of God's self-revelation in and through the Incarnation that to alter this language is to suggest, even if only implicitly, that one speaks instead of a different deity. Divine self-revelation, then, requires the glad retention of God as Father, Son, and Holy Spirit.

Fourth, one last caution will be mentioned. For revisionist feminism, it may be granted that biblical language speaks of the triune God as Father, Son, and Holy Spirit. But, these revisionists continue, those same Scriptures also employ the language of God as creator, redeemer, and Sustainer. May we not use in the church this other biblical language of God and by so doing both honor God's self-revelation and avoid the illicit equation of God with masculinity that the traditional masculine language risks? While the terms *creator, redeemer,* and *sustainer* are biblical terms for God, they cannot function as substitutes for the persons of the Godhead named as Father, Son, and Holy Spirit.

There are at least three reasons why this substitution is unacceptable. First, one risks a modalistic understanding of God when He is first creator and then changes to the next historical phase of redeemer and likewise then to sustainer. The phases and aspects of activity can easily be seen as historical modes of the manifestation of the one God, as has been advocated by Sabellius and other modalists.

Second, since these terms refer to God's relationship to the world, this substitution implies that the world is eternal, not temporally finite, and that God's redemptive work is necessary, not free. The church's affirmation of God as "Father, Son, Spirit" is a claim not merely of His economic manifestation as the Father of the incarnate Son in the power of the Spirit (though this is true, in part), but also of the immanent trinity[14] who is *eternally* Father, Son, and Spirit. The Father, then, is the *eternal* Father of the Son; the Son is the *eternal* Son of the Father. Now, if we substitute "creator, redeemer, sustainer" as names for these *eternal* realities, it requires that we see God as eternal creator, implying an eternal creation, and as eternal redeemer, implying necessary redemption. It is clear that while "Father, Son, Spirit" work well as names of the immanent and economic trinitarian persons, "creator, redeemer, sustainer" are merely economic and functional designations. As such, they simply cannot substitute for the language of Scripture and church tradition for the eternal God who is in Himself (i.e., immanently and eternally) and in relation to creation (i.e., economically) Father, Son, and Spirit.

Third, the personal names of Father, Son, and Holy Spirit simply do not reduce to the supposed functional substitutes of creator, redeemer, and sustainer.[15] Is the Father and the Father alone the Creator? Is the Son alone the Redeemer? Is the Spirit alone the Sustainer? Biblical teaching instructs us that each of these activities is accomplished by all three divine persons working together. Yes, the Father creates, but He does so through the power of His Word (John 1:3) who acts as implementer of His creative design (Col. 1:16). The Spirit, likewise, energizes the formation of the creative work of the Father through the Son (Gen. 1:2). Redemption, likewise, is destroyed altogether if the work of redemption is reduced to that of the second person of the Trinity. Biblically, redemption only occurs as the Father sends the Son into the world to receive the wrath of the Father against Him for our sin (2 Cor. 5:21). And, of course, the Son accomplishes this work only by the power of the Spirit who rests on Him and empowers Him to go to the cross (Heb. 9:14) and raises Him from the dead (Rom. 8:11). Likewise, sustaining and sanctifying is the work of the Father (1 Thess. 5:23-24) and the Son (Eph. 5:25-27) and the Holy

---

[14]In most contemporary discussions of the Trinity, "immanent trinity" refers to the eternal ontological existence and intra-trinitarian relationships of the three divine persons within the Godhead, apart from creation; "economic trinity" refers to the temporally framed relations of the three divine persons to the created order.

[15]Karl Barth, *Church Dogmatics*, 4 vols. in 13 parts (Edinburgh: T. & T. Clark, 1936-1969), I.2., 878-879, writes: "The content of the doctrine of the Trinity . . . is not that God in His relation to man is Creator, Mediator and Redeemer, but that God in Himself is eternally God the Father, Son and Holy Spirit. . . . [God] cannot be dissolved into His work and activity."

Spirit (2 Cor. 3:18) to preserve believers and move them toward the holiness of life and character designed for them from all eternity (Eph. 1:4). One realizes that the substitution of "creator, redeemer, and sustainer" for "Father, Son, and Holy Spirit" not only fails as a functional equivalent of the traditional and biblical trinitarian formula, but worse, if followed it would result in such major theological distortions that the faith that would result would bear only a superficial resemblance to the faith of true biblical and Christian religion. In the words of Geoffrey Wainwright, "Consideration of creation, redemption, and sanctification shows that an account of them that is true to the biblical narrative will also imply and depend on the trinitarian communion and cooperation of Father, Son, and Holy Spirit."[16]

EVANGELICAL FEMINISM'S REJECTION OF ETERNAL FUNCTIONAL SUBORDINATIONISM WITHIN THE TRIUNE GOD

Evangelical Feminism's Embrace of Masculine Trinitarian Language and Rejection of Inner Trinitarian Functional Subordination

Evangelical feminists, otherwise known as egalitarians, have generally favored retaining traditional masculine trinitarian language. For reasons given above, particularly because Scripture is for egalitarians God's inspired Word and self-revelation, the vast majority of egalitarians have sought to defend masculine God-language against the criticism of many of their feminist colleagues.[17] In the process, however, they deny that such masculine God-language has any implications either 1) of superiority of what is masculine over feminine, or 2) that the eternal relations of Father, Son, and Holy Spirit indicate any kind of eternal functional hierarchy within the Trinity.

Let it be said clearly that non-egalitarian, complementarian[18] evangelicals agree wholly with the first of these denials. Because God created the man and the woman fully in His image (Gen. 1:26-27), it is clear that no use of masculine language for God is meant to signal some

---

[16]Wainwright, "Doctrine of the Trinity," 123.

[17]Not all egalitarians are so convinced. See, e.g., Ruth A. Tucker, *Women in the Maze* (Grand Rapids, MI: Baker, 1992), 20-21, where Tucker encourages Christians to call God "Mother" in private, but not in public, worship.

[18]The term *complementarian* is the self-designation of the evangelical constituency that would see God's created design for men and women as comprising male headship in the created order, reflecting itself in the requirement of a qualified male eldership in the church and the husband's overarching responsibility in the leadership of the home. The single best volume describing and defending a complementarian vision is John Piper and Wayne Grudem, eds., *Recovering Biblical Manhood and Womanhood* (Wheaton, IL: Crossway Books, 1991).

supposed greater value, dignity, or worth of men over women. Furthermore, that women and men alike are redeemed by the Savior and that the believing husband is to grant his believing wife honor as "a fellow heir of the grace of life" (1 Pet. 3:7) further indicates the full equality of personhood and worth vested in women and men, through both creation and redemption, by our gracious God. Egalitarian and complementarian evangelicals agree, then, that the Bible's masculine God-language in no way indicates the essential superiority or greater value of male over female. Both men and women are, in creation and redemption, prized, sought, and loved by God equally; women with men stand before God equal in standing, dignity, worth, and human personhood.

Concerning the second denial, however, there is significant reason to challenge the egalitarian position. If, as egalitarians argue, the masculine language of God in Scripture is not a concession to a patriarchal culture but represents rather God's own chosen means of self-disclosure, what *is* conveyed by this masculine terminology? Does this masculine language not intentionally link God's position and authority as *God* with the concept of *masculinity* in distinction from femininity? Furthermore, what *does* it mean that the Father is the eternal *Father* of the Son, and that the Son is the eternal *Son* of the Father? Is not the Father-Son relationship within the immanent Trinity indicative of some eternal relationship of authority *within* the Trinity itself?

Egalitarians reject these implications.[19] They see clearly that if an eternal relationship of authority and obedience is grounded in the eternal, immanent, inner-trinitarian relations of Father, Son, and Holy Spirit, then this gives at least *prima facie* justification to the notion of creational human relations in which authority and submission inhere.[20] And yet both features of the orthodox view mentioned above might seem to suggest such a correspondence. That is, both the predominant masculine language for God and the eternal nature of the Father-Son

---

[19]See, e.g., Gilbert Bilezikian, "Hermeneutical Bungee-Jumping: Subordination in the Godhead," *Journal of the Evangelical Theological Society (JETS)*, 40/1 (March 1997), 57-68; and Stanley J. Grenz, "Theological Foundations for Male-Female Relationships," *JETS* 41/4 (December 1998), 615-630; Royce G. Gruenler, *The Trinity in the Gospel of John: A Thematic Commentary on the Fourth Gospel* (Grand Rapids, MI: Baker, 1986); and Millard Erickson, *God in Three Persons: A Contemporary Interpretation of the Trinity* (Grand Rapids, MI: Baker, 1995).

[20]Some egalitarians acknowledge the eternal inner-trinitarian Father-Son relation, yet do not understand this as implying or entailing relations of authority and submission in the created order. See Craig Keener, "Is Subordination Within the Trinity Really Heresy? A Study of John 5:18 in Context," *Trinity Journal* 20 NS (1999), 39-51.

relationship within the Godhead could lead one to think that authority and obedience is rooted in the Trinity and that authority in some special way corresponds to masculinity.

To counter these lines of thought, egalitarians argue fundamentally along three lines. First, they assert that the predominant masculine references to God in no way convey some corresponding authority attaching to the male. As already seen in the previous section, the appeal to woman and man being created fully in the image of God indicates no such subordination of the female to the male. Equality (only) characterizes their relation as human persons. As Paul Jewett has put it, to affirm the functional subordination of women to men in any respect cannot avoid the charge that women are thereby inferior to men.[21] But the creation of woman and man in the image of God renders this impossible. Masculinity is never inherently superior, though it is, admittedly, the gender in which God has chosen to name Himself most commonly.

Second, they assert that any suggestion of subordination within the Godhead, even the claim of a functional subordination of the Son to the Father, cannot avoid at least an implicit Arianism.[22] The early church theologians, it is argued, rejected all talk of subordination regarding any member of the Trinity to any other. Full equality of Father, Son, and Holy Spirit precludes any and all types of subordinationism. Since the Son is *homoousios* with the Father, we are wrong ever to speak of the Son's subordinate status to the Father and by so doing undermine the orthodoxy won by Athanasius at Nicea and affirmed ever since by the church.

Third, they claim that all of Scripture's language of the authority of the Father and submission of the Son is only rightly accounted for within the incarnational mission of the Son. Here, as God having taken on human flesh, precisely because Christ was the second Adam and fully human, it was necessary for Him to subject Himself to the will of

---

[21]See, e.g., Paul K. Jewett, *Man as Male and Female: A Study of Relationships from a Theological Point of View* (Grand Rapids, MI: Eerdmans, 1975), where he asks, "how can one defend a sexual hierarchy whereby men are over women . . . without supposing that the half of the human race which exercises authority is superior in some way to the half which submits?" (71). He continues by asking further whether anyone can "establish the mooted point—woman's *subordination to* the man—by underscoring the obvious point—woman's *difference from* the man—without the help of the traditional point—woman's *inferiority to* the man? The answer, it appears to us, is no" (84).

[22]Bilezikian, "Hermeneutical Bungee-Jumping," 67 says, e.g., that any talk about subordination "smacks of the Arian heresy."

244 BIBLICAL FOUNDATIONS FOR MANHOOD AND WOMANHOOD

the Father. Thus, as Gilbert Bilezikian states, "Christ did not take upon himself the task of world redemption because he was number two in the Trinity and his boss told him to do so or because he was demoted to a subordinate rank so that he could accomplish a job that no one else wanted to touch."[23] Furthermore, when the mission of redemption was completed, the Son resumed His former stature and full equality within the Trinity, leaving forever behind the role in which He had to submit Himself in obedience to the Father. As Bilezikian again comments, "Because there was no subordination within the Trinity prior to the Second Person's incarnation, there will remain no such thing after its completion. If we must talk of subordination it is only a functional or economic subordination that pertains exclusively to Christ's role in relation to human history."[24] So while masculine language predominates in the biblical depiction for God, and while the divine Father-Son relationship is eternal, none of this indicates a relationship of authority and obedience in the Godhead or a corresponding relationship of authority and submission in human relationships, according to egalitarian reasoning.

Response to the Egalitarian Embrace of Masculine Trinitarian Language and Rejection of Inner Trinitarian Functional Subordination

First, it appears that egalitarianism is in a difficult position. It affirms the predominance of masculine biblical references for God, and yet it seems incapable, logically, to explain this divinely chosen use of masculine language. Granted, one can argue, as we have seen earlier with Achtemeier, that referring to God in feminine language would result in a confusion between the Creator and creation. But must this be so? Even Achtemeier admits it need not, while she is convinced it likely will. But if God Himself thought and believed as egalitarians do, could He not overcome this supposed faulty Creator-creature confusion that might be drawn if He chose, deliberately, to employ masculine and feminine metaphors in equal proportion? Certainly He could make clear, as He has, that He is Spirit and so not a sexual or gendered being. Furthermore, He could make clear that when He refers to Himself as Mother, He is not by this conveying an ontological connection with the world. So I find it difficult to accept this as a full or adequate answer to

---

[23]Ibid., 59.
[24]Ibid., 60.

the question of why God chose to name Himself in masculine, but never feminine, terms.

Another obvious reason exists, one that egalitarians seem to bump up against regularly without acknowledging it for what it is. For example, in Wainwright's musing over God as "Father" he notes that "'Father' was the name that the second person in his human existence considered most appropriate as an address to the first person." But why is this? To this question, Wainwright can only say that *"there must be . . . something* about human fatherhood that makes Father a suitable way for Jesus to designate the one who sent him. In trinitarian terms, the crucial point is that Father was the address Jesus characteristically used in this connection."[25] However, just what the "something" is, Wainwright does not tell us. But is it not obvious? Jesus said over and again throughout His ministry that He was *sent* to do the will of His *Father* (e.g., John 4:34; 5:23, 30, 37; 6:37-38, 57; and 12:49). Clearly, a central part of the notion of "Father" is that of fatherly authority. Certainly this is not all there is to being a father, but while there is more, there certainly is not less or other. The masculine terminology used of God throughout Scripture conveyed within the patriarchal cultures of Israel and the early church the obvious point that God, portrayed in masculine ways, had authority over His people. "Father," "king," and "Lord" conveyed, by their masculine gender referencing, a rightful authority that was to be respected and followed. Malachi 1:6, for example, indicates just this connection between "father" and authority: "'A son honors his father, and a servant his master. If I am a father, where is the honor due me? If I am a master, where is the respect due me?' says the LORD Almighty" (NIV). God as Father is rightfully deserving of His children's honor, respect, and obedience. To fail to see this is to miss one of the primary reasons God chose such masculine terminology to name Himself.

Second, while the early church clearly embraced the full essential equality of the three trinitarian persons (because each of the three divine persons possesses fully and simultaneously the identically same infinite divine nature), nonetheless the church has always affirmed likewise the priority of the Father over the Son and Spirit. Since this priority cannot rightly be understood in terms of essence or nature (lest one fall into Arian subordinationism), it must exist in terms of

---

[25]Wainwright, "Doctrine of the Trinity," 120 (italics added).

relationship.[26] As Augustine affirmed, the distinction of persons is constituted precisely by the differing relations among them, in part manifest by the inherent authority of the Father and the inherent submission of the Son. This is most clearly seen in the eternal Father-Son relationship, in which the Father is eternally the Father of the Son, and the Son is eternally the Son of the Father. But, some might wonder, does this convey an eternal authority of the Father and eternal submission of the Son? Hear how Augustine discusses both the essential equality of the Father and Son and the mission of the Son who was sent, in eternity past, to obey and carry out the will of the Father:

> If however the reason why the Son is said to have been sent by the Father is simply that the one is the Father and the other the Son then there is nothing at all to stop us believing that the *Son is equal to the Father* and consubstantial and co-eternal, and yet that the Son is sent by the Father. Not because one is greater and the other less, but because one is the Father and the other the Son; one is the begetter, the other begotten; the first is the one from whom the sent one is; the other is the one who is from the sender. For the Son is from the Father, not the Father from the Son. In the light of this we can now perceive that *the Son is not just said to have been sent because the Word became flesh, but that he was sent in order for the Word to become flesh*, and by his bodily presence to do all that was written. That is, we should understand that *it was not just the man who the Word became that was sent, but that the Word was sent to become man*. For he was *not sent in virtue of some disparity of power or substance or anything in him that was not equal to the Father*, but in virtue of the Son being from the Father, not the Father being from the Son.[27]

---

[26]For a discussion of evidence that early church theology upheld the simultaneous eternal equality of essence *and* the functional relationship of authority and obedience among the persons of the triune Godhead, see also Robert Letham, "The Man-Woman Debate: Theological Comment," *Westminster Theological Journal* 52 (1990), 65-78; and Stephen D. Kovach and Peter R. Schemm, Jr., "A Defense of the Doctrine of the Eternal Subordination of the Son," *JETS* 42/3 (September 1999), 461-476. In limited space, Kovach and Schemm cite examples from Hilary of Poitiers, Athanasius, the Cappadocian fathers, and Augustine, with supporting commentary from John Calvin, Philip Schaff, Jaroslav Pelikan, J. N. D. Kelly, Charles Hodge, and W. G. T. Shedd, and they cite (471) the conclusion of Paul Rainbow, "Orthodox Trinitarianism and Evangelical Feminism," 4 (unpublished paper based on his dissertation, "Monotheism and Christology in 1 Corinthians 8:4-6" [D.Phil. dissertation, Oxford University, 1987]), in which Rainbow concludes, "From the earliest form of the creed we can see that the Father and the Son are united in being, but ranked in function."

[27]St. Augustine, *The Trinity*, trans. Edmund Hill, Vol. 5, *The Works of St. Augustine* (Brooklyn: New City Press, 1991), IV.27 (italics added).

Notice two observations from Augustine's statement. First, Augustine sees no disparity between affirming, on the one hand, the full *equality* of the Son to the Father, and on the other hand, the Son's eternal position as *from* the Father, whose responsibility it is to carry out the will of the Father as the one *sent* from all eternity from the Father. Jewett's claim that functional subordination entails essential inferiority is here denied by Augustine. Second, notice that Augustine denies Bilezikian's claim that all subordination of the Son to the Father rests fully in the Son's incarnate state. To the contrary, Augustine affirms that "the Son is not just said to have been sent because the Word became flesh, but that he was sent in order for the Word to become flesh." In other words, the decree to send the Son occurred in eternity past in order that the eternal Word, sent from on high from the Father, might take on human flesh and then continue His role of carrying out the will of His Father.

As P. T. Forsyth writes, the beauty of the Son's simultaneous equality with and obedience to the Father expresses the willing service God intends His people to render. Forsyth asserts that "subordination is *not* inferiority, and it *is* Godlike. The principle is imbedded in the very cohesion of the eternal trinity and it is inseparable from the unity, fraternity and true equality of men. It is not a mark of inferiority to be subordinate, to have an authority, to obey. It is divine."[28] And in another place Forsyth makes clear that the Son's obedience to the Father was indeed an eternal obedience, rendered by an eternal equal, constituting an eternal subordination of the Son to do the will of the Father. He writes:

> Father and Son co-exist, co-equal in the Spirit of holiness, i.e., of perfection. But Father and Son is a relation inconceivable except the Son be obedient to the Father. The perfection of the Son and the perfecting of his holy work lay, not in his suffering but in his obedience. And, as he was eternal Son, it meant an eternal obedience. . . . But obedience is not conceivable without some form of subordination. Yet in his very obedience the Son was co-equal with the Father; the Son's yielding will was no less divine than the Father's exigent will. Therefore, in the very nature of God, subordination implies no inferiority.[29]

---

[28]P. T. Forsyth, *God the Holy Father* (1897; reprint, London: Independent Press, 1957), 42.

[29]P. T. Forsyth, *Marriage, Its Ethic and Religion* (London: Hodder and Stoughton, 1912), 70-71.

Third, the egalitarian denial of any eternal submission of the Son to the Father makes it impossible to answer the question why it was the "Son" and not the "Father" or "Spirit" who was sent to become incarnate. And even more basic is the question why the eternal names for "Father" and "Son" would be exactly *these* names. John Thompson has indicated a trend in much modern trinitarian discussion to separate Christology from trinitarian formulations. He writes that "Christology and the Trinity were virtually divorced. It was both stated and assumed that any one of the three persons could become incarnate. . . . There was thus only an accidental relation between the economy of revelation and redemption and the eternal triune being of God."[30] It appears that contemporary egalitarianism is vulnerable also to this criticism. Since nothing *in God* grounds the Son's being the Son of the Father, and since every aspect of the Son's earthly submission to the Father is divorced altogether from any *eternal relation* that exists between the Father and Son, there simply is no reason why the *Father* should send the *Son*. In Thompson's words, it appears that the egalitarian view would permit "any one of the three persons" to become incarnate. And yet we have scriptural revelation that clearly says the Son came down out of heaven to do the will of His Father. This sending is not *ad hoc*. In eternity, the Father commissioned the Son who then willingly laid aside the glory He had with the Father to come and purchase our pardon and renewal. Such glory is diminished if there is no eternal Father-Son relation on the basis of which the Father sends, the Son willingly comes, and the Spirit willingly empowers.

And finally, what biblical evidence exists for the eternal functional subordination of the Son to the Father? A running theme in the history of this doctrine (as seen above in Augustine and Forsyth) is that the Son was commissioned by the Father in *eternity past* to come as the incarnate Son. As Jesus declares on well over thirty occasions in John's Gospel, He was *sent to the earth* by the Father to do the Father's will. Could this be reduced merely to the sending of the *incarnate* Son to fulfill the Father's mission for Him now that He has already come into the world? Or should we think of this sending, this commissioning, as having taken place in *eternity past*, a commissioning that then is fulfilled in time? Scripture, it seems clear, demands the latter view.

Consider, for example, Peter's statement in his Pentecost sermon

---

[30]John Thompson, *Modern Trinitarian Perspectives* (New York: Oxford University Press, 1994), 22.

recorded in Acts 2. Concerning Christ, he says, "This man was handed over to you by God's set purpose and foreknowledge; and you, with the help of wicked men, put him to death by nailing him to the cross" (Acts 2:23, NIV). The crucifixion of Christ fulfilled God's "set purpose" that He established far in advance of the actual incarnation. Though this verse alone does not tell us exactly how far back God's plan was set, we know from numerous biblical prophecies (e.g., Ps. 22; Isa. 9:6-7; 53; Mic. 5:2, to name a select few of the most notable) that God had planned and predicted, long before the Incarnation, precisely the birth, life, death, and ultimate triumph of the Son. If Christ's coming fulfilled God's "set purpose," and this purpose was established long in advance of the Incarnation, then it is clear that the commissioning of the Son occurred in Christ's relation with the Father in the immanent Trinity and not after He had come as the incarnate Son.

Consider another of Peter's claims. In regard to Christ's redemptive work, Peter writes, "He [Christ] was chosen before the creation of the world, but was revealed in these last times for your sake" (1 Pet. 1:20, NIV). If we wonder how far back this commissioning of the Son took place, this verse settles the question. Before the world was made, the Father chose (literally, "foreknew") the Son to come as the Redeemer. The Son's coming in time to shed His blood reflects not an *ad hoc* decision or a toss of the trinitarian coin but the eternal purpose of the *Father* to send and offer His *Son*.

Ephesians 1:3-5 and Revelation 13:8 confirm this understanding. In Ephesians 1, Paul gives praise to God the *Father* for choosing His own *in Christ* before the foundation of the world, and for predestining them to adoption as sons *through Jesus Christ* to Himself:

> *Blessed be the God and Father of our Lord Jesus Christ, who has blessed us with every spiritual blessing in the heavenly places in Christ, just as He chose us in Him before the foundation of the world, that we would be holy and blameless before Him. In love He predestined us to adoption as sons through Jesus Christ to Himself, according to the kind intention of His will.*

Since Paul specifically 1) gives praise to the *Father* for this election and predestination, 2) designates *Christ* as the one toward whom our election and predestination is directed, and 3) states that the Father's elective purpose and plan occurred before the creation of the world, it follows that the Father's commissioning of the Son is based in eternity past, and that the Son's submission to the Father is rooted in their eternal relationship within the Godhead. Revelation 13:8 likewise indicates that "the book of life" in which believers' names have been recorded is 1) "from the *foundation of the world*" and 2) is "*of the Lamb who has been slain.*" Again we see clear evidence that the Father's purpose from eternity past was to send His Son, the Lamb of God, by which His own would be saved. The authority-obedience relation of Father and Son in the immanent Trinity is mandatory if we are to account for God the Father's eternal purpose to elect and save His people through His beloved Son.

But will Christ one day, as Bilezikian argues, be elevated to the same status or equality of role as that of the Father? Consider Paul's discussion of the consummation of Christ's reconciling work in a day yet future. In 1 Corinthians 15:27-28 he writes:

> *For he [the Father] "has put everything under his [Christ's] feet."
> Now when it says that "everything" has been put under him, it is clear
> that this does not include God himself, who put everything under
> Christ. When he has done this, then the Son himself will be made
> subject to him who put everything under him, so that God may be all
> in all.* (NIV)

Because Christ was commissioned in eternity past to come, in time and history, to carry out the will of His Father, when this work is completed, Christ will place Himself in the very position He had with the Father previously. While possessing again the full glory of the Father (John 17:5), He will put Himself in subjection to the Father (1 Cor. 15:28). The relation of the Father and Son in eternity past, in Christ's historic and incarnate life, and in eternity future, then, is the same.[31] Christ is fully equal in essence with the Father, yet subordinate in role. Scripture clearly upholds these truths, and we in the church should likewise do the same.

---

[31]In light of this discussion, recall again the astonishing words of Gilbert Bilezikian, quoted earlier: "Because there was no subordination within the Trinity prior to the Second Person's incarnation, there will remain no such thing after its completion. If we must talk of subordination it is only a functional or economic subordination that pertains exclusively to Christ's role in relation to human history" ("Hermeneutical Bungee-Jumping," 60).

CONCLUSION

We have examined two areas where significant and widespread revisionism is currently taking place in the doctrine of the Trinity: mainline feminism's rejection of Scripture's predominantly masculine trinitarian language, and evangelical feminism's rejection of the eternal inner-trinitarian relations of authority and obedience. Each of these areas calls for great care by thoughtful and prayerful Christian people. Because we have God's inspired Word, and because God has, in this Word, made His own triune life known, we must with renewed commitment seek to study, believe, and embrace the truth of God as made known there. Where we have been misled by the history of this doctrine, may Scripture lead to correction. But where contemporary revision departs from Scripture's clear teaching, may we have courage to stand with the truth and for the truth. For the sake of the glory of the only true and living God, who is Father, Son, and Holy Spirit, may we pledge to Him alone our fidelity, obedience, and love.

ADDENDUM: POINTS OF PRACTICAL APPLICATION

1. *Embrace rightful authority structures.* Because the structure of authority and obedience is not only established by God but is, even more, possessed in God's own inner trinitarian life, as the Father establishes His will and the Son joyfully obeys, therefore we should not despise but should embrace proper lines of authority and obedience. In the home, believing community, and society, rightful lines of authority are good, wise, and beautiful reflections of the reality that is God Himself. This applies to those in positions of God-ordained submission and obedience who need, then, to accept joyfully these proper roles of submission. It applies equally to those in God-ordained positions of authority who need to embrace the proper roles of their responsible authority and exercise that authority as unto the Lord.

2. *View both authority and submission as Godlike.* With P. T. Forsyth, we need to see not only authority but also submission as Godlike. We more readily associate God with authority, but since the Son is the *eternal Son* of the Father, and since the Son is *eternally God*, then it follows that the inner-trinitarian nature of God honors both authority and submission. Just as it is Godlike to lead responsibly and well, so

it is Godlike to submit in human relationships where this is required. It is Godlike for wives to submit to their husbands; it is Godlike for children to obey their parents; it is Godlike for church members to follow the directives of their godly male eldership. Consider Philippians 2:5-11, and see the pattern of Godlike submission demonstrated there. We honor God as we model both sides of the authority-submission relationship that characterizes the trinitarian persons themselves.

3. *Revive the wholesome and biblical concept of God as Father.* As Jesus instructed us in His model prayer (i.e., the Lord's prayer), we are to pray to "our Father which art in heaven" (KJV). The concept and reality of God as Father is so very glorious, and we dare not lose this article of the church's faith and practice because of abusive fatherhood or cultural confusion over what fatherhood is. "God as Father" invokes two counterbalancing and complementary ideas: *reverence* (e.g., "hallowed be thy name") and *reliance* (e.g., "give us this day our daily bread"). God as Father deserves our highest and unqualified respect and devotion, and He deserves our absolute trust and dependence. Devotion to and dependence on God as Father captures, at heart, the whole of what our life before Him is to be.

4. *Our common adoption into God's family is as sons.* All of us, as children of God, need to embrace God's rightful authority over our lives. We are all sons of God (*uioi theou*) through faith in Jesus Christ (Gal. 3:26), and as sons we must see our role, as with the role of the eternal Son, always and only to submit to the will of our Father. Paradoxically, when we obey fully, we enter fully into life as God created it to be. As Jesus said, "If you keep My commandments, you will abide in My love, just as I have kept My Father's commandments and abide in His love. These things I have spoken to you so that My joy may be in you, and that your joy may be made full" (John 15:10-11). We are to obey without reservation, fully, and with great anticipation of blessing, for as we obey, we enter into full and lasting joy.

5. *Our worship is of the Triune God, equal in essence, yet distinct in role.* The beauty and harmony of God's created design of diversity in unity (as seen, e.g., in marriage and in the body of Christ) is rooted eternally and immutably in God Himself. We only worship God when we uphold Him *as He is.* If, in our relationships, we despise unity and "celebrate diversity" that is fragmented and disjointed or despise diversity by insisting on a uniformity that denies created and God-ordained dif-

ferences, we will not value God for *who* He is, and so we will not honor Him *as* he is. In God, diversity of persons serves a unity of purpose, method, and goal. The will of the Father is gladly carried out by the Son. When the Spirit comes, it is His joy to do the will of the Son. In purpose they are united, in roles they are distinct, and in *both* (purpose and role) there is glad acceptance. Together the three persons model what our diversity in unity of relationship should look like and how our lives together are to be lived.

IV

STANDING AGAINST
THE CULTURE

9

SEXUAL PERVERSION: THE NECESSARY FRUIT OF NEO-PAGAN SPIRITUALITY IN THE CULTURE AT LARGE

Peter R. Jones

———

INTRODUCTION: THE GATHERING PAGAN STORM IN ONCE-"CHRISTIAN" AMERICA

The most radical American Revolution took place not in 1776 but in the last generation of the twentieth century. In those last thirty or so years we witnessed the First Great Awakening—of Paganism. It deconstructed western Christendom and produced a radical transformation of once-"Christian" America.

At the street level, the marginal student revolutionaries of the sixties, who rejected the American political system, took political power in the nineties, and their extremist ideas are now mainstream "moderate." They defined sin as social oppression and sought redemption in social structures. This search liberated the individual from personal guilt. For many, redemption became synonymous with sexual liberation. Radical feminists demanded that their sisters be "sinarticulate," have the "courage to sin," and "liberate the inner slut." Sexuality was liberated from its traditional conjugal confines, with the inevitable explosion of the divorce rate; now over 40 percent of first marriages end in divorce.[1] Rampant divorce has virtually destroyed normative

---

[1] See *Time* (Sept. 25, 2000), 76-77.

marriage and the two-parent family. Barbara Dafoe Whitehead has written *The Divorce Culture*[2] to describe modern America. The University of Chicago issued a report (November 24, 1999) showing that in 1972, 46 percent of Americans lived in traditional families (two parents with children). Currently only 26 percent do. Cohabiting couples have increased 700 percent since 1970.[3] Presently one third of all babies are born out of wedlock.

A University of Michigan study indicates that living together without benefit of marriage is now the norm in the United States.[4] Cohabitation has gone from involving just 10 percent of households in 1965 to more than 50 percent in 1994.[5] We now have a whole generation of liberated sluts and cads, freed from the chains of marriage, responsible to no one—democracy gone nuts! Said a college student: "The sexual revolution is over and everyone lost."[6] The only winner is the pagan agenda!

Professor Lawrence Stone of Princeton observes:

> The scale of marital breakdowns in the West since 1960 has *no historical precedent* that I know of. There has been nothing like it for the last 2000 years and probably longer.[7]

IDEOLOGICAL REVOLUTION: A WAR OF FUNDAMENTAL IDEAS

To measure the nature of the struggle for the culture, we must realize that we are not dealing with an unfortunate social aberration that can be fixed with more family-based movies out of Hollywood. Two ideological plates have collided: the Modern Rationalist world and the Postmodern Irrationalist world. The Postmodern has won.

Since the eighteenth-century Enlightenment, the great enemy of the Christian Faith has always been Rationalism, whether in the form of atheistic humanism, materialistic Marxism, or rationalistic "Christian" liberalism. But the Rationalist edifice is now crumbling under its own weight. In the fifties and sixties, critics from within the system began to doubt the truths of the modern world and the ability

---

[2]Barbara Dafoe Whitehead, *The Divorce Culture* (New York: Vintage Books, 1998).

[3]Glenn T. Stanton, *Why Marriage Matters: Reason to Believe in Marriage in a Postmodern Society* (Colorado Springs: Pinon Press, 1997), 24.

[4]"'Living in Sin' Now the Norm," *UPI* (Feb. 7, 2000), 17.

[5]Ibid.

[6]Gerard Reed, *Readings* 97 (Point Loma, CA: January 2000), 3.

[7]Cited in Glenn T. Stanton, *Why Marriage Matters*, 20.

of reason to make true statements. Postmodernism has given rise to a relativization of rational truth and to a proliferation of individual truths, whereby truth has become power exercised on others for the sake of personal agendas. Truth has become pluralistic, and so have morals. In such a climate, how can anyone tell others how to run their lives? If there is any "truth," it is to be found in nonrational, personal spirituality. Atheistic evolutionists have become deep ecologists, and Marxists like Mikhail Gorbachev and Vaclav Havel have shown interest in theosophy and Buddhism. The true measure of the *culture wars* is that they are (as they have always been) *spirit wars*.

The hard truth is that America is no longer a "Christian" nation. Orthodox rabbi Daniel Lappin, in his book *America's Real War*, states: "One of the most profound truths about [modern] America is that we are no longer one nation under God."[8] This subtle anti-Christian shift in modern society recently came out as a sociological "fact." Said sociologist Alan Wolfe to a group of journalists during a visit to Washington in the spring of 1998: "We've gone from a predominantly Christian country to one of religious toleration, and that's never been reported as a news story."[9] "We used to be a Christian nation. Recently we have become a nation tolerant of all religions."[10] Wolfe recently produced a sociological study of the American middle class. He believes that there is no culture war because most Americans will not choose sides. Moderation and tolerance are the norms. "Americans are reluctant to pass judgment on how other people act and think. . . . Middle-class Americans have added an Eleventh Commandment: 'Thou shalt not judge.'"

Such tolerance and refusal to judge is the seedbed of syncretism, and syncretism is the motor of modern paganism. This much-touted tolerance is not progress toward a more enlightened society, but the postmodern failure to recognize that there is objective truth. If rationalism is dead, the world stands before two "spiritual" answers—the spirituality of the Bible or the spirituality of paganism, but the tide is with paganism, which fits the postmodern paradigm.

---

[8]Daniel Lappin, *America's Real War* (Sisters, OR: Multnomah, 1999), 46.

[9]Julia Duin, "Morality Matters to Middle Class; Tolerance More So; Few Use the Language of Absolutes," *The Washington Times* (March 10, 1998).

[10]Alan Wolfe, *One Nation After All* (New York: Viking, 1997), 12.

PAGANISM'S CORE BELIEFS

The unifying program of unity and wholeness is another form of monism, or "one-ism." This is why monism loves the symbolism of inclusive circles.[11]

All Is One and One Is All

In the Disney movie *Lion King,* everything in the universe is a part of a mass of energy. There is no Creator: The circle of life swallows up God. Many non-Christian faiths use circles as a means of expressing this All-Is-One philosophy. Hinduism, goddess worship, New Age/Taoist physics, witchcraft, and the Parliament of the World's Religions all show universal unity with circles. This circular, All-Is-One notion inspires deep ecology and the worship of bewitching, encircling Mother Earth.

Humanity Is One

This second principle of monism flows naturally from the first. If all is one and one is all, then humanity is a part of God, an expression of divine oneness. Humans are a kind of concentrated cosmic energy who create their own reality. Belief that humans are divine, and essentially good, explains today's quest for personal spiritual discovery and the hope that we can create heaven on earth. This monistic humanism becomes a path to religious utopia.

By finding God in themselves, monists hope to break down the divisions in our world and to accomplish God's loving work by uniting with one another. If we are little holograms of divinity—smaller, cloned versions of the great divine circle—then we are uncreated and eternal. We are as old as God! We are outside the jurisdiction of any authority—a kingless generation. What need have we to submit to outside rule? If we are God, if we are as old as God, then we can make our own rules.

All Religions Are One

Monism hates a system that creates categories and makes distinctions. In Chicago, delegates to the Parliament of the World's Religions held hands and danced around the room to the sound of a Native American

---

[11]This analysis of monism can also be found in Peter Jones, *Gospel Truth, Pagan Lies: Can You Tell the Difference?* (Mukilteo, WA: WinePress, 1999).

Indian shaman's drum. Six thousand delegates shared their experience of the divine within. If all humanity is one, then all religions are one.

Mystical oneness is at the heart of spirituality for the monist. All religions share a common, mystical experience. True believers in any religion will arrive at the same *unio mystica* (mystical union with God in which we become divine). All religions are pie slices that join at the center. If you believe in this oneness, you must throw away rationality, for mystical union is an irrational affair. If you believe in this oneness, you must throw off doctrine. It doesn't matter if you are a Christian, a Jew, a Hindu, or a witch; you are a part of the same whole, which is *God*. You can find union with that whole—and the way to union is experience. Just bite into the pie! This view is becoming as American as apple pie!

At Harvard Divinity School, studies are now dominated by the feminist perspective. In a semi-humorous but well-documented article entitled "What's up at Harvard Divinity School?" Jewish social commentator Don Feder recounts that Buddhist chanting and meditation are now more popular than hymn singing, and the Christian calendar is passed over in favor of pagan holidays. According to Feder, feminist goddess worship is the grill through which religion, Christian theology, and the Bible are now interpreted.[12]

This non-doctrinal, mystical unity of religions will increase in the years ahead. Technology has brought our world together. In addition, many religious organizations (the World Council of Churches, the United Religions, the Parliament of the World's Religions, and the Interfaith Movement, for example) are working hard to bring about a one-world reality. Leading "Christian" scholars believe that the Spirit's present work is to shape all the world's religions into a single truth.

One Problem: Wake Up

Monism believes that the real problem is lack of knowledge—the knowledge of ourselves as divine. We have forgotten our true nature; we have been lulled into metaphysical amnesia or spiritual sleep by the illusions of the external, physical world. The Hindus call it *maya*—illusion. Thus the monist points an accusing finger at structures we once considered natural, such as a father's loving authority in his home or a husband's loving leadership of his wife. These illusions turn us away from our true selves.

---

[12]Don Feder, "What's up at Harvard Divinity School?" *Conservative Chronicle* (April 1994), 28.

Monists identify old-fashioned, black-and-white thinking with western Christian culture. They find the Bible full of patriarchy (male/fatherly authority) and hierarchy (authority structures), and they accuse Christians of making many other such distinctions that they claim tear the world apart and obscure the truth about ourselves as essentially spiritual beings with no ties to the visible world. In the fog of *maya* we make unfortunate distinctions.

One successful emerging form of monism today is Buddhism. Buddhist philosophy specifically teaches that distinctions are illusory.

> Like the Buddha 2500 years ago, Buddhists today work for the liberation of all beings from the illusion of separation. When there is an "other," there is an Auschwitz . . . a ravaged and raped woman, a clear-cut forest, an abused and abandoned child, a young boy with fear and hate in his eyes and a gun in his hand. . . .
>
> The basic vows that we take as Buddhists remind us that there is no "other." The most basic practices . . . of Buddhism . . . point to the fact that there is no "other." The fundamental teachings of the Buddha tell us that there is no "other."[13]

Monism's message of hope is clear: Rid the world of distinctions, and humanity can realize the mystical unity of all things.

One Solution: Go Within

Monists tell us to complete the circle by looking into ourselves. Your self sits at the center. Spiritual understanding dawns when you eliminate distinctions and rational controls to take your place in the unity of all things. Sixties rebels discovered themselves through drugs. Today meditation has replaced dangerous drugs as the path to the discovery of self and God. Meditation allows you to detach from your body's limitations and discover a connection with the whole through a mystical experience of true knowledge (*gnosis*). As more individuals find their divine identity, the planet will supposedly shift into a unified, altered state of consciousness.

But there is more to a spiritual high than trancelike ecstasy. To go beyond the limitations of the mind also entails going beyond rational definitions of right and wrong. Everything about you is okay. All your

---

[13]Roshi Joan Halifax, "Excerpts from *Buddhist Peacework: Creating Cultures of Peace*," *Boston Research Center for the Twenty-First Century: Newsletter* 14 (Winter 2000), 10-11.

instincts are valid. As the sixties hippies said: "If it feels good, do it." Or as C. G. Jung said, our instincts are spiritual *archetypes* that we must accept in order to be fully integrated persons. When we go within, notions like right and wrong, guilt and bad conscience disappear. In this way, embracing evil, pagan spirituality produces a temporary, counterfeit euphoria of *virtual redemption*.

SEXUALITY IN THE PAGAN WORLDVIEW

Do you want to capture a civilization? Change its perceptions of sexuality. Very few are into New Age Eastern spirituality with its chakras, crystals, astral travel, and channeling. Everybody, without exception, is into being a male or a female—which is what makes a civilization function. The pagan agenda is the elimination of the distinction between male and female.

Methodology: Crisis, Deconstruction, and Reconstruction

Take, for instance, the program for unity of the world's religions, which first warns of the ecological crisis, then calls for a deconstruction of the orthodox Christian view of creation. Finally theological syncretism offers to reconstruct an ideal ecosystem and save the planet. Similarly, the new sexuality identifies the evils of patriarchy as a social crisis and proceeds to deconstruct traditional sex and gender roles. Sexual identity is then reconstructed according to the monistic ideal of androgyny.

The Sexual Crisis: Patriarchy

According to Scripture, patriarchy is responsible male leadership in the home and the church. But in theologian Rosemary Ruether's feminist universe, patriarchy has taken the place of sin. Such an affirmation cannot be established from the founding texts of Genesis 3. These texts must themselves be characterized as the adopted myths of patriarchal religion.[14] According to Ruether, patriarchy is the work of the devil, the Mark of the Beast, the Great Babylon,[15] the evil land of Egyptian slavery from which the church should organize a modern-day exodus, an inner reality that produces prostitution.[16]

---

[14]Rosemary Radford Ruether, *Women-Church: Theology and Practice* (San Francisco: Harper and Row, 1985), 131.

[15]Ibid., 280-281.

[16]Ibid., 132.

Once an influential evangelical writer, Virginia Mollenkott now blames what she calls "heteropatriarchy" for virtually all social ills, including racism and classism. As a practicing lesbian she adds that "compulsory heterosexuality is the very backbone that holds patriarchy together."[17] She realizes that homosexuality will break that backbone. "If society is to turn from patriarchy to partnership, we must learn that lesbian, bisexual, and gay issues are not just private bedroom matters of 'doing whatever turns you on.' They are wedges driven into the superstructure of the heteropatriarchal system."[18]

On a much less radical level, evangelical egalitarian feminism makes a similar move. Gretchen Gabelein Hull, a board member of the Council for Biblical Equality, speaks of the "sin of patriarchy": "[To] Christianize patriarchy is to end it and its abuses against women and minorities."[19] According to Hull, one does not reform patriarchy in the light of the Christian revelation of God as Father of our Lord Jesus Christ;[20] rather, one eliminates it! The end-result—where egalitarian Christians refuse to go—is the elimination of the God of Scripture, the great Patriarch from whom all families derive their name (Eph. 3:14). The Jewish feminist Naomi Goldenberg implicitly fingers God the Father, author of the Judeo-Christian Scripture, as the architect of the patriarchal society. "We women are going to bring an end to God."[21] How are they doing?

Sexual Deconstruction Through Feminism

The Curriculum Commission has recommended to the California State Board of Education that homosexual couples be presented in the public schools' health curriculum as having an alternate acceptable family lifestyle.[22] Is it mere happenstance that liberalism's conversion to monistic spirituality coincides with major changes in sexual practice,

---

[17]Virginia Ramey Mollenkott, *Sensuous Spirituality: Out from Fundamentalism* (New York: Crossroad, 1992), 12.

[18]Ibid., 13.

[19]*Christians for Biblical Equality: Books, Reprints and Tapes Catalogue*, August 1991. See also Rebecca M. Groothuis, *Women Caught in the Conflict: The Culture War between Traditionalism and Feminism* (Grand Rapids, MI: Baker, 1994), who believes that patriarchy is the result of sin, which the Bible progressively shows must be rooted out (115).

[20]Groothuis, ibid., 122 too denies the possibility that patriarchy can be reformed along Christian lines.

[21]Naomi Goldenberg, *Changing of the Gods: Feminism and the End of Traditional Religions* (Boston: Beacon Press, 1979), 5.

[22]*Good News, Etc.* (July 1992), 3.

gender roles, and family structures? The sexuality of western civilization has been deconstructed in just one generation. The role of women
has changed drastically, representing a mega-shift in the perceptions of
human sexuality. Feminism has opened doors to many other changes
as well. Oddly, not many are willing to consider feminism as a major
driving force of the neo-pagan ideal,[23] though the radicals do at every
occasion. For example, Naomi Goldenberg ties the feminist movement
directly to an attack on Judeo-Christian foundations: " . . . when feminists succeed in changing the position of women in Christianity and
Judaism, they will shake these religions at their roots."[24] In 1971 when
she first met feminists she remembers thinking, "Such women will
change the world."[25]

Liberal theology can run the gamut from the white, straight, male
Harvard professor of theology to the lesbian ecofeminist witch who has
severed all ties with biblical Christianity. But the twain do meet. Mary
Daly, who screams blasphemies on every page of her recent books promoting witchcraft and erotic "spiritual" lesbianism, receives accolades
from Harvey Cox, respected liberal theologian and the Victor S.
Thomas Professor of Divinity at Harvard Divinity School. Daly dis-
misses the incarnation of the eternal Son as the "symbolic legitimation
of the rape of all women and all matter" and describes as "bull . . . the
apostles creed."[26] Cox considers her "a woman who makes a Big
Difference" of whom he is a self-styled "fan."[27]

Sexual Deconstruction Through Homosexuality

The proof of this mega-shift and of its radical implications is the
growing acceptance and power of the homosexual community,

---

[23]Few Christian books on the New Age broach this subject, so that great sections of the church
have been swept along by a more modified, sanitized form.

[24]Goldenberg, *Changing of the Gods*, 5.

[25]Ibid., 2. William Oddie, *What Will Happen to God? Feminism and the Reconstruction of Christian
Belief* (San Francisco: Ignatius Press, 1984), 11-15 makes remarks to the same effect.

[26]"Mary Daly in Cahoots with Jane Caputi," in Mary Daly's and Jane Caputi's *Websters' First New
Intergalactic Wickedary of the English Language* (Boston: Beacon Press, 1987), 78, 186.

[27]Donna Steichen, *Ungodly Rage: The Hidden Face of Catholic Feminism* (San Francisco: Ignatius
Press, 1991), 330. See Leila Prelec, "BC Campus Scene of Small Daly Protests," *National Catholic
Register*, April 30, 1989, 1. See also Cox's endorsement of Daly's latest book, *Outercourse: The Be-
Dazzling Voyage Containing Recollections from My Logbook of a Radical Feminist Philosopher* (San
Francisco: Harper, 1992) in the 1992 Harper/San Francisco Catalogue *Religious Studies*, 17. This
book by Daly is a further promotion of ecofeminist erotic lesbian witchcraft. In 1988 Cox is sur-
prised by the reemergence of witchcraft (see his *Many Mansions* [Boston: Beacon Press, 1992],
195). Four years later he is the enthusiastic supporter of a witch/philosopher.

which has many average citizens convinced that heterosexuality may not be the norm. "We are no longer seeking just a right to privacy and a protection from wrong," says a leading spokesman for the movement. "We have a right . . . to see government and society affirm our lives."[28]

The project is succeeding in modern-day America in spite of the millions of Americans who oppose it. The boundaries move every day. Today one of the major debates is the place of gay groups on high school, junior high, and even elementary campuses.[29] When the Los Angeles Unified School District sponsored an end-of-year prom for gay students, the news report tried to get readers to believe there was nothing more natural for the progress of American democracy than a teenage boy making himself a lace dress to wear at that dance![30]

In academia, feminism and homosexuality have urged each other to more and more radical positions, as the well-researched and finely titled article "Coming Out Ahead: The Homosexual Movement in the Academy" demonstrates.[31] The author reports that "at many colleges, gay/lesbian/bisexual student associations are among the most active . . . on campus, funded by student fees and by institutional funds from the university's Office of Multiculturalism." He notes that at Harvard each dorm has a designated gay tutor; at Columbia University, the chairman of the English Department is committed to "hiring, tenuring and working with" gay and lesbian scholars. Many universities, including Stanford, the University of Chicago, the University of Iowa, and Pitzer College, offer spousal benefits to homosexual partners of faculty members.[32]

---

[28]A speech by Jeff Levi in 1987 to the National Press Club in Washington, cited in Joseph P. Gudel, "That Which Is Unnatural: Homosexuality in Society, the Church and Scripture," *Christian Research Journal* (Winter 1993), 10.

[29]See the article "Gay Rights Moves on Campus" on the front page of the *L.A. Times* (January 10, 1994).

[30]Ibid.

[31]By Jerry Z. Muller, Associate Professor of History at the Catholic University of America, in *First Things* (August/September 1993), 17-24. "Most important in measuring the influence of homosexual thought in the academy is its impact upon women's studies, by far the fastest growing area within the humanities and social sciences, both institutionally and in terms of publications. It is estimated that there are now five hundred women's studies programs, thirty thousand courses, and fifty feminist institutes" (18). One of the leading ideas in academic feminism is that lesbianism is the most "authentic form of feminism."

[32]Ibid.

Sexual Reconstruction: Androgyny, the New Spiritual Human

PAGAN ESCHATOLOGY

Many believe that the liberated woman may well be instrumental in the realization of a unified humanity and a global religion. But doesn't feminism have to do only with social conditions and democratic rights? What does it care about religion? Wrong. Feminists see themselves as called to transform both society and religion. Roman Catholic theologian Paul Knitter is a thinker committed to the development of one worldwide religion. He is also the general editor of the series *Faith Meets Faith* whose recent offering is entitled *After Patriarchy: Feminist Transformations of the World Religions*.[33] This book argues that since the "second class status, if not the outward oppression, of women . . . [is] rooted in the theologies . . . of world religions," it is feminism's globalized vision of gender and sexual liberation that will transform all the world's religions. At that point emancipation will be won for all. This rosy religious future on earth will come about because a new and higher form of humanity is in the process of taking control of the planet.

This new spiritual human being is of indeterminate sexuality or, in many cases, specifically homosexual. It should come as no surprise that the *revival of pagan religion* in our day should be accompanied by a stark *reappearance of pagan homosexuality*.[34] In other words, homosexuality is not merely biological destiny (though many believe it is). Its extension and acceptance are not merely the good and just applications of democratic and human civil rights (though most would see it in that light). If the connection with pagan spirituality is correct, homosexuality has a deeply religious component, whether or not any particular homosexual is aware of it and whatever the causes of such a lifestyle.[35]

A particular religious commitment is always accompanied by a par-

---

[33]Paula M. Cooey, ed., *After Patriarchy: Feminist Transformations of the World Religions* (Maryknoll, NY: Orbis Books, 1991).

[34]Much of what follows is drawn from my more scholarly article dealing with the same theme, "Androgyny: The Pagan Sexual Ideal," *Journal of the Evangelical Theological Society (JETS)* (September 2000), 443-469.

[35]This can be seen in the apparently innocuous statement of a contemporary homosexual academic who affirms "the fact that human sex is not a strictly binary category"—see Martti Nissinen, *Homoeroticism in the Biblical World: A Historical Perspective* (Minneapolis: Fortress Press, 1998), 12. From the fact of physical and sexual perversions, Nissinen actually argues for moral and spiritual relativism.

ticular sexual theory and practice. One does not need to invent a scarlet, conspiratorial thread to explain this unusual agreement. There is a logical and theological inevitability that monistic belief will work itself out in all domains of human existence, and especially in the domain of sexuality.[36] Homosexuality is not just biology. Says a gay spokesman, "being a gay man or lesbian entails far more than sexual behavior alone . . . [it entails] a whole mode of being-in-the-world."[37]

HOMOSEXUALITY AND SPIRITUALITY IN HISTORICAL PERSPECTIVE

Homosexuality has been identified with pagan spirituality in many ages and many places. An androgynous priesthood was associated with the worship of the goddess Istar in the Sumerian age (1800 B.C.),[38] as well as in Syria and in Asia Minor during the first millennium B.C.[39] From the Roman Empire at the beginning of the Christian era, the Great Mother under the names of Atargatis or Cybele had androgynous priests, called *Galli*, who castrated themselves as a permanent act of devotion to the goddess. This organic connection is documented in the modern world in ancient religions that persist today. The Siberian shamans, known as Chukchi, and the shamans of Central Asia engage in ecstatic rituals and dress as androgynes.[40] This is true also of Amazonian shamans and celtic priests (ancient and modern), as well as the Indian *hijras*. The *hijras*, who go back into the mists of Hinduism, are a religious community of men who "dress and act like women and

---

[36]C. G. Jung, *Mysterium Coniunctionis: An Inquiry into the Separation and Synthesis of Psychic Opposites in Alchemy*, Bollingen Series XX, trans. R. F. C. Hull (Princeton, NJ: Princeton University Press, 1970), 244-245 identifies this same phenomenon, though not directly associated with sexuality. He states: "Anyone familiar with the spirit of alchemy and the views of the Gnostics in [the writings of the church father] Hippolytus will be struck again and again by their inner affinity." But he notes that the alchemists "could have known nothing of Hippolytus, as his *Philosophumena,* long believed lost, was rediscovered only in the middle of the nineteenth century in a monastery on Mount Athos." It is interesting that in this same context Jung states his indebtedness to the alchemists as those "who first put me on the track of a psychological interpretation"; ibid., 249.

[37]J. Michael Clark, "Gay Spirituality," *Spirituality and the Secular Quest*, ed. Peter H. Van Ness (New York: Crossroads/Herder, 1996), 335.

[38]Nissinen, *Homoeroticism*, 28. For what follows of this older period, I am greatly indebted to this study. According to Helmer Ringgren, *Religions of the Ancient Near East*, trans. John Sturdy (Philadelphia: Westminster Press, 1973), 25, naked "eunuchs" were associated with the cult to the Sumerian goddess Inanna, including an *hieros gamos* ("holy marriage") rite (ibid., 12).

[39]Ibid., 31. According to Nissinen, ibid., 149, n. 73, there is evidence of *Galli*, androgynous priests, in the third century B.C.

[40]Mircea Eliade, *Shamanism: Archaic Techniques of Ecstasy* (Princeton, NJ: Princeton University Press, 1972), 125. See also Nissinen, *Homoeroticism*, 34.

whose culture centers on the worship of Bahuchara Mata, one of the many versions of the Mother Goddess worshipped throughout India."[41]

A recent book tracing the history of gay male spirituality argues that "gender-variant men have fulfilled a sacred role throughout the millennia."[42] In American Indian religious practice, homosexual transvestite males—*berdaches*—have often functioned as shamans. For example, among the Navajo the *nadle*, a feminized male, served as a reconciler of conflict. According to an expert in the field, the "asexual priest-shamans . . . true hermaphrodites, dressing and behaving like women," have a priestly function because "they combine the two cosmological planes— earth and sky—and also from the fact that they combine in their own person the feminine element (earth) and the masculine element (sky). We here have ritual androgyny, a well-known archaic formula for the . . . *coincidentia oppositorum* ["the joining of the opposites"]."[43] The same phenomenon in different garb is appearing in our time.

A disturbing trend is now being identified—young people declaring themselves "homosexual" at earlier and earlier ages. Bisexuality is cool on many high-school campuses, to keep options open.[44] The *Utne Reader*, promoting the Gay Straight Alliance, which is active in schools to encourage children as young as thirteen to "come out" as gays or les-

---

[41]See Serena Nanda, *Neither Man Nor Woman: The Hijras of India* (Belmont, CA: Wadsworth Publishing, 1990), xv. cited in Nissinen, *Homoeroticism*. According to Tal Brooke, *Avatar of Night* (Berkeley, CA: End Run Publishing, 1999), 331, Sai Baba, a leading Hindu guru and Goddess-worshipper (see 193, 200), with whom Brooke was closely associated before his Christian conversion, was androgynous and practiced homosexuality with a number in his inner circle.

[42]Robert M. Baum, "Homosexuality and the Traditional Religions of the Americas and Africa," in Arlene Swidler, *Homosexuality and World Religions* (Valley Forge, PA: Trinity Press International, 1993), 15. See also Edward Carpenter, "On the Connection between Homosexuality and Divination, and the Importance of the Intermediate Sexes Generally in Early Civilizations," *Revue d'ethnographie et de sociologie*, 11/12 (1910), 310-316 and *Intermediate Types Among Primitive Folk* (London, 1914); Walter Williams, *The Spirit and the Flesh: Sexual Diversity in American Indian Culture* (Boston: Beacon Press, 1986).

[43]Mircea Eliade, *Shamanism*, 352.

[44]*Lambda Report* (January-February 1998), 5. See an article on Kate Bornstein's *My Gender Workbook* in *The Washington Blade* (February 13, 1998), 13, where sexual fluidity is the subject: "I hated my body for 50 years," says Bornstein. "As a boy, part of the reason I hated it was because it was a boy body and it had a penis and everything. I was anorexic from high school on, seriously anorexic, hospitalized and all that. Then I lived for a year as a woman. Then I learned to hate my body as a woman body. When I finally stopped being a woman and started being a transsexual Lesbian, I learned to hate my transsexual Lesbian body. . . . I'm just starting to say, 'Yeah, my body's six feet tall, my arms are long, my jaw is kind of square, I have stubble on my face because I couldn't afford all my electrolysis, I've got a pot belly from time to time— but you know what? I like my body.' Most people think I'm attractive and that stuns me." This newfound self-acceptance, Bornstein says, is "amazing," adding, "I think it comes from frying my brain enough that I don't have to listen to social standards. That's what I hope all the questions in the workbook will do, is fry people's brains so they don't have to bow down to what anyone else says about them."

bians, says that for young people, "sexual identity can be fluid . . . it's not so absolute . . . this means rejecting the labels of male *and* female. If you erase those lines, then the whole thing changes."[45] What they are erasing is Genesis 1:27: "So God created man in his own image . . . male and female he created them." The "whole thing" is quite simply the redefinition of human society and personal sexual identity.

Is this abnormal? Is this socially and historically revolutionary? Recently a coalition of medical, mental health, and religious organizations produced a booklet, *Just the Facts About Sexual Orientation and Youth*, and mailed it to the heads of all 14,700 public school districts. The booklet declares with disarming moral certitude that homosexuality is not abnormal. Ken Jennings, executive director of the Gay, Lesbian and Straight Education Network, was surely right, however, when he observed: "I think this is a history-changing moment."[46] Changing the moral sensibilities of the next generation will certainly change history. Though rarely pointed out, the *actual fact* is both how much this social trend erases the 4,000-year-old Judeo-Christian and western understanding of reality and gives expression to an essential notion of pagan spirituality.

The "ascended Masters" of contemporary occultism are having a grand old time. One of them, the spirit-guide of a prominent New Age writer, Barbara Marx Hubbard, reveals that sexual identity confusion in young people is a good thing, because in the New Age, people will be androgynous. Androgyny is part of the neo-pagan utopian vision and fits with the beliefs and hopes of Wiccan feminists. Emily Culpepper, an ex-Southern Baptist and now a lesbian pagan witch, sees gays and lesbians, in her words, as "shamans for a future age."[47] Virginia Mollenkott, calling herself "an evangelical lesbian feminist," describes gays and lesbians as "God's Ambassadors."[48] Rosemary Ruether believes androgyny is the sexual ideal.[49]

The pagan vision seems to be progressing according to plan.

---

[45]Andy Steiner, "Out Early," *Utne Reader* (January-February 2001), 17.

[46]Erica Goode, *New York Times News Service* (November 23, 1999). Ironically, the booklet opposes reparative therapy (changing homosexuals into heterosexuals) because that can cause guilt and anxiety and because of homosexuality's religious nature. Thus the Coalition will oppose the discussion of the value of reparative therapy on church/state constitutional grounds! Incredibly, the religious group supporting this "moral" progress is the Interfaith Alliance Foundation.

[47]Emily Culpepper, "The Spiritual, Political Journey of a Feminist Freethinker," in Paula M. Cooey, ed., *After Patriarchy*, 164.

[48]Virginia Mollenkott, *Sensuous Spirituality*, 42, 166.

[49]Donna Steichen, *Ungodly Rage*, 302: "Androgyny is her model for a human species liberated from 'dualistic' gender into 'psychic wholeness.'"

Traditional values are not winning.[50] On the cutting edge of culture and in the high schools of the land, they are losing big-time. In a moral climate where democratic theory has recently freed itself of transcendent values and theistic underpinnings in favor of polyvalent pagan practice, nothing short of a spiritual revival can stop the rot.

Though often pushed as an agenda of civil rights of the same nature as civil rights for minority races, the homosexual/androgynous revival is surely deeply connected to the revival of pagan esoteric spirituality in our time. What is the relationship? Why call homosexual androgyny pagan?

The Pagan Religious Significance of Androgyny/Homosexuality

Androgyny, the joining of male and female in the same person, reflects and confirms the experience at the heart of pagan monism—namely, a mystical moment where distinctions disappear and opposites are joined together. This is not to suggest that everyone engaging in such activity thinks about the ultimate spiritual stakes.[51] For most people, ignorance is bliss. However, the link between androgynous sexuality and spirituality is explicitly established by influential pagan theorists in both the ancient and the modern world. Their explanations, though separated by vast distances and great periods of time, are strikingly similar and thus independently testify to the coherent connection this chapter seeks to underline. Eliade saw androgyny in many traditional religions as ". . . an archaic and universal formula for the expression of wholeness, the co-existence of the contraries, or *coincidentia oppositorum* . . . symboliz[ing] . . . perfection . . . [and] ultimate being."[52]

The *basir*, "asexual priest-shamans . . . true hermaphrodites, dressing and behaving like women," have a priestly function because they combine earth and sky, feminine and masculine in a ritual androgyny, a well-known archaic formula for the *coincidentia oppositorum*.[53]

The androgyne is the physical symbol of the pagan spiritual goal, which is the merging of two distinct entities, the self and God, and a mystical return to the state of godhead prior to the mistake of physical

---

[50]The University of Chicago has just issued the results of a study showing that in 1972 46 percent of Americans lived in a traditional, two-parent/children family. Today only 26 percent do; see *The New York Times* (November 24, 1999), B3.

[51]After I had given a lecture on this theme, a homosexual thanked me for showing him (for the first time) where his sexual drive was taking him spiritually and religiously.

[52]Mircea Eliade, *Myths, Dreams and Mysteries* (New York: Harper and Row, 1975), 174-175 and *Patterns of Comparative Religion* (New York: New American Library, 1974), 420-421.

[53]Mircea Eliade, *Shamanism*, 352.

creation. On the sexual plane, the homosexual androgyne affirms his power by willingly joining what God has put asunder. A gay leader at a Pagan Spirit Gathering in 1985 made this spiritual claim: "We feel there is a power in our sexuality . . . [a] queer energy that most cultures consider magical. It is practically a requirement for certain kinds of medicine and magic."[54]

The physico-theological mechanism seems to function as follows: Androgynous persons, whether homosexual or bisexual, are able to express within themselves both sexual roles and identities. In the sex act they engage *both* as male and female and thus taste in some form or other both physical and "spiritual" androgyny.[55] As in classic monistic spirituality, they have, on the physical plane, joined the opposites, "proving" and experiencing that there are no distinctions. Just as the distinctions inherent in heterosexuality point to the fundamental the-istic notion of the Creator/creature distinction, so androgyny in its var-ious forms eradicates distinction and elevates the spiritual blending of all things, including the idolatrous confusing of the human and the ani-mal with the divine, as Paul showed in Romans 1:18-27.

Contemporary gay thinkers make the same point. J. Michael Clark, professor at Emory University and Georgia State University, a gay spokesman, turns to Native American animism for an acceptable spiri-tual model. Specifically, the *berdache*, an androgynous American Indian shaman, born as a male but as an adult choosing to live as a female, con-stitutes a desirable gay spiritual model. The *berdache* achieves "the reunion of the cosmic, sexual and moral polarities"[56] or the "joining of the opposites." How interesting that the *berdaches* were known as "sacred Balancers," unifying the polarities to "nurture wholeness."[57] One can-not help but recall that the great vocation of Anakin Skywalker in the *Star Wars* series is to balance the two sides of the force.[58]

CONCLUSION

It is evident that sexual perversion and the elimination of sexual dis-tinctions are not incidental footnotes of pagan religious history but rep-

---

[54]Cited in George Otis, *The Twilight Labyrinth* (Grand Rapids, MI: Baker, 1997), 180.

[55]Mircea Eliade, *The Two and the One* (New York: Harper, 1969), 112 mentions homosexual practice in ritual androgynous initiation.

[56]Ibid., 342.

[57]Ibid.

[58]In George Lucas's film *The Phantom Menace*.

resent one of paganism's fundamental ideological commitments. As we have noted, the pagan priesthood is identified, across space and time, with the blurring of sexual identity via homosexual androgyny.[59] If history is a wise teacher, we may surely conclude that paganism will always give enormous priority to destroying God-ordained monogamous heterosexuality and to promoting androgyny in its varied forms.

Though we must be concerned with the scriptural interpretations and practices of our evangelical egalitarian brothers and sisters in order to show the clarity and importance of the biblical message about creational sex, it is nevertheless true that the real opponent in the *Sex Wars*,[60] as in the *Spirit Wars*,[61] is not Christian feminism but the fiercely anti-Christian religious paganism that now surrounds us on every side.

Joseph Campbell, one of the spiritual creators of Anakin and *Star Wars*,[62] was an apostate Roman Catholic who sought wisdom in the pagan myths and delivered much of it on public television.[63] He describes the calling of every human being, though born in one sex or the other, to transcend duality. This is to be done, as in the ancient mystery religions, by undergoing a series of initiations (or mystical experiences), whereby the individual "realizes that he is both mortal and immortal, male and female."[64] This is a socially explosive message in a time of sexual and religious chaos. How explosive? We can get some idea of the power of this modern paganism by measuring the worldwide success of the Lucas movies—and then realizing that this is just a drop in a bucket of constant indoctrination going on in the media, in the public schools, and on the university campuses. As our modern world more and more brings together western material success and eastern spirituality and unites the globe around the twin notions of economic well-being and the spiritual unity of all religions, it is not difficult to see that the next great opponent of Christian truth will be triumphant, globalist paganism—in both its spiritual and sexual forms.

---

[59]See my article "Androgyny: The Pagan Sexual Ideal," mentioned above, for an extended documentation of this fact.

[60]See my forthcoming book on pagan and biblical sexuality.

[61]See my book *Spirit Wars: Pagan Revival in Christian America* (Mukilteo, WA: WinePress, 1997), to appear in revised form as *Pagans in the Pews* (Ventura, CA: Regal, 2001).

[62]George Lucas recognized Campbell as one of his spiritual mentors, and Campbell was a constant guest at the Skywalker Ranch.

[63]In a PBS series, shown in the late 1980s. One must not miss the irony of taxpayer money being used to promote a deeply religious, anti-Christian, proselytizing apology for pagan spirituality.

[64]Joseph Campbell, *The Power of Myth* (New York: Doubleday, 1991), 58.

10

The Unchangeable Difference: Eternally Fixed Sexual Identity for an Age of Plastic Sexuality

Daniel R. Heimbach

Abstract: "Plastic sexuality" is the idea that sexual identity has no fixed meaning and that anyone can shape his or her sexual identity any way he or she chooses. This view, now sweeping academic circles and over-flowing into popular culture, is growing because it denies there is any objective basis for fixed gender roles in any sort of human relationship—in work, in play, in the family, in religion, or even in procreation. Christians can oppose this by showing the Bible teaches that differences in human sexual identity are fixed for eternity.

Christians have always believed that the meaning of human sexual identity involves something more than biological reproduction. Even outside the church, few have disputed the idea that who we are as sexual beings involves something more than physical form. Yet, when we start looking at what this "something more" might be, agreement breaks down rather rapidly because we find deep differences of opinion about whether or to what degree sexual identity is fundamental to actually being human. This will be clear after asking a few simple questions.

Is sexual identity something basic to humanity itself, or is it simply peripheral? Do sexual differences matter even at the most fundamental level of human existence, or is sexual being ultimately irrelevant at the core of human identity? Does basic human identity lie beyond whatever differences divide men from women and women from men? Or is the division between male and female humanity essential to who we are as human beings? In theological terms the issue has to do with whether differences in sexual identity will characterize human existence eternally. Or will they someday come to an end? Will sexual being remain when we who know Jesus Christ are raised to a state of sinless immortality at the return of Christ, or will it pass away along with pain, suffering, and death when the present order is replaced by a new heaven and earth (Rev. 21:1-4)?

After commenting on the relevance of an opposing way of thinking now arising in contemporary western culture, I will present arguments to support why I believe Scripture teaches there is an eternal dimension to the difference that distinguishes male from female human beings. These arguments will also serve to explain why I think this particular biblical doctrine is pivotal for Christians right now as we battle the culture over the meaning of male versus female gender identity and the morality of gender roles in relationships between men and women.

I. CONTEMPORARY RELEVANCE OF THE ISSUE: THE RISE OF "PLASTIC SEXUALITY"

Today the "essential" or "fixed" nature of human sexual identity is under fire mainly because it stands in the way of the social and moral deconstructionism that underlies hardline feminism and homosexual militancy. The essentialist view of human sexual identity is the view associated with traditional Christian morality. It refers to thinking there is some objective reality that establishes a fixed, unchangeable meaning to the difference between men and women. It involves the conviction that while men and women share a common humanity, there is something fundamental about human sexual identity that is not the same when men as men are compared to women as women. And not only is this difference real, it also is terribly important because it is rooted in nature or in creation or in the will of God.

In recent years a growing number of social scientists have started promoting a very different view concerning human sexual identity. This view, sometimes referred to as the "constructionist" view, is based on the idea that human sexual identity is something conditioned entirely by the social and cultural history of a people and by personal choice. Constructionists claim there are no fixed features that define or restrict who we are as sexual beings, and so of course there can be no moral boundaries that depend on thinking sexual differences are actually real.

Constructionist scholars writing for academic journals and books are now saying that human sexuality is "plastic," by which they mean individuals are free to "shape" their sexual identities any way they choose. Adrian Thatcher explains that "plastic sexuality" is the idea that human sexuality is something "malleable," something "able to adjust to changing circumstances"; that is, a person's sexual identity is something "in his or her control."[1] And social scientist Milton Diamond claims a person can "develop and express his or her potential in any direction, on all levels of sexuality, without attaching a negative value to any variation just because it is different."[2]

In a similar vein, Andrea Dworkin, in *Woman Hating*, argues that the categories "man" and "woman" are in fact "fictions, caricatures, [or] cultural constructs" that are "demeaning to the female, [and a] dead-end for male and female both."[3] John Stoltenberg, in *Refusing to Be a Man*, goes so far as to claim that physical, biological differences we think distinguish male from female and female from male are culturally determined as well.[4] And Anthony Giddens, in *The Transformation of Intimacy*, asserts:

> "Sexuality" today has been discovered, opened up and made accessible to the development of varying life-styles. It is something each of us "has," or cultivates, no longer a natural condition which an individual accepts as a preordained state of affairs. Somehow, in a way that has to be investigated, sexuality functions as a malleable feature of self, a prime connecting point between body, self-identity and social norms.[5]

---

[1]See Adrian Thatcher, "Postmodernity and Chastity," in *Sex These Days: Essays on Theology, Sexuality and Society*, eds. Jon Davies and Gerard Loughlin (Sheffield, England: Sheffield Academic Press, 1997), 127-130.

[2]Milton Diamond, "Human Sexual Development: Biological Foundations for Social Development," in Frank A. Beach, ed., *Human Sexuality in Four Perspectives* (Baltimore: Johns Hopkins University Press, 1977), 58.

[3]Andrea Dworkin, *Woman Hating* (New York: Dutton, 1974), 174.

[4]John Stoltenberg, *Refusing to Be a Man: Essays on Sex and Justice* (Portland: Breitenbush Books, 1989), 28.

[5]Anthony Giddens, *The Transformation of Intimacy: Sexuality, Love & Eroticism in Modern Societies* (Stanford, CA: Stanford University Press, 1992), 15.

Such thinking naturally rejects all fixed gender roles. In fact, the logic of plastic sexuality deconstructs all normative standards—whether moral, cultural, or even biological—that depend on thinking differences between male and female are real. Of course, whatever sexual ethic comes from such thinking has to wreak havoc with all efforts aimed at generating or maintaining deeply human relationships between men as men and women as women. Any ethic based on the idea of plastic sexuality must naturally despise the notion of complementary difference in sexual union; and it must ridicule evidence that good might result from cooperation between fixed differences in sexual identity. This means the idea of plastic sexuality in the end destroys the social and moral foundations upon which the institution of marriage depends. So proponents of plastic sexuality actually praise the demise of traditional marriage as if it were some kind of moral goal.[6] Indeed, what they seek is realization of an ironic notion of "sexual equality." The notion is ironic because while motivated by a desire to improve human sexual relationships in the name of "equality," their goal, if realized, actually dehumanizes human sexuality by reducing sexual identity to distinctionless, monolithic sameness incapable of sustaining any meaningful relationship.

Ultimately the sort of moral thinking that arises from a plastic notion of human sexual identity must be characterized by intentional, self-conscious rebellion against God. Why? Because any moral perspective that denies there is any real or meaningful difference between men and women at all has to result in an ethic that disdains the will and work of the Creator.

Yet, even as the nonessentialist, plastic view of human sexuality gains popularity in the culture, arguments justifying the position remain weak.[7] No anthropology denying the essential nature of human sexuality can explain the mysterious depth involved in relationships

---

[6]Adrian Thatcher says, "In a world of plastic sexuality . . . monogamy has to be 'reworked' [and] . . . 'fidelity' has no meaning," "Postmodernity," *Sex These Days*, 129.

[7]The growing popularity of such thinking in the culture can be measured in the way colleges and universities across the nation have been multiplying courses in a new and rapidly growing field that goes under the name of "sexuality studies." Most, if not all, courses being developed for this new field either affirm or assume the constructionist or plastic view of human sexuality. Here are several excerpts taken from various college and university catalogs around the nation. A course in "Queer Histories" at Yale University is an:
   Examination of analysis for gender studies and study of sexuality within a historical framework. Readings look at different aspects of what is "queer," including gender and sexual nonconformity, compare past and present notions of nonconformity and examine how historical perspective can influence understanding of modern categories.

joining men as men with women as women. Nor can it explain the persistent power for both good or evil generated by interaction between the sexes, a power that very obviously persists even where biological reproduction is completely out of the picture.

Universal human experience leans another way, and even without the Bible common experience warns Christians that perhaps we should look more closely at what the culture is busy rejecting. While some Christians seem beguiled by the song of sirens promoting a view of sexual equality that denies the importance of sexual differences, evangelicals must resist the trend by examining what gives meaning to differences in human sexual identity.

II. THE IMPORTANCE OF DISTINGUISHING BEING AND FUNCTION

Before looking at direct evidence in Scripture, we should set the stage with a little philosophical discussion. What I have in mind is something just assumed in the Bible, but that we must make explicit in order to avoid confusing influences arising from our culture. So before looking at what the Bible says about the permanent nature of sexual being, we need to understand the importance of distinguishing between sexual being per se and functions that are assigned to men and women as sexual beings. If we fail to see this distinction, we can easily misread Scripture and might fail to appreciate how consistent the Bible is in all it says about norms that govern the way men relate with women and women with men.

Any serious examination of the essential nature of human sexual identity has to start by assuming that we can distinguish conceptually between sexual being per se and sexual functions that relate to specific sexual identity. It starts by understanding there is a conceptual difference between our existence as sexual beings and our acting on the basis of either one of two specific sexual identities–either as male or female.[8]

A course in "Queer Lives" at Hampshire College in Massachusetts is offered as:

An introduction to thinking about lives and work of lesbians, gay men, transsexuals and transgendered people (groups currently allied politically under the term "queer") mainly through their autobiographies and their work as artists and activists. The course will trace the social and cultural history of queer people from the end of the 19th century to the queer liberation movement of the present day, stressing race and class issues as well as gender.

And a degree in "Lesbian, Gay and Bisexual Studies" offered at the University of California at Riverside promises to address such issues as: sexual identity and orientation; gay, lesbian and bisexual representation; gay, lesbian and bisexual perspectives on the arts; sexuality and cultural diversity; intersections of sexualities and ethnic identities.

[8]For further treatment of this distinction, see Helmut Thielicke, *Theological Ethics*, trans. John W. Doberstein, Vol. 3: *Sex* (Grand Rapids, MI: Eerdmans, 1979), 20-26.

Indeed, one way to understand the basic division that separates complementarians (Christians who teach the Bible requires respect for gender roles) from egalitarians (Christians who deny there is any legitimate basis for gender roles) is that egalitarians follow the culture in refusing to distinguish between sexual being and sexual function, while complementarians oppose the culture by insisting they are different. On this specific matter, egalitarians side with the thinking of contemporary social scientists who promote "plastic sexuality," while complementarians do not.

By the *being* of human sexual existence we refer to men and women insofar as both sexes are centers of transcendent worth, are creatures uniquely privileged to bear the image of God, are moral beings responsible for their own actions, and are persons worthy of being "ends in themselves" and never just means to an end. By *functions* in connection with human sexuality we refer to men and women insofar as each acts in ways shaped by his or her specific gender identity and is assigned responsibilities in relationships with other sexual beings that are specific to their gender identities. Sexual functions affect matters that go beyond the sexual being of mere individuals. They are what defines human sexuality to the degree it involves interaction and relationship between persons in ways defined by specific sexual identity. These interactive functions or relationships shape the meaning of human sexuality in the context of community. They concern the meaning of human sexuality as it has to do with reproductive capacities, assignments, achievements, and goals—what the Bible calls being "united" (Gen. 2:24) and being "fruitful" (Gen. 1:28).

Because human sexual existence involves both being and function, ways of understanding human sexuality that focus on one and not the other, ways that fail to distinguish one from the other or that reduce the whole meaning of special identity to one at the expense of the other, must be deficient. But failure to accept both together risks something more than deficiency. It also invites perversion. The result will be wrong not just because someone might dislike it, but because it actually *dehumanizes* human relationships.

On the one hand, ways of understanding human sexuality that emphasize function over being lead to the perversion of slavery. Slavery is abhorrently perverted precisely because a person's inherent worth as a human being is denied. He or she is valued only in reference to function with no reference to his or her value as a human being per se. On the other hand, understanding human sexuality in a way that focuses exclusively on the common value of sexual being with no place for functional differences tends to leave relational aspects of human sexual existence (sexual union and fruitfulness) barren and shallow to the point of dysfunction. As a result, failing to distinguish between sexual being and sexual function, or focusing on one at the expense of the other, can only lead human sexual relationships into social, moral, and spiritual confusion. If nothing defines functional differences between male and female, then relationships involving gender identity are perverted and quickly degenerate into a mere struggle for power.

While distinguishing between sexual being and sexual function helps us guard against slavery and relational confusion, it also removes rational objections to the essentialist view of human sexuality. If we can distinguish being from function, then there is nothing at all inconsistent with thinking that sexual being may endure while functions may change. Sexual being can be something fixed and unchanging, even if some specific sexual functions cease (for example, the functions of marriage and procreation) and others might be modified (perhaps the function of headship).

III. BIBLICAL EVIDENCE THAT SEXUAL IDENTITY IS ETERNAL

Having set the stage by clarifying the difference between sexual being and sexual function—something the Bible just assumes when it presents the equality of men and women but goes right on discussing gender roles without any sense of contradiction—we now will consider some direct evidence given in the Bible that lends strong support to the essentialist view. Specifically we are going to find that the gender identity aspect of sexual being—the identity of men as men and women as women—is something so profound, so very important to God, that it is going to last throughout all eternity. And if God says the gender identity aspect of human sexual being is eternal, then it cannot be something culturally relative or plastic. Instead, it must be something very real that must of course remain fixed throughout life on earth.

Looking at what the Bible teaches about human sexual identity and whether it will cease or not is not an entirely new question. At least we should not think we are the first Christians to examine Scripture for answers. Augustine, in the fourth century, studied the question and concluded that the Bible teaches that both men and women will keep their specific gender identities beyond the resurrection and into eternity. In his case Augustine was responding to some who were saying women would cease to be women after the resurrection. "There are some," he said, "who think that in the resurrection all will be men and that women will lose their sex. . . . For my part, I think that those who believe that there will be two sexes in the resurrection are more sensible."[9]

How did Augustine reach this conclusion? Using Augustine's work for a guide and expanding upon his initial efforts, I will now lay out and explain four biblically sound theological reasons for asserting that God in the Bible clearly gives us an essentialist view of human sexuality. Two of these reasons come from the record of creation, and two come from the promise of bodily resurrection and future eternal life in an embodied state.

First, in the record of creation we understand that when God created Adam and Eve, He created embodied spirits. God did not first create nonmaterial beings and then in a second, separate action place them into material bodies. Rather, each was created whole in a single divine act of creation. Thus the being of each is presented as something we might call "materialized spirit." In other words, the creation record teaches that men and women are beings who exist spiritually and physically at the same time. "The LORD God formed the man from the dust of the ground and breathed into his nostrils the breath of life, and the man became a living being" (Gen. 2:7). Also, "the LORD God made a woman from the rib he had taken out of the man, and he brought her to the man" (Gen. 2:22). Not only is human existence spiritual—it also requires embodiment to be whole. So, if embodiment includes sexual identity and if embodiment is essential to being human, then sexual identity must be essential to human existence. Put another way, it is only logical to assume that because God in creation made sexual identity essential to embodied human life, then absent specific revelation to the contrary we must assume that sexual identity will always remain essential to embodied human existence.

Second, the Bible supports an essentialist view of human sexuality because when God created Adam and Eve, He demonstrated the fact that human sexual identity has absolutely nothing to do with sin. Of course, what we now experience of human sexuality certainly is affected by sinful human nature. But human sexual identity has as such never actually depended on being sinful. Indeed, Augustine saw that

---

[9]Augustine, *The City of God*, 19.22.17.

since Adam and Eve were sexual beings before the Fall, we have to conclude that sinful sexual desire does not have any necessary connection with what it means to be a sexual being.[10] And because human sexuality existed without sin before the Fall, there is at least no moral reason for opposing the idea that we shall continue to be sexual creatures after God does away with all moral corruption—that is, after the entire created order (including human beings) is released from the curse imposed by God as a consequence of sin (Rom. 8:20-21).[11]

Third, the essentialist view of human sexuality is presumed in the biblical hope of bodily resurrection because there is a restorative and not just a reconstructive purpose in God's promise of bodily resurrection. In the resurrection we will experience a continuity of being and personal identity that links the new with what was old. We are told that we will be "changed" (1 Cor. 15:51-52). But it is still "we" who shall be changed. The subject remains the subject. At the resurrection, Paul says, "the perishable must clothe itself with the imperishable, and the mortal with immortality" (1 Cor. 15:53). Yet it is those same beings who once were mortal who will then at the resurrection "clothe" themselves with immortality. And since we know there will be continuity of personal identity, and because sexuality has always been part of that identity, Augustine was led to say, "He, then, who created both sexes will restore both."[12]

Augustine first saw that because human sexuality existed before the coming of mortality and the Fall (Gen. 2:25; cf. 2:17), we know sexual being is not incompatible with human life in a state of sinless perfection. But he did not stop there. Augustine also understood from creation that human sexual identity is not merely good in the sense of being sinless. It also is good in a constructive sense. That is, the good of sexual being has to do with more than something it avoids, excludes, or merely is not. It is also has to do with accomplishing something commendable—something truly worthy that would or could never be at all apart from God's creation of sexual identity. In other words, God

---

[10]Of our future state Augustine says, "There shall be no lust, which is now the cause of confusion. For before they sinned, the man and the woman were naked, and were not ashamed. From those [sexual] bodies, then, vice shall be withdrawn, while [sexual] nature shall be preserved. And the sex of woman [as well as of man] is not a vice, but nature" (*The City of God*, 19.22.17).

[11]We have yet to discuss the statement Jesus made about human marriage ceasing or become irrelevant in heaven. At this point we are only removing the idea of some essential moral objection to the possibility of sexual being in heaven.

[12]Ibid.

generated sexual being *as* good but also *for* good. At creation, human sexual identity not only is without sin—it is also created for the purpose of achieving something good. When God made Adam and Eve male and female, He had in view the achievement of some very good thing that can be achieved no other way—not even in the relationship between human beings and God Himself. By creating male and female human beings in two distinctly separate acts, God focused attention on some good thing that can be achieved only because human life is sexually differentiated. "The LORD God said, 'It is not good for the man to be alone. I will make a helper suitable for him'" (Gen. 2:18). In this statement, God revealed that human sexuality not only is a good thing in itself—it is also *for* something good. It realizes some good thing that does not exist apart from a relationship that consists of unifying the sort of corresponding differences involved in human sexual identity.

This point adds even greater support to the principle we noted earlier—the principle that absent specific revelation to the contrary, we should assume that human sexual identity is eternal. If God says human sexual identity is necessary in order to realize something He declares good, and if He reveals no reason to think any good thing will be left behind, then surely the resurrection must include the specific sort of good for which God says complementary differences in human sexual identity are intended. Of course, the meaning and purpose of human sexuality may in that day rise to some higher level of significance and completion, but it would not be logical to think it would ever be worthless. While its worth may be enhanced, it can never be worth nothing.

The argument that God's promise of bodily resurrection presumes the essential nature of human sexual identity has additional scriptural validation in accounts given by those who recognized Jesus after His resurrection. It also finds validation in Paul's revelation of an immediate connection or relationship between sexual activity and the bodies we have now and the purity of the eternal bodies we look forward to having after the resurrection. Following Jesus' resurrection, the disciples recognized the same male human being they knew and loved before the crucifixion. Peter boldly declared that "God has raised this Jesus [i.e., the very same man] to life, and we are all witnesses of the fact" (Acts 2:32). After Jesus' resurrection, angels also testified to His continuing male identity when they said, "This same Jesus, who has been taken from you into heaven, will come back in the same way you have seen him go into heaven" (Acts 1:11).

These accounts show that all who saw Jesus after His bodily resurrection just assumed that He remained a male human being. As strong as this evidence may be, we must acknowledge that it is indirect. The evidence is based on natural assumption with no clear evidence to the contrary. But there is further evidence in the New Testament that goes beyond conjecture. We also have direct evidence of continued sexual identity after the resurrection in something Paul explains to new believers in Corinth. Writing to the Corinthians Paul says something about a link that is both strong and direct:

> *The body is not meant for sexual immorality, but for the Lord, and the Lord for the body. By his power God raised the Lord from the dead, and he will raise us also. Do you not know that your bodies are members of Christ himself? Shall I then take the members of Christ and unite them with a prostitute? Never!*
>
> —1 COR. 6:13B-15

Here by divine inspiration Paul links sexual sin involving the bodies we have now with the purity that must and certainly will characterize the bodies we will have after the resurrection. Our sexual organs themselves, in Paul's bold language, are said to be "members of Christ" and thus are parts of our future resurrection bodies—bodies that in their entirety God "will raise" from the dead—bodies that in their entirety God wants us to use now for His glory and that someday He will also perfect for His glory through the resurrection. The logical connection Paul makes here between our pre- and post-resurrection bodies makes absolutely no sense (there is no logical lever connecting one with the other) unless human sexual identity does in fact continue to characterize human embodiment on both sides of the resurrection.

Fourth and last, the essentialist view of human sexuality is expressed and thus affirmed in the way Jesus answered a group of Sadducees who tried to stump Him with a question about marriage after the resurrection. The Sadducees did not believe in a physical resurrection and thought they could confound Jesus with a question about seven brothers who were each in succession married to the same woman (Matt. 22:23-32). Whose wife would she be after the resurrection? If human sexuality is limited only to this life, then Jesus only needed to explain that their question was irrelevant. If sexual identity ceases after the resurrection, then any question about marriage following the resurrection simply does not matter. For marriage along with any other sort of relationship involving sexual identity would just be impossible.

However, Jesus did not respond that way. He did not respond by saying the question was completely irrelevant because marriage would be impossible, but only that present practices will cease. "You are in error," he said, because "at the resurrection people will neither marry nor be given in marriage." They will, in that regard, "be like the angels in heaven" (vv. 29-30). Indeed, the form of response given by Jesus should be understood as confirming the ongoing existence of human sexual identity per se.

So, for example, if there had been a conversation about toll roads, and Jesus had said, "Come the resurrection, you will no longer pay tolls," the statement denying tolls would also be affirming the continuing presence of highways. In the same way, by not denying the *possibility* but merely denying the *practice* of marriage, the answer Jesus gave points rather strongly toward the continuing presence of sexual identity even while denying further need (after the resurrection) for the institution that now defines and protects its present function.

This is exactly what Augustine said in his day to refute some who were claiming that female sexual identity will not continue after the resurrection. Against this claim, Augustine argued that Jesus actually

> affirmed that the [female] sex should exist [after the resurrection] by saying, "They shall not be given in marriage," which can only apply to females; "Neither shall they marry," which applies only to males. There shall therefore be those who are in this world accustomed to marry and be given in marriage, only they shall there make no such marriages.[13]

This is not to say God has revealed an eternal purpose that explains the value of sexual differences after the resurrection. But since God never acts without purpose, and because we know marriage practices will cease, we can only surmise that lasting sexual differences after the resurrection indicate God must have some very profound eternal purpose for manhood and womanhood. And it must be also that this last-

---

[13]Ibid. Here Augustine quotes Matt. 22:30.

ing purpose transcends present functions that require protection by marriage.

While God has not revealed what it will mean to be male and female after the resurrection, we should certainly trust His goodness and should take comfort in knowing that His plans for eternal resurrected life without sin will far exceed every blessing and joy we have known in this fallen world. At the same time we must resist speculating beyond what God actually reveals in Scripture. For on this subject speculation can be as harmful as it is tempting, and if God thought we should know more, he would certainly have told us.

IV. PLASTIC SEXUALITY AND THE EGALITARIAN POSITION

We have considered a new way of thinking now emerging in our culture that promotes the idea that human sexual identity is not fixed but is instead malleable or plastic. I in turn have argued that Christians must prepare to resist such thinking by studying reasons in the Bible for believing that human sexual identity is something so deeply profound and important to God it will last through eternity, and if it is eternal, then it certainly cannot be culturally relative or plastic. I have also noted how the idea of plastic sexuality reconfigures sexual ethics and is especially opposed to gender roles. And in doing this I have also pointed out how egalitarians and the advocates of plastic sexuality share a common view of equality—one that fails to distinguish between sexual *being* and sexual *function*.

As we close, I will add some comments about similarities I see, and about which I think we should all be deeply concerned, between egalitarian teaching in the church on the one hand and the promotion of plastic sexuality in the culture on the other. In view of biblical doctrine concerning the eternally fixed nature of human sexual identity, promotion of plastic sexuality amounts to a wager that erases sexual boundaries at the cost of real significance and meaning. It promises freedom from moral limitations at the price of perpetual shallowness. And although Christian egalitarians continue to proclaim faith in the authority of Scripture, and although they have never been so extreme as those who openly espouse plastic sexuality, the egalitarian position takes on this same wager. Egalitarians also sacrifice the meaning of sexual difference for the sake of monolithic sameness.

The idea of plastic sexuality with its ethical ramifications is the inevitable result of humanistic thinking when views about sexual identity are severed from objective truth about who we are as sexual beings. If the meaning and definition of human sexual identity is separated from all fixed references and is left to arbitrary personal choice, we should not be surprised that advocates then claim human sexuality is arbitrary. Ironically, the idea of plastic sexuality requires a very profound commitment to believing there is nothing at all profound about sexual identity. Plastic sexuality is simply sex without purpose, and one without purpose has no moral limits other than insisting that all moral limits have to be rejected.

Christian egalitarians still believe human sexuality has some purpose, but they so reconstruct what that purpose means that sexual differences are all but irrelevant. For example, egalitarian Stanley Grenz writes that "The basic purpose of our existence as sexual creatures is related to the dynamic of bonding." And he claims the problem for which God made Eve as a solution was just the problem of "solitude."[14] But "bonding" for the purpose of companionship solving the problem of solitude does not require sexual difference. Defined this way, human sexuality fulfills its revisionist purpose whether sexual differences exist or not. Thus, for egalitarians, sexual differences distinguishing men from women are marginalized to the point of becoming unnecessary or meaningless. In this way egalitarians end up arguing a position not so very different from that taken by cultural advocates promoting plastic sexuality.

Whether it is social scientists advocating plastic sexuality or evangelicals promoting egalitarianism, both seem beguiled by a view of sexual "equality" that leaves no room for deeply meaningful distinctions in human sexual identity. Both pursue a view of equality that refuses to accept complementary differences. Neither allows the sort of equality that has room for corresponding differences in function that do not compromise the equal value of men and women as sexual beings. Both insist on an idea of equality that focuses exclusively on monolithic sameness. But if gender differences in human sexual identity really do not matter—if in fact what we think are differences are actually just transitory, cultural, or perhaps even unreal—then the idea of difference based on separate sexual gender identities can sustain no real moral value either. Then the idea that gender-based sexual differences sustain or define any sort of normative standard must be rejected. Thus, it

[14]Stanley J. Grenz, *Sexual Ethics: An Evangelical Perspective* (Louisville: Westminster/John Knox, 1997), 32.

turns out, a way of thinking used by egalitarians to justify opposition to gender roles is shared by advocates of plastic sexuality who use it to deny that heterosexual marriage should be treated as a standard.

Convictions about the reality of enduring, meaningful difference in human sexual identity—a difference so profound it can define and sustain normative moral relations between men as men and women as women—lies at the center of a colossal social, ethical, and ultimately religious struggle now straining American life and culture. If fixed and permanent differences in human sexual identity are ultimately unreal, then God is a deceiver, and the Bible perpetrates enormous evil. But if sexual differences are fixed and real, then the God of Scripture is true, and Christian teachers must firmly oppose the tide of culture no matter how strong it gets. Scripture cannot be shaped to accommodate the goals and assumptions of plastic sexuality, and teaching based on the influence of plastic sexuality in our culture has no place in the life of the church.

APPENDIX:
THE DANVERS STATEMENT

———◦◦◦———

The "Danvers Statement" summarizes the need for the Council on Biblical Manhood and Womanhood (CBMW) and serves as an overview of our core beliefs. This statement was prepared by several evangelical leaders at a CBMW meeting in Danvers, Massachusetts, in December of 1987. It was first published in final form by the CBMW in Wheaton, Illinois in November of 1988.

RATIONALE

We have been moved in our purpose by the following contemporary developments which we observe with deep concern:

1. The widespread uncertainty and confusion in our culture regarding the complementary differences between masculinity and femininity;

2. the tragic effects of this confusion in unraveling the fabric of marriage woven by God out of the beautiful and diverse strands of manhood and womanhood;

3. the increasing promotion given to feminist egalitarianism with accompanying distortions or neglect of the glad harmony portrayed in Scripture between the loving, humble leadership of redeemed husbands and the intelligent, willing support of that leadership by redeemed wives;

4. the widespread ambivalence regarding the values of motherhood, vocational homemaking, and the many ministries historically performed by women;

5. the growing claims of legitimacy for sexual relationships which

have Biblically and historically been considered illicit or perverse, and the increase in pornographic portrayal of human sexuality;

6. the upsurge of physical and emotional abuse in the family;

7. the emergence of roles for men and women in church leadership that do not conform to Biblical teaching but backfire in the crippling of Biblically faithful witness;

8. the increasing prevalence and acceptance of hermeneutical oddities devised to reinterpret apparently plain meanings of Biblical texts;

9. the consequent threat to Biblical authority as the clarity of Scripture is jeopardized and the accessibility of its meaning to ordinary people is withdrawn into the restricted realm of technical ingenuity;

10. and behind all this the apparent accommodation of some within the church to the spirit of the age at the expense of winsome, radical Biblical authenticity which in the power of the Holy Spirit may reform rather than reflect our ailing culture.

PURPOSES

Recognizing our own abiding sinfulness and fallibility, and acknowledging the genuine evangelical standing of many who do not agree with all of our convictions, nevertheless, moved by the preceding observations and by the hope that the noble Biblical vision of sexual complementarity may yet win the mind and heart of Christ's church, we engage to pursue the following purposes:

1. To study and set forth the Biblical view of the relationship between men and women, especially in the home and in the church.

2. To promote the publication of scholarly and popular materials representing this view.

3. To encourage the confidence of lay people to study and understand for themselves the teaching of Scripture, especially on the issue of relationships between men and women.

4. To encourage the considered and sensitive application of this Biblical view in the appropriate spheres of life.

5. And thereby

—to bring healing to persons and relationships injured by an inadequate grasp of God's will concerning manhood and womanhood,

—to help both men and women realize their full ministry potential through a true understanding and practice of their God-given roles,

—and to promote the spread of the gospel among all peoples by fostering a Biblical wholeness in relationships that will attract a fractured world.

AFFIRMATIONS

Based on our understanding of Biblical teachings, we affirm the following:

1. Both Adam and Eve were created in God's image, equal before God as persons and distinct in their manhood and womanhood.

2. Distinctions in masculine and feminine roles are ordained by God as part of the created order, and should find an echo in every human heart.

3. Adam's headship in marriage was established by God before the Fall, and was not a result of sin.

4. The Fall introduced distortions into the relationships between men and women.

—In the home, the husband's loving, humble headship tends to be replaced by domination or passivity; the wife's intelligent, willing submission tends to be replaced by usurpation or servility.

—In the church, sin inclines men toward a worldly love of power or an abdication of spiritual responsibility, and inclines women to resist limitations on their roles or to neglect the use of their gifts in appropriate ministries.

5. The Old Testament, as well as the New Testament, manifests the equally high value and dignity which God attached to the roles of both men and women. Both Old and New Testaments also affirm the principle of male headship in the family and in the covenant community.

6. Redemption in Christ aims at removing the distortions introduced by the curse.

—In the family, husbands should forsake harsh or selfish leadership and grow in love and care for their wives; wives should forsake resistance to their husbands' authority and grow in willing, joyful submission to their husbands' leadership.

—In the church, redemption in Christ gives men and women an equal share in the blessings of salvation; nevertheless, some governing and teaching roles within the church are restricted to men.

7. In all of life Christ is the supreme authority and guide for men and women, so that no earthly submission—domestic, religious, or civil—ever implies a mandate to follow a human authority into sin.

8. In both men and women a heartfelt sense of call to ministry

should never be used to set aside Biblical criteria for particular ministries. Rather, Biblical teaching should remain the authority for testing our subjective discernment of God's will.

9. With half the world's population outside the reach of indigenous evangelism; with countless other lost people in those societies that have heard the gospel; with the stresses and miseries of sickness, malnutrition, homelessness, illiteracy, ignorance, aging, addiction, crime, incarceration, neuroses, and loneliness, no man or woman who feels a passion from God to make His grace known in word and deed need ever live without a fulfilling ministry for the glory of Christ and the good of this fallen world.

10. We are convinced that a denial or neglect of these principles will lead to increasingly destructive consequences in our families, our churches, and the culture at large.

We grant permission and encourage interested persons to use, reproduce, and distribute the Danvers Statement without charge. Or you may visit the CBMW webstore (www.cbmw.org) or contact us (888-560-8210) to place an order for printed copies, which are available for a small fee.

SCRIPTURE INDEX

AUTHOR INDEX

Subject Index